D1587559

For Those In Peril

For Those In Peril

The Lifeboat Service of the United Kingdom and the Republic of Ireland, Station by Station

Nicholas Leach

· MARITIME HERITAGE ·
from
The NOSTALGIA *Collection*

© Nicholas Leach 1999

All rights reserved. No part of this publication may be reproduced, stored in a retrieval system or transmitted, in any form or by any means, electronic, mechanical, photocopying, recording or otherwise, without prior permission in writing from Silver Link Publishing Ltd.

First published in June 1999

British Library Cataloguing in Publication Data

A catalogue record for this book is available from the British Library.

ISBN 1 85794 129 2

Silver Link Publishing Ltd
The Trundle
Ringstead Road
Great Addington
Kettering
Northants NN14 4BW

Tel/Fax: 01536 330588
email: sales@slinkp-p.demon.co.uk

Maps drawn by Christina Siviter

All photographs by the author unless otherwise credited

For high-quality photographic prints from any of the pictures by Rick Tomlinson, please phone 01703 458450

Printed and bound in Great Britain by Butler & Tanner Limited, Frome and London

Acknowledgements

Many people have contributed towards this book in various ways. Their help is most appreciated, for without it I would not have been able to complete the work. At RNLI Headquarters in Poole, Edward Wake-Walker, Public Relations Officer, provided support and generously made available RNLI records for my inspection and use; Shelley Woodroffe was extremely helpful in providing answers to numerous questions and supplying much information; and Alan King and Derek King have also assisted. The files of the late Grahame Farr, held at the RNLI's library in Poole, have also proved invaluable during the research for this book.

I am particularly indebted to Jeff Morris, the Honorary Archivist of the Lifeboat Enthusiasts' Society, who has been of immense assistance checking information, answering many queries and whose excellent station history books were regularly consulted. Tony Denton, Colin Dingle and John Maddock also helped to check various parts of the text.

My gratitude extends to Rick Tomlinson, Tony Denton, Jim Wallbridge and Gary Markham for kindly supplying many excellent photographs for possible inclusion. I am also grateful to the following for making their photographs available to me: Andy Anderson, Alasdair Barker, Vladimir Dasiukevich, Steve Dutton, Peter Edey, Kevin Escott, Martin Fish, Steve Guscott, Stuart Ladd, Chris Lambert, Leon Goldwater, Brian J. Green, Stuart Ladd, Ian Leask, John Maddock, A. R. McKerlich, Jeff Morris, Michael O'Gorman, Jack O'Grady, Paul Richards, Mark Roberts, Paul Russell, Sam Shiels, Aine Stafford, Tony Smith, Craig Taylor, Graham Taylor, John Truran, Turtle Photography, Michael Webb, Phil Weeks and Bob Williams. John Leach, of A. H. Leach & Co Ltd, supplied high quality photographic prints.

On a personal note, my thanks to Sarah Ford, for support, help and companionship; to Peter Bendall, for grammatical accuracy; to Susan Leach, for patience and assistance in checking through draft versions of the text; and to Peter Townsend, my publisher, who has enabled this book to become a reality.

Finally, I am extremely appreciative of the help I have received from officials, coxswains, crews and others at so many of the lifeboat stations that I have visited. Those to whom I have talked have proved to be helpful and co-operative, patiently answering my questions and enabling me to take many of the photographs included in this book. They are the heroes of the lifeboat service – I have the utmost respect and admiration for the magnificent work they do.

Contents

Foreword by Andrew W. Freemantle MBE, Director RNLI

I feel very privileged to have taken over the helm of the Royal National Lifeboat Institution in such an exciting year as 1999. Not only because we are celebrating the 175th anniversary of our founding on 4 March 1824 with a myriad of events around the United Kingdom and Republic of Ireland, but also because we can look forward to the Second Millennium and all the new possibilities that brings.

We must, of course, look at the past during this year, and Nicholas Leach's book *For Those In Peril* will be an excellent record in years to come of all the lifeboats that were on station in 1999; it will also act as a time capsule for the lifeboat fleet on 4 March 1999. Collating all the information must have been a tremendous feat of dedication, and Nicholas is to be congratulated. I thoroughly recommend *For Those In Peril* to lifeboat supporters everywhere.

When Lt Col Sir William Hillary launched his *Appeal to the Nation* in

1824 he had the foresight and imagination to believe that a lifesaving service could be organised using volunteers to crew the lifeboats. The fact that this holds true today, in a material world, is particularly striking.

It is also remarkable that while the technology we use has advanced beyond all expectations, the volunteer spirit, which drives our whole organisation, has remained constant. The dedication of thousands of volunteers who give up their time to raise funds to support the organisation is another example of this. In short, the RNLI's volunteers embody many of the qualities that we are all looking for in society today: dedication, compassion and courage.

The aim of the RNLI's 175th anniversary in 1999 is to remind everyone, particularly the young, that the RNLI is a modern, efficient and reliable service, free and available to all, and as essential

today as it was 175 years ago. The lifeboat service needs the support of young people to keep it functioning into the 21st century. I hope this book will help to fire the enthusiasm of the young today – our future crew members and fundraisers.

Foreword by Brian Miles CBE, Director RNLI 1988-98

I am delighted to be invited by Nicholas Leach, a fellow Lifeboat Enthusiast, to provide a brief Foreword for his book. In his Foreword, Andrew Freemantle, the new Director, concentrated on the future of the Institution, which I am sure will be as challenging and as successful as the past. Nicholas has asked me to look back over the last 175 years, although I hope he has not assumed that I have been involved for quite that long!

On great occasions like the 175th anniversary, I believe it is entirely appropriate to review the past and take pride in all that the Institution has achieved. Over 175 years momentous change has taken place, with some of the more far-reaching changes being implemented in the fairly recent past. Following the founding of what was ultimately to

become the RNLI in 1824 by Sir William Hillary, the service depended on various designs of pulling and sailing lifeboats to fulfil its lifesaving role until well into the following century. Even in those early days some innovative and imaginative ideas were put forward in terms of new lifeboat designs, but oar and sail predominated.

The development of power-driven lifeboats at the beginning of the 20th century must have seemed a revolutionary change to those concerned, and I am sure that these people were saying that things would never be the same again. First steam, then petrol, and finally diesel – the introduction of these new techniques must have presented a tremendous challenge, but surely a period of change to rival the transition from pulling and sailing to power-driven

lifeboats commenced at the beginning of the 1960s when faster lifeboats started to be introduced. As an Inspector on the coast, as Coxwain of the lifeboat 70-002 for over a year and from the vantage point of several staff appointments at Head Office, I witnessed the transition at first hand and the improvements in the service that resulted: the advent of the Waveney, early trials and developments of the ILB fleet, Aruns, Merseys, Tynes and, more recently, the Severns and Trents. The RNLI will never stand still and the new generation Fast Slipway Boat and lifeboats beyond 2000 are just around the corner.

At the very heart of all the change I have referred to have been the people, primarily those who have served as crew members through the generations. I can only confirm that my own respect and admiration for those men and women who serve as crew members remains undiminished. How proud I shall always be to say that I know and counted as friends Patsy Sliney, Dick Evans, Dan Kirkpatrick, Matt Lethbridge and more recently Derek Scott, Brian Bevan and Hewitt Clark. There are so many other names I could mention, but I will end up writing the book!

I am really delighted that Nicholas is providing this further opportunity to honour our lifeboat stations and those who serve at them both ashore and afloat. I commend the book to all its readers and wish it and them well.

Introduction

There is a strong tradition of saving life at sea in the United Kingdom and Ireland, and the Royal National Lifeboat Institution (RNLI) is justifiably proud of its 175-year history. The sole purpose of the RNLI is to rescue life at sea by providing, manning and maintaining lifeboats at strategic positions on the coasts of the United Kingdom and Republic of Ireland. Throughout its history, the lifeboat service has been ready to assist those in difficulty at sea, impelled by a humane spirit of compassion and charity that makes the lifeboat service and the lifeboat crews special in the eyes of the public.

Today, the lifeboat service is dedicated to continuing this tradition, and operates some of the best lifeboats ever built. These boats are incredibly strong, seaworthy, technologically advanced and very fast, capable of speedily reaching casualties in any weather – but they are only as good as the men and women who operate them. The crews that man the boats are, as they always have been, volunteers. For no personal gain, they are prepared to go to sea to save the lives of others, often in the worst of weathers.

The volunteer crews willingly give up their time for service calls, exercises, training, and the day-to-day running of the station. They come from all walks of life, including fishermen, shopkeepers, builders and teachers, and are willing to exchange the comfort of their homes for the danger and discomfort of saving lives at sea. Usually the only full-time member of the crew at all-weather lifeboat stations is the mechanic, whose job it is to maintain the lifeboat and its gear. There is one completely full-time crew, at the busy Humber station in Yorkshire, where the men and their families live on the isolated Spurn Point peninsula.

Each of the RNLI's lifeboat stations operates with a degree of autonomy, but under the regulations and supervision of the Institution. Each station has an honorary secretary who is responsible for the general running of the station. If a lifeboat is needed, the honorary secretary authorises the launch and the volunteer crew are alerted by pagers, telephone or maroons. Once a call has been made, the crew will immediately leave what they are doing, whether at home or work, and make for the lifeboat station. In many cases a lifeboat will be at sea in less than 4 minutes from the time the crew were alerted. Once at sea, the coxswain or helmsman is in sole charge of the boat and will make the decisions about how best to tackle the rescue situation that faces the lifeboat and its crew.

This book is intended as a guide to and directory of all of the RNLI's operational lifeboat stations at the time of the Institution's 175th anniversary, 4 March 1999. Every station is unique and each has its own idiosyncrasies, its own history and its own feats of bravery by the lifeboat crews – it is hoped that this uniqueness will be reflected in the main part of the book. But at the same time, all are brought together under the RNLI's auspices and all share the same aim – that of saving life at sea. The combination of lifeboat and crew ensure that the RNLI maintains its tradition of providing a comprehensive sea rescue service.

175 years of lifesaving by the RNLI

The Royal National Institution for the Preservation of Life from Shipwreck (RNIPLS) was founded on 4 March 1824 at a meeting in London, mainly as a result of the exertions of Sir William Hillary. In 1823, Hillary, of Douglas in the Isle of Man, wrote and published 'An Appeal to the British Nation on the Humanity and Policy of forming a National Institution for the Preservation of Lives and Property from Shipwreck'. In this he set out his ideals for forming a national body whose sole responsibility would be the preservation of life from shipwreck. By this time many lifeboat stations had already been established, but there was no co-ordination on a national basis and their management and funding involved essentially local arrangements.

Before Hillary's pioneering efforts, attempts had been made to establish lifeboats near the busiest shipping lanes. These attempts began during the last quarter of the 18th century, when Britain's industrial revolution was taking shape. Shipwrecks had occurred before this time, but remedies had not included the building of a boat specifically designed to be operated from the shore and employed to save those in distress at sea. Navigational aids, such as lighthouses, had been built at strategic points to assist ships, but no concerted efforts had been made to improve the passage of ships around the coast.

The first recorded lifeboat was at Formby, in Lancashire, and was set up and financed by the Liverpool Docks Commissioners. Although specific details of the boat, such as its name, are lacking, it was in operation in the 1770s and, together with another funded by the Commissioners that was placed at Hoylake in 1803, protected the entrance to the River Mersey. Liverpool was the fastest-growing port on the West Coast, hence the need for a lifeboat. On the East Coast, the fastest-growing port was

Newcastle. It is no surprise, therefore, that the first boat known to be designed and built specifically for lifesaving has its origins in that city. It was built by Henry Greathead in 1790 at South Shields, on the south bank of the mouth of the River Tyne, and operated from there for several decades.

During the early years of the 19th century many lifeboats were funded and built through the initiatives of shipowners' groups, such as those at Sunderland, Montrose, Aberdeen, Hartlepool, Ayr and Arbroath. Other lifeboats, such as those at St Andrews, Scarborough, Lowestoft, Whitby and Redcar, were established as a result of philanthropy, either by an individual or a group of subscribers. In 1806 a Humane Society was formed in Suffolk, which, among other activities, financed local lifeboat societies, and during the first half of the 19th century associations based in specific districts and regions were formed.

Many of the early lifeboat stations were helped by Lloyd's insurance agency, in London, which set up a fund to encourage the building and operating of lifeboats to counter ship losses. This fund provided an impetus to early lifeboat building, and helped pay for almost 30 lifeboats up to the 1820s. Yet despite assistance from Lloyds, the establishment of lifeboat stations was still somewhat fragmented, and it was this lack of co-ordination that led Hillary to push for the founding of a National Institution.

Initially, the national body was quite successful and provided a new impetus for coastal rescue provision as the number of lifeboats in operation increased. As well as its own stations, it encouraged independent organisations to place lifeboats on the coast, although these independent societies adopted different stances towards the central body, varying from full co-operation to indifference. But from the 1830s its fortunes started to fluctuate through lack of funds, and few new

lifeboats were built. Annual income dwindled further during the 1840s and, with no public appeals made for over a decade, reached its lowest level in 1850.

The deterioration of the nation's lifeboats was highlighted by a number of events, notably a disaster at the mouth of the Tyne in December 1849 when one of the local Society's lifeboats capsized with the loss of 20 of the 24 lives on board in sight of land. Change was needed, and improvements in the national service began after the fourth Duke of Northumberland became President of the Institution in 1851. At this time there were said to be 95 lifeboats in existence, although many were in a poor state of repair. The Duke set about instituting many reforms, including organising a national competition to find a new design of lifeboat. In addition, in 1854 a new title for the service was adopted – the Royal National Lifeboat Institution (RNLI). The old title, often shortened to National Shipwreck Institution, was deemed inappropriate as well as inaccurate.

Throughout the latter half of the 19th century the Institution gradually went from strength to strength as the number of lifeboats and stations in existence rose steadily. In the course of time almost all of the independent societies joined the RNLI, and by the 20th century the operation of more or less every lifeboat station in the United Kingdom and Ireland was the responsibility of the RNLI.

The maximum number of operational stations was reached in 1895 when there were 308 of the RNLI's lifeboats around the coast, plus about a dozen under the auspices of other organisations. This was in the heyday of the 'standard' self-righting lifeboat, which had been gradually improved since its introduction in the 1850s so that by the 1880s it was almost the only type of lifeboat in use and was by then used throughout almost the whole world. It was primarily a rowing boat, only 34 or 35 feet in length,

The standard self-righter *Richard Ashley* (ON.584) being launched over the beach at Ferryside, with the lifeboat house to the right. *Richard Ashley* served at Ferryside from 1907 until 1941. *From an old photo supplied by a Shoreline member*

The standard 34ft ten-oared self-righter, characterised by the high airtight boxes at bow and stern, typical of the RNLI's late-19th-century lifeboats. This example, *Elinor Roget* (ON.348), is on the stone slipway outside the lifeboat house at Clovelly where she served from 1893 to 1907. *From an old photo supplied by a Shoreline member*

The Rye Harbour lifeboat *John William Dudley* (ON.453) on the beach at Winchelsea, where the station was located. This photo shows the boat in the process of being recovered, with skids laid on the beach over which the lifeboat will be hauled. A drogue can be seen towards the stern of the boat; this was used to slow down the lifeboat (or any other vessel) in a following sea, and prevent waves breaking over the stern. *From an old photo supplied by a Shoreline member*

and its radius of action was rather limited. For this reason, two lifeboats were operated at many stations at one time, and at some three or more boats were in service.

The lifeboats of the late 19th century were often launched from a carriage off an open beach. This could cause many difficulties for the lifeboat crew, and especially for the launchers. Because they were light enough to be carriage-launched, and because sailing against the wind in a vessel relying solely on manpower was slow and exhausting work, these lifeboats would sometimes be taken further afield to a site for a launch that would enable the casualty to be reached more easily.

The lifeboatmen of the 19th century performed many heroic and courageous acts using this type of boat. One of the most remarkable rescues that involved the lifeboat being moved overland before being launched occurred in January 1881 when the brig *Visiter*, carrying coals to London, was grounded in rough weather close to the small village of Robin Hood's Bay, Yorkshire. The nearest lifeboat was at Whitby, but in the driving snow and huge seas rowing the lifeboat several miles to the wreck would have been virtually impossible. It was thus decided to manhandle the lifeboat over 8 miles of hills, through fields and snowdrifts for launching at Robin Hood's Bay. Almost everybody in the town of Whitby helped, and after three hours of concerted effort, the lifeboat was launched to the aid of the *Visitor*. In spite of the freezing conditions, the casualty was reached successfully and all of its crew were saved in a truly extraordinary rescue.

Although it was used extensively and had been involved in effecting many rescues, the self-righting type of lifeboat had its problems. In order to right in the event of a capsize, it had a relatively narrow beam, and this made it less stable than a non-self-righting lifeboat and thus more prone to capsize in the first place. There were a number of accidents throughout the late 19th century involving this type of lifeboat, many of which were fatal. One of these disasters occurred on 9 December 1886, when lifeboats from Lytham, Southport and St Annes put out to the aid of the same ship. Two of the boats, those from St Annes and Southport, capsized with the loss of 27 lifeboat men.

Following this tragedy, the RNLI re-examined the design of its lifeboats and a new type was introduced that had been designed by George Lennox Watson, the newly appointed Consulting Naval Engineer. Watson's boat sacrificed the self-righting principle in favour of stability – his design was larger, steadier and far less likely to capsize under sail. The new type was seen as comparatively sophisticated compared to the smaller self-righting lifeboat, and with its greater radius of action the number of stations was reduced. However, the future lay with motor-powered lifeboats, but as steam was poorly suited to the job, despite a number of steam lifeboats being built, the newly invented internal combustion engine pointed the way ahead.

Petrol-driven engines were developed during the second half of the 19th century, and were used to power motor vehicles in the 1880s. By the 1900s, therefore, it was inevitable that this new motor power would become a vital element in lifesaving. In 1904 a lifeboat was fitted with an engine for the first time. Although there were many technical problems to be ironed out to operate an engine successfully on board a lifeboat, the numerous setbacks were gradually overcome. In 1908 the first lifeboat to be built with an engine was completed, and by 1914 the number of motor lifeboats in service was well into double figures.

Further advances in design and development were delayed

The 38ft Watson *John Fortune* (ON.523) outside the lifeboat house at Port Errol on Scotland's east coast. *John Fortune* was stationed here until 1921, when the station was permanently closed, one of many closed during the first half of the 19th century. The site of the station can still be seen, but only the boathouse walls and slipway remain intact. *From an old photo supplied by a Shoreline member*

The 47ft Watson *Frederick Edward Crick* (ON.970) moored in the Yacht Basin at Lowestoft. The station provides cover for the notorious sandbanks off the East Anglian coast, and a lifeboat with protected propellers is needed to ensure that the boat can take the ground, if necessary, without damage. *From an old postcard, author's collection*

considerably due to the World War of 1914-18. However, following the cessation of hostilities the RNLI adopted a policy of modernisation that resulted in many new motor lifeboats being built to replace the pulling, sailing and steam lifeboats. As the motor lifeboat had a greater range than its pulling counterpart, the need for multiple stations close together was obviated, and consequently there was a gradual reduction in the number of stations in operation.

Further advances in design suffered delay due to the two World Wars, but there were several valuable improvements during the inter-war years, notably the introduction of twin engines. As the RNLI gained greater experience in the operation of motor lifeboats, more reliable engines were developed to power larger boats that were able to cover greater areas. In the 1920s James Barnett, the RNLI's Consulting Naval Engineer, designed a 60-foot lifeboat that employed twin engines

and twin propellers, eliminating the need for the auxiliary sails that single-engined motor lifeboats carried. In 1932 a diesel engine was fitted to a lifeboat for the first time.

By the outbreak of the Second World War almost the whole of the lifeboat fleet had been motorised as a result of the modernisation programme pursued by the RNLI. However, although relatively well-equipped, the lifeboat service was severely affected by the war. Fund-raising became more difficult, and

One of the earliest motor lifeboats was *Helen Smitton* (ON.603), a small 38ft Watson. This photo shows her leaving the harbour at St Abbs, where she was stationed from 1911 to 1936. She was fitted with a single 34hp petrol engine, which gave her a maximum speed of just over 7 knots. *From an old photo supplied by a Shoreline member*

ST ABBS LIFEBOAT "HELEN SMEATON" LEAVING HARBOUR.

The 52ft Barnett *Joseph Hiram Chadwick* (ON.898) in Padstow harbour. The hull of the Barnett design was similar in shape to that of the first Watson sailing lifeboat built in 1890, albeit somewhat larger. The Barnetts were the first lifeboats in which twin engines and twin propellers were incorporated. *From an old photo supplied by a Shoreline member*

lifeboats were forced to operate in conditions more hazardous than ever. Even routine services were more difficult than in peacetime, so under such conditions it is perhaps not surprising that during the course of the war some of the most outstanding rescues and courageous acts ever performed by lifeboat coxswains and crews took place.

While placing greater demands on lifeboat crews, the war also effectively halted lifeboat construction and development, so that after 1945 there was a need to start building new lifeboats again. Embarking on the building programme for new boats, all of which had twin engines and twin propellers, the RNLI shared the hopes for a better and brighter future that swept the nation in the immediate postwar years. However, despite such optimism, there were a number of notable and tragic lifeboat disasters that prompted greater efforts to improve the design of lifeboats still further.

In April 1947 catastrophe overtook the Mumbles lifeboat, and her entire crew were lost as they went to the aid of a steamship. In February 1953 the lifeboat stationed at Fraserburgh, on the north-east coast of Scotland, was overwhelmed and capsized close to the harbour

entrance, with six of her seven crew lost. Further capsizes occurred at Bridlington in 1952, Arbroath in 1953, Scarborough in 1954 and Seaham Harbour in 1962, all with fatal consequences. As a result of these capsizes, the RNLI reviewed its policy on self-righting lifeboats and increased its efforts to find a better design of lifeboat that would minimise the risks to its crews.

The situation that existed in the 1950s was the result of a combination of historical preferences and an inability to overcome the century-old problem of designing a boat that would self-right if capsized, but also had a high degree of lateral stability to make capsize unlikely in the first place. The majority of the motor lifeboats built up to the mid-1960s were based on Watson's non-self-righting hull shape. The way forward was for lifeboats to be self-righting and yet retain the same lateral stability as the non-self-righting designs.

The answer to the problem was provided by Richard Oakley, the RNLI's Consulting Naval Architect. In the 1950s Oakley designed a lifeboat 37 feet in length that employed a system of water ballast transfer that would right the boat in the event of a capsize. This design, the 37-foot Oakley, entered service in

1958 and represented a major breakthrough because it was the first design of lifeboat that had a high degree of inherent stability, yet would also self-right in the event of a capsize. It represented a significant technological advance, and can thus be regarded as the first of the modern generation of self-righting motor lifeboats.

Although new self-righting lifeboats had been introduced, the chances of a non-self-righting lifeboat capsizing remained, and sadly there were further capsizes. At Longhope and Fraserburgh in 1969 and 1970 respectively, non-self-righting lifeboats capsized in very heavy seas off the coast of Scotland with tragic loss of life. The entire crew of eight from the Longhope boat was lost, while at Fraserburgh it was the second lifeboat disaster in less than two decades. The change to self-righting lifeboats thus became more urgent. The disasters prompted the RNLI to rethink its building policy so that there would be an increase in the construction programme of self-righting lifeboats. Watson and Barnett lifeboats would be fitted with air-bags that would give a once-only self-righting capacity, and this would be part of a policy whereby the fleet of offshore lifeboats would all be self-righting by 1980.

In addition to lifeboats that were self-righting, during the 1960s a completely new type of lifeboat was introduced – the inshore rescue boat. As a result of the growth of the leisure industry, the number of inshore incidents to which lifeboats were called was increasing. The conventional lifeboats were not well suited to such work, and it was clear that a simple, fast rescue craft was required for working inshore. In 1962 the RNLI bought an inflatable boat for extensive trials, and a delegation visited France, where similar boats were in operation, to obtain further advice and see the boats in service. Following these initial steps, the first inshore rescue boats were introduced during the summer of 1963. Such was their success that in each of the subsequent years more and more stations began to operate the boats.

By 1966 the number of inshore rescue boats on station had risen to 72, of which 32 remained on station throughout the year, the rest operating only during the summer. Some of the stations that had been established during the 19th century, but closed following the advent of the motor lifeboat, were re-opened

to operate an inshore lifeboat (as they became known). At other places the ILBs were used to complement the existing offshore lifeboat and undertake rescues close to the shore. The inshore lifeboats were, and still are, hugely successful and carry out a great many rescues every year.

However, by the late 1960s there was a further requirement for a larger inshore lifeboat capable of night operation and greater range, yet retaining the advantages of the standard ILB. After various rigid hulls had been tested, one developed at Atlantic College in South Wales was deemed the most suitable. The boat had a rigid wooden hull with an inflatable sponson attached to it, and had twin outboard engines that enabled a speed of over 30 knots to be achieved, while the sponsons gave the boat great stability. Named the Atlantic 21, the new design was developed and refined by the RNLI, and in 1972 the first went on station at Hartlepool. The advantages of the design soon became apparent and more and more stations now operate Atlantic rigid-inflatables. The importance to the RNLI of these small, fast boats cannot be overstated.

As well as the introduction of the inshore lifeboat, during the 1960s further developments in lifeboat design took place. Following the International Lifeboat Conference at Edinburgh in 1963, the RNLI purchased a 44-foot steel-hulled lifeboat from the United States Coast Guard service for trials around Britain. This boat, self-righting by virtue of its watertight wheelhouse, was faster than and completely different from the conventional lifeboat designs then in service. When it was taken on a tour of stations throughout the British Isles, lifeboat crews' reaction to it was so positive that a building programme was embarked upon. The type was given the class name Waveney and the boats were well-liked at the stations where they served.

The faster a lifeboat, the less time it takes to reach casualties, reducing the chances of a situation deteriorating and making a rescue more difficult. Increased speed was therefore the next goal as the demands on lifeboats continued to change. The Waveney, capable of speeds in excess of 14 knots, was the first of the modern generation of 'fast' lifeboats, but it was soon

Relief D class inflatable lifeboat *Sarah Helena* (D-419) on exercise off Cromer. Small inflatable inshore lifeboats such as this were first introduced into service by the RNLI in 1963 and now form an integral and essential part of the lifeboat service. They are the most numerous type of lifeboat currently in service. *Paul Russell*

Top 44ft Waveney *Barham* (ON.1065), which was stationed at Great Yarmouth & Gorleston between 1980 and 1996, on exercise off the harbour entrance. The Waveney was a radical departure from the conventional displacement-hulled motor lifeboats in service until the 1980s. It had a semi-planing hull, which partly lifted from the water at speed, enabling it to achieve 15 knots, almost twice the speed of existing lifeboats then in service.

Middle The second 52ft Arun to be built, *Sir William Arnold* (ON.1025), moored in the harbour at St Peter Port, where she was stationed between 1973 and 1997. She had a similar hull shape to later Aruns, but had a unique superstructure with the flying bridge aft; the majority of Aruns had the flying bridge further forward and a slightly larger superstructure.

followed by other 'fast' types. During the early 1970s a new 52-foot type was designed and built, and given the class name Arun; it has proved to be one of the finest lifeboat types ever developed for use by the RNLI. Capable of a speed between 18 and 20 knots, the Arun was completely different from anything that had gone before.

During the 1980s two new classes of 'fast' lifeboat were introduced: the 47-foot Tyne and 12-metre Mersey, intended for stations that practised slipway and carriage launching. Both designs are capable of speeds of more than 16 knots, are self-righting and provide fully enclosed protection for both crew and survivors. With the introduction of 'fast' lifeboats that could be slipway and carriage launched, in 1986 a target date of 1993 was set by when it was intended to have 'fast' lifeboats operating from every station equipped with an all-weather lifeboat. Fast all-weather lifeboats are now the norm, and the RNLI extended its declared area of coverage from 30 to 50 miles offshore during the 1990s. The change from slower displacement to the fast lifeboats, of which the Waveney was the first, is as significant a development as the

Bottom Newbiggin's Atlantic 75 *CSMA 75th Anniversary* (B-745) in Newbiggin Bay.

Top Fleetwood's 47ft Tyne *William Street* (ON.1156) leaving her station on exercise.

Middle Humber's 17m Severn *Pride of the Humber* (ON.1216) at Spurn Point after arriving on station in 1998, with Coxswain Brian Bevan at the wheel.

Bottom 14m Trent *Henry Hayes Duckworth* (ON.1213) on exercise off Gorleston harbour. The Trent, one of the latest classes of fast lifeboats, is capable of speeds of up to 25 knots.

introduction of the motor lifeboat during the first half of the 20th century.

The demand on the RNLI's services increased considerably during the last two decades of the 20th century: during the 1990s lifeboats launched more than 6,000 times a year and saved on average 1,500 lives. To meet this demand, a new generation of even faster all-weather lifeboat was designed, and the 14m Trent and 17m Severn classes were introduced in the 1990s, intended to operate from stations where they will lie afloat on moorings. The new designs reach speeds of up to 25 knots as well as operating in the worst of weathers. They share similar hull characteristics, the smaller being a scaled-down version of the larger, and are constructed of fibre-reinforced composite, which is an exceptionally strong, yet light, material.

As the RNLI prepares for the 21st century, the Institution can look back on the last 175 years with pride and satisfaction at what has been achieved in the field of lifesaving at sea. Since its inception, RNLI lifeboats have launched 171,282 times on service and saved 132,758 lives. No doubt Sir William Hillary, who had the foresight to found a national lifeboat service in 1824, would be proud of the service today. The coverage of the coast is better than it has ever been, the lifeboats are more sophisticated, and the equipment used more effective. The voluntary crews remain as dedicated as they always were, and the lifeboat men and women, who are prepared to stop whatever they are doing at a moment's notice to put to sea, demonstrate most ably that Sir William's vision has been realised.

Explanatory notes to the entries

Key dates

Due to the vagaries of history and the continued improvements in lifeboat design, keeping track of the opening and closing of each of the RNLI's lifeboat stations is not a straightforward task. Many stations were opened, closed, then re-opened in response to the changing pattern of casualties, then closed again. Many stations have had neither an all-weather lifeboat nor a motor lifeboat, although it is indicated if a station had either but no longer has them.

Opened   The year in which the lifeboat station was established, when a lifeboat was first operated.

RNLI   The year when a station came under the management of the RNLI; if this date is the same as the 'Opened' year, it follows that the RNLI was responsible for the station's opening. If the date is before 1854, the RNIPLS (as the RNLI was known up to that time) would have been responsible for the station's establishment.

Motor LB   The year when a station began to operate a motor lifeboat.

AWLB withdrawn   The year that the all-weather lifeboat was withdrawn; many stations that operated these lifeboats, which included pulling and sailing lifeboats, were closed when the lifeboat was withdrawn but have since re-opened as inshore lifeboat stations.

Fast LB   The year that a 'fast' lifeboat went on station; 'fast' lifeboats are those capable of speeds of 13 knots and over. These craft are described in their historical context in the previous section, and their technical details are listed in Appendix 3.

Inshore LB   The year that an inshore lifeboat first went on station; some stations operate two or three ILBs.

ro   The year a station was re-opened.

Current lifeboat details

The details of the lifeboat or lifeboats operated at each station are accurate as of 4 March 1999. The entries contain the following information:

Type   Information about the different lifeboat types can be found in Appendix 3.

Official Number   The number allocated to every new lifeboat built by the RNLI.

Operational Number   The first two digits indicate the class of lifeboat, and refer to the type's hull length; for example, 52-?? indicates a 52ft Arun, while 12-?? indicates a 12m Mersey (recently the numbers indicating the class have been in metric measurements). The number after the hyphen, unique to the individual lifeboat, indicates the number of that boat within its class; for example 52-42 indicates the 42nd boat of the 52ft Arun class; 17-06, the 6th boat of the 17m Severn class, and so on. A zero is added, giving three digits after the hyphen, to differentiate between a steel-hulled boat and a non steel-hulled (wood, glass fibre, etc) boat; for example, lifeboats of the 47ft Tyne class (built of steel) are numbered 47-009, 47-018, and so on. Lifeboats constructed of other materials are numbered with only two digits; for example, lifeboats of the 14m Trent class (built of fibre-reinforced composite) are numbered 14-08, 14-16, and so on.

Year built   The year the lifeboat was built.

Name   The name of the lifeboat; this is usually chosen by the lifeboat's donor, who may be an individual, an organisation or a fund-raising branch of the RNLI. Some lifeboats are named after famous individuals who have been involved with the RNLI in some capacity.

Donor   The individual, organisation or other group who provided the funding for the lifeboat.

Placed on station   The date that the lifeboat was officially placed on station; with modern lifeboats, this is usually some days or weeks after the boat has actually arrived at its station, as the crew have to train on the new boat and become familiar with the equipment on board.

Launch   The method of launching employed to get the boat afloat. Descriptions of the different launching methods are given below.

Location history

The location history gives a résumé of the different sites and boathouses of a particular station. Some stations have been located at several different places. Their relocations may have come about as a result of the adoption of a different launch method or a new lifeboat being operated. Major alterations to boathouses have usually been included, but it has not been possible to include details of every alteration.

Where an old lifeboat house is still in existence, details have been included. Where a current station had links with or took over the area covered by an adjacent station that has since been closed, details of the closed station have usually been given. It should be noted that details of only a few closed lifeboat stations have been included, while many have had to be omitted.

Medals and awards

Although the history of the RNLI's medals is a complex subject in itself that cannot be dealt with fully here, the following brief explanations should assist readers in interpreting information in the entries for individual stations.

The presenting of medals to reward acts of outstanding bravery performed by lifeboat crews and meritorious actions by anyone saving lives at sea began with the founding of the Institution. The idea was first suggested by the Institution's founder, Sir William Hillary. In his Appeal to the British Nation, published in 1823, Hillary suggested that a medal or badge 'might have a very powerful effect [in inducing men] to render their utmost aid to the shipwrecked of every land, in the moment of their extreme distress.'

The Gold and Silver Medals were introduced at the founding meeting of the Institution, at which a Resolution was passed stating 'that Medallions or Pecuniary rewards be given to those who rescue Lives in cases of shipwreck'. The first medals for gallantry to be awarded by the newly formed National Institution for the Preservation of Life from Shipwreck (renamed RNLI in 1854, see above) were voted at a meeting of the Institution's Committee of Management on 10 July 1825. At that meeting a Gold Medal was voted to Commander Charles Freemantle, and three Silver Medals were voted to seamen William Rowe and James Freeman, and Master Mariner Charles Watts, for rescues in which they had been involved. Since then, the RNLI has continued to reward the bravest acts of lifesaving at sea with medals. Between 1824 and 4 March 1999, 120 Gold Medals, 1,549 Silver Medals and 770 Bronze Medals were awarded by the RNLI for gallantry. There have also been honorary awards of 29 Gold and eight Silver Medals.

The Gold Medal is the RNLI's highest award for gallantry, and its award 'will be recommended for a rescue which has been effected as the result of an act in which outstanding courage, skill and initiative has been shown. It may also be recommended when life has not been saved if altogether exceptional courage has been shown.' The Silver Medal is awarded 'for an act of outstanding merit which just falls short of the standard required for the Gold Medal.' The Bronze Medal, which

was not introduced until 1917, is awarded 'for an act of conspicuous gallantry and courage which just falls short of the standard required for the Silver Medal.' The Thanks of the Institution Inscribed on Vellum (Thanks on Vellum) is a framed certificate on parchment signed by the current President and Chairman of the Institution, and is accorded to individuals when a rescue, although meritorious, does not warrant the award of a medal.

In addition to recognising outstanding acts of bravery performed by its own lifeboat crews, the RNLI awards medals in instances when a rescue has been performed without the involvement of a lifeboat. Such rescues are termed shore rescues or shore-boat rescues, as they have been performed either by persons from the shore, using equipment such as rocket line-throwers to reach the casualty, or by persons using small craft or boats not designated as rescue boats but the only craft available at the time.

Some medals have been awarded to individuals for long service, and there have been a number of Honorary Gold and Silver Medals awarded for a variety of reasons. For example, some foreign lifeboat societies have been presented with medals on their centenaries, HM Coastguard was awarded the Gold Medal in 1972 to mark its 150th anniversary, and various individuals, such as Presidents of the RNLI, have been given honorary awards. Information about these honorary awards has not been included in the entries as such awards are not associated with any particular station.

Notable rescue

The notable rescue described is often only one of many outstanding rescues that the lifeboat men and women of a particular station have performed. Unfortunately, space precludes descriptions of more than one such rescue for each station. The

official number (ON) of all-weather lifeboats involved in rescues can be found in the Index.

Launch methods

There are three main ways of launching an all-weather lifeboat: from an afloat berth or mooring, down a slipway, or from a carriage pushed across the beach.

Launching an afloat boat is fairly straightforward; it involves the crew boarding the boat, dropping the mooring and putting to sea. This is how the majority of lifeboats are launched, and it is the RNLI's preferred method of launching all-weather lifeboats.

Where it is not possible for a lifeboat to be kept afloat, it is either launched down a slipway or from a carriage. For a slipway launch, the lifeboat is kept at the head of a slipway in a boathouse, above the water. To launch, the lifeboat is released from the securing chains and runs freely down the slipway into deep water. To recover, the lifeboat is manoeuvred until the keel is on the bottom of the slipway, then a cable is attached to the keel. Once this is secure, the boat is hauled stern-first up the slipway by a winch and into the boathouse where the securing chains are attached.

Where the only way to launch a boat is across a beach or through a harbour that is dry at low tide, the lifeboat is floated by means of a specialised carriage that is pushed by a waterproofed caterpillar-tracked tractor. The lifeboat is secured on the carriage by chains that are released once the carriage is in sufficient depth of water for the lifeboat to float. Some beaches are very steep and a launch can take place at the shoreline, as at Dungeness; other beaches are very shallow and the lifeboat has to be pushed for a considerable distance until the water is deep enough for it to be launched, as at Hoylake.

There is one exception to the

THE MARGATE LIFEBOAT, 'NORTH FORELAND'. (*Civil Service No. 11.*)

THE LIFEBOAT WALMER

Above left The spectacular sight of a slipway launch is one of the most enduring images from the RNLI's history. Here, the 46ft 9in Watson *North Foreland (Civil Service No.11)* (ON.888) hits the water after leaving the lifeboat house at Margate. *From an old postcard, author's collection*

Above 42ft Beach *Charles Dibdin (Civil Service No.32)* (ON.948) on the launching cradle at the top of Walmer beach. At several stations the lifeboat was launched over the beach from a cradle, with skids laid to ease the passage into the water. This practice was discontinued in 1993. *From an old postcard, author's collection*

Left 12m Mersey *Doris M. Mann of Ampthill* (ON.1161) being recovered on the beach at Wells-next-the-Sea. The Mersey class was designed to serve at stations that practised carriage launching. The propellers were protected by bilge keels and partial tunnels so that when the boat was beached they would not suffer any damage. *Paul Russell*

above three methods of launching. At Workington the lifeboat is lowered into the water by a unique launching crane. The lifeboat rests on a cradle mounted on rails, and is moved out of the boathouse on this cradle to a position beneath the launching crane. It is then lifted up by the gantry, rather like a container crane, and lowered into a tidal basin where there is sufficient depth of water to launch the boat at all states of the tide.

Several different ways are employed to launch inshore lifeboats (ILBs). Many Atlantic rigid-inflatable ILBs are launched from a drive-on drive-off ('do-do') carriage that is hauled across an open beach by specially designed and constructed launching tractors.

At most stations one of two types of waterproofed tractor are used to

launch Atlantics: the Biglands Talus 4WH is a specially designed hydrostatic tractor that provides a fully enclosed watertight position for the driver, and the Biglands Talus MB-764, which is based on the Ford County agricultural tractor. Where conditions are most severe, such as at Minehead and Aberdovey, where the beach is unusually steep, a more powerful Case 1150B tractor is used. At a few stations where a relatively sheltered launch site is available, standard agricultural tractors, which do not need to be waterproofed, are employed.

At three stations, Atlantics are kept in floating boathouses, in which the lifeboat is kept clear of the water by a cradle that is lowered and raised to launch and recover the boat.

D class inflatable ILBs are floated by more varied means. Many are pushed into the water on a trolley, which is either manhandled to the

launch site or towed there by a Honda quadbike. Where the beach is too exposed for such launching, an ordinary agricultural tractor is used to push the ILB into the water. At some stations the ILB is towed on its trolley by a Land Rover, which can take the boat to the launch site nearest to the casualty; this may involve travelling by road, which is often faster than through the water. This makes the ILBs very mobile and enables them to cover large areas, such as a river estuary.

Many ILBs are launched by davit. The ILB is kept in a boathouse on a trolley, which is moved into position beneath the davit. The ILB is then attached to the davit by means of strops, and the davit lifts the boat off the trolley, swivels over the water, and the ILB is lowered down until it floats. Both D class and Atlantic 21/75 ILBs can be davit launched.

Part 1
East Coast of England:
Berwick to Hastings

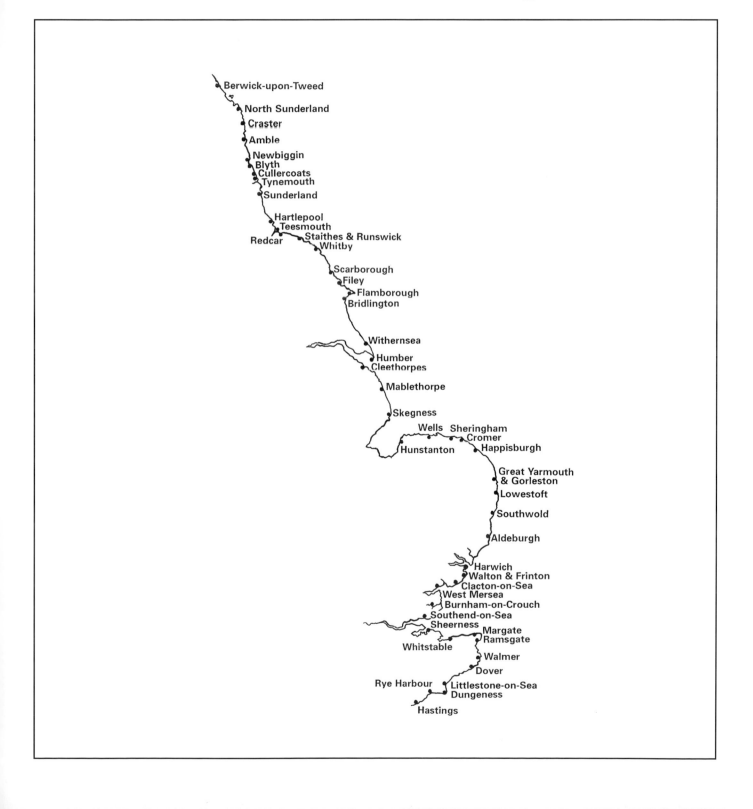

Key dates

Opened	1835
RNLI	1855
Motor LB	1930-76 and 1993
AWLB withdrawn	1976-93
Fast LB	1993
Inshore LB	4.1967-93 and 1995

Current lifeboat details

All-weather lifeboat

Type	Mersey
Official Number	1191
Operational Number	12-32
Year built	1993
Name	Joy and Charles Beeby
Donor	Legacy of Mr Charles Beeby, of Long Itchington, Warks
Placed on station	5.2.1993
Launch	Slipway

Inshore lifeboat

Type	D class inflatable
Official Number	D-494
Name	Sunrise
Donor	Bequest of Mr Charles Beeby
Placed on station	30.3.1996
Launch	Davit

Location history

1835 The first lifeboat house was located on the south side of the Rivern Tweed at Spittal beach, near the Coastguard station.

1859 A new lifeboat house was built at Spittal by the RNLI, who took over the station in 1855; this enabled a launch into the outer harbour. This house was used until 1901 and has since been converted into a garage.

1901 The lifeboat was moved to the Berwick side of the river owing to the difficulty experienced in obtaining a crew at Spittal; a new lifeboat house was built at Ferry Landing and this was used until 1930; it is still standing, and is used as a private residence.

1930 The station was moved back to the south side of the river and a new boathouse with a roller slipway on concrete pillars was built near Spittal beach.

1939 The 1930 boathouse was moved to Carr Rock Jetty, and was altered for the first motor lifeboat.

1967 An inshore lifeboat station was established in April; the ILB was kept in a small house at Spittal, close to the 1859 boathouse and the Sailing Club, until 1976.

1976 The all-weather lifeboat was withdrawn on 17 September and an Atlantic 21 was placed on station; it was kept in the 1930 boathouse, which was converted to accommodate it, until 1993.

1993 The Atlantic 21 was withdrawn on 5 February and the station reverted to operating an all weather-lifeboat; the 1930 house was converted to house a 12m Mersey class lifeboat; this included the removal of the existing winch and installation of a new Bigland hydraulic winch, the construction of an external housing for the winch engine, a new access stair and viewing gallery, and the installation of a new fuel storage tank.

1995 A D class inshore lifeboat was supplied in May, and a new house for the ILB was built on Carr Rock Jetty, close to the 1939 lifeboat house.

Medals and awards

Eight medals have been awarded, one Gold, six Silver and one Bronze.

Notable rescue

On 29 March 1913 the lifeboat *Matthew Simpson* was launched to the Swedish barque *Jacob Ruers*, of Gothenburg, which had been stranded on rocks.

She arrived at the casualty just as attempts by the rocket brigade were being abandoned. The lifeboat veered down to the casualty, over which heavy seas were breaking, until a rope could be passed. Using the lifebuoy, 11 men were hauled from the barque to the safety of the lifeboat.

For this rescue, the Silver Medal was awarded to Coxswain Robert Burgon, who, together with Second Coxswain James Jamieson, also received Swedish Government Silver Medals.

12m Mersey *Joy and Charles Beeby* (ON.1191) in the River Tweed in 1995, with Berwick's three distinctive bridges in the background.

Key dates

Opened	1827
RNLI	1859
Motor LB	1936
Fast LB	1991
Inshore LB	1964

Current lifeboat details

All-weather lifeboat

Type	Mersey
Official Number	1173
Operational Number	12-16
Year built	1990
Name	*Grace Darling*
Donor	Provided by the Grace Darling

150th Anniversary Appeal, together with other special gifts and legacies

Placed on station	7.8.1991
Launch	Carriage

Inshore lifeboat

Type	D class inflatable
Official Number	D-529
Name	*Martin, John and Ann*
Donor	Gift of J. G. Lynch, Edinburgh
Placed on station	4.11.1997
Launch	Trolley

Location history

1827 The station was established by the Crewe Trustees; a stone lifeboat house was built during the early 1830s in the fishing village of Seahouses, close to the harbour; this house was rebuilt in 1879, and was used until 1935; it was demolished in the 1960s.

1935 A new lifeboat house was built at the north end of Seahouses harbour; this house was used until 1993 and was then demolished.

1964 An inshore lifeboat station was established in May; an ILB house was built adjacent to the 1935 house; it was used until 1993.

1993 A new lifeboat house for the 12m Mersey class lifeboat and inshore lifeboat was built on the site of the 1935 house, which was demolished; it includes toilets, showers, a kitchen, crew room, drying room, a new workshop and a souvenir sales outlet.

Medals and awards

Four medals have been awarded, three Silver and one Bronze.

Notable rescue

Early on the morning of 18 February 1908 the lifeboat *Forster Fawsett* was launched to the steamship *Geir*, of Bergen, which had stranded on Knavestone Rock, Farne Islands, in a northerly gale and very heavy seas.

In approaching the casualty, great care was needed because of the number of rocks and the strong currents. The rocks made it impossible for the lifeboat to go alongside the casualty so she was taken by her Coxswain, James Robson, to a small rock near the steamer.

The lifeboat men managed to get the lifeboat alongside the rock where some were landed. They took a lifebuoy and ropes with them, after which the lifeboat moved away to a safer position and dropped anchor.

The crew of 14 from the steamer were then transferred on to the rocks by means of lines fired by the lifeboat men; then one by one they got into the lifebuoy and were hauled through the sea to the lifeboat. Coxswain Robson was the last to leave the rock.

For this rescue the Silver Medal was awarded to Coxswain Robson; he was also awarded a Silver Medal by the King of Norway.

Background information

The station is perhaps most famous for its connection with Grace Darling, as it is the nearest operational lifeboat station to the Longstone Lighthouse. Men from Seahouses made an attempt to rescue the survivors of the steamship *Forfarshire*, which had been wrecked on 7 September 1838 on the Farne Islands. Seven fishermen put out to the wreck, only to find that the survivors had already been rescued by William and Grace Darling, who had set out from the Longstone Lighthouse.

12m Mersey *Grace Darling* (ON.1173) at sea off Seahouses harbour during the station's annual Lifeboat Day in 1994.

The lifeboat house built for the Mersey lifeboat in 1991 in Seahouses harbour, on the site of the previous house.

Current lifeboat details

Inshore lifeboat

Type	D class inflatable
Official Number	D-542
Name	A B One
Donor	The John Bagley Appeal
Placed on station	3.2.1999
Launch	Trolley

Location history

1969 An ILB station was established in August, and an ILB house built in the harbour.

1992-3 A new ILB house was built on the same site as the previous house, on the landward side of the coast road, at the edge of the harbour.

Medals and awards

No medals have been awarded.

Notable rescue

On 1 May 1982 the D class inshore lifeboat D-228 was launched to three fishermen who were stranded after their dinghy had been blown on to the Embleston Rocks in a west-north-westerly gale force 7 wind and rough seas. The ILB had to travel at reduced speed because of the seas, but once the men had been sighted it was taken in to the rocks and the three men were safely taken on board. The survivors were landed at Newton Haven Bay and the ILB returned to station.

Only 15 minutes later the ILB was again launched, this time to a dinghy that had capsized off Newton Haven after hitting a submerged rock and a man had been thrown into the water. The ILB arrived on the scene and began a search of the area, encountering high seas in the force 7 wind that was still blowing. After discovering that the man had got ashore safely, the ILB returned to station.

For these rescues a framed letter of appreciation signed by the Chairman of the RNLI, the Duke of Atholl, was presented to Helmsman Neil Robson and crew member Keith Williams for the skill and determination they displayed in carrying out this difficult service.

The inshore lifeboat house built in 1993 in the harbour for the D class inflatable.

Location history

1842 The first lifeboat was kept in a house located close to the beach, which also had living accommodation above; the lifeboat was removed in 1856, but the house still stands in use as a private residence.

1939 The station was re-opened with a motor lifeboat, but no boathouse was built as the lifeboat was kept afloat at moorings, Amble Harbour having been well dredged by the Air Ministry. The lifeboat is still kept afloat, moored alongside Radcliffe Quay at the seaward end, on the south side of the river Coquet.

1966 An inshore lifeboat station was established in May; the ILB was housed in the yacht club premises.

1985-6 A new ILB house was built at Radcliffe Quay and a new berth was built adjacent for the all-weather lifeboat.

Medals and awards

Four medals have been awarded, all Bronze.

Notable rescue

On 29 September 1969 the D class inshore lifeboat D-51 was launched to the RAF pinnace No 1386, which had capsized half a mile from Amble North Pier while attempting to turn into a heavy breaking swell. The ILB proceeded at full speed towards the casualty, followed by the lifeboat *Millie Walton*.

Once on the scene, the ILB spotted and immediately picked up two survivors who were clinging to a lifebuoy. They then began to search for other survivors from the pinnace. After radioing for further assistance,

Key dates

Opened	1842-56; ro1939
RNLI	1939
Motor LB	1939
Fast LB	1986
Inshore LB	5.1966

Current lifeboat details

All-weather lifeboat

Type	Waveney
Official Number	1004
Operational Number	44-005
Year built	1967
Name	Margaret Graham
Donor	An anonymous gift to record the friendship of William H. Cavenaugh, Hazel M. Dugan, Theodore L. and Margaret N. Harley with the donor
Placed on station	9.6.1986
Launch	Afloat

Inshore lifeboat

Type	D class inflatable
Official Number	D-447
Name	Thomas Campbell
Donor	Bequest of Mr Edwin Ramsden
Placed on station	2.6.1993
Launch	Davit

Above 44ft Waveney *Margaret Graham* (ON.1004) moored alongside Radcliffe Quay in 1989.
Tony Denton

Right The ILB house built in 1986 at Radcliffe Quay, close to the all-weather lifeboat moorings.

the ILB returned to the harbour, where the two survivors were landed.

It was feared that three of the crew were still trapped under the upturned craft, so efforts were made to reach them by skin-divers. This proved impossible due to the tide and heavy swell. The lifeboat was taken alongside the casualty, and picked up one survivor who was clinging to the hull. She then towed the wreck into the harbour where RN divers using cutter gear cut through the bottom of the pinnace and freed one more survivor.

Despite establishing that there were no more men inside the hull, three of the crew were still missing. A search for them continued throughout the night, with both Newbiggin and Amble lifeboats involved. Sadly, the three bodies

were later found among rocks by shore searchers.

For this rescue, Bronze Medals were awarded to Coxswain William Henderson and crew members James Stewart, Andrew Scott and Robert Stewart; the Thanks on Vellum was accorded to Second Coxswain John Connell, Acting Bowman Ronald Falcous, Mechanic Ronald Sabiston, Assistant Mechanic Hugh Matthews, and crew member Hugh R. Matthews; framed letters of appreciation signed by the Chairman were presented to skin-divers J. B. Sample and E. Bramhan.

This was the first service performed using an inshore lifeboat for which medals were awarded by the RNLI.

Background information

The lifeboat station at Amble was re-established in 1939 following the closure of the station at Hauxley 2 miles to the south. The latter had been established in 1852 and the lifeboat was launched by carriage across the beach. The lifeboat house used throughout the life of the station still stands and is used as a private residence. The official closure date was 17 January 1939, with a record of 81 launches and 246 lives saved.

Key dates

Opened	1852
RNLI	1853
Motor LB	1938-81
AWLB withdrawn	26.2.1981
Inshore LB	3.1981

Current lifeboat details

Inshore lifeboat

Type	Atlantic 75
Official Number	B-745
Name	CSMA 75th Anniversary
Donor	Civil Service Motoring Association and Frizzell Financial Services
Placed on station	5.8.1998
Launch	Tractor and do-do carriage

Location history

1852 A lifeboat house was built at the eastern end of the Promenade, near Church Point overlooking Newbiggin Bay, with doors at either end; this boathouse has been used, with various additions and alterations, throughout the life of the station.

1937 The lifeboat house was extensively altered for the station's first motor lifeboat; it was lengthened, the rear doors were removed and a mechanic's workshop was built.

1949 A tractor house was built on to the east wall of the lifeboat house.

1964 The lifeboat house was adapted to accommodate a 37ft Oakley class lifeboat; this included raising the main door lintel, lengthening the doors, and the provision of a toilet.

1981 The lifeboat house was adapted to accommodate an Atlantic 21 lifeboat and launching tractor; the extension to the boathouse was also converted to provide improved crew facilities.

1998 The lifeboat house was extensively modified, and a new crew building was built on the east side.

Medals and awards

Ten medals have been awarded, nine Silver and one Bronze.

Notable rescue

On 4 February 1940 the lifeboat *Augustus and Laura* was launched, with Second Coxswain George R. Taylor in command, to the motor vessel *Eminent*, which had been driven ashore near Newbiggin Point.

Unable to make any headway through the breaking sea and gale-force winds, the boat was re-carriaged and taken overland to another beach from which she was successfully launched. On this occasion she reached the casualty safely, and using the lines thrown on board, saved the motor vessel's crew of 11.

For this service Second Coxswain Taylor was awarded the Silver Medal, and the Thanks on Vellum was accorded to the launchers, many of whom were women, who had helped to drag the lifeboat across moors and sand dunes to enable it to be launched.

Atlantic 75 *CSMA 75th Anniversary* (B-745) on the do-do carriage in front of the refurbished lifeboat house, being launched at the end of her Naming Ceremony on 2 August 1998.

Blyth

Northumberland

Location history

1808 A lifeboat was first established by Sir Matthew Ridley; he funded a boat and a boathouse, built close to the High Light on the south side of the River Blyth, near the high-water mark. The lifeboat was wrecked on service on 31 March 1810.

1826 Another lifeboat was stationed at Blyth, funded by the Port of Newcastle Shipwreck Association, and from 1845 managed by the Blyth Lifeboat Association. The boat was kept in a boathouse on the 1808 site; this house was found to be in a poor state when the RNLI took over the station in 1866.

1866 The first boathouse was renovated and lengthened; it was used until 1898.

1898 The first boathouse was demolished during harbour improvements, and a new lifeboat house was built in the South Docks, with a launchway into the Dock; this house was used until 1920, and is still standing.

Key dates

Opened	1808-10 and 1826
RNLI	1866
Motor LB	1921
Fast LB	1982
Inshore LB	5.1965

Current lifeboat details

All-weather lifeboat

Type	Trent
Official Number	1204
Operational Number	14-06
Year built	1994
Name	Windsor Runner
	(Civil Service No.42)
Donor	Civil Service, Post Office and British Telecom Lifeboat Fund, named to mark the success of the half marathons, with other legacies and RNLI funds
Placed on station	21.12.1995
Launch	Afloat

Inshore lifeboat

Type	D class inflatable
Official Number	D-464
Year built	1994
Name	Wren
Donor	Sinclair Roche & Temperley
Placed on station	20.7.1994
Launch	Slipway

1920 A new lifeboat house and slipway were built near to the Pilot Watch House, at what is now the North gate of the South Harbour; this house was used for the all-weather lifeboat until 1982, and has been converted to house the inshore lifeboat.

1965 An inshore lifeboat station was established in May; the ILB was kept in a small house adjacent to the 1920 boathouse until 1979.

1979 A new ILB house was constructed; this house was used until the ILB was moved into the 1920 boathouse.

1982 A permanent mooring in the River Blyth, upstream from the 1920 boathouse, was taken up.

Medals and awards

Eleven medals have been awarded, eight Silver and three Bronze.

Notable rescue

On 18 November 1962 the coaster *Paulgate* got into difficulties off the Blyth Fairway Buoy in a severe gale. The lifeboat *Winston Churchill (Civil Service No.8)* was launched under the command of Coxswain Thomas Fawcus and battled her way out of the harbour into some exceptionally heavy seas to go to the aid of the coaster.

On reaching the scene, the Coxswain assessed the situation, as the coaster's cargo had shifted and the vessel had developed a list. The lifeboat was then taken alongside the coaster, and despite its unpredictable rolling, two men were taken off, although the lifeboat sustained some damage.

The master was still on board, and he requested an escort so that he could head south for the safety of the River Tyne, although his ship was in danger of capsizing. The lifeboat escorted the coaster south, but at the mouth of the Tyne the *Paulgate* ran out of fuel, and was in grave danger of being washed on to the rocks.

The lifeboat was taken alongside again, and the Bowman, John Kerr, was put on board the coaster. He secured a line to the lifeboat, which managed to hold the casualty clear of the rocks until a tug arrived. Another lifeboat man, Signalman C. Hurst, was also put on board the casualty to assist with the towing operation.

For this rescue the Silver Medal was awarded to Coxswain Fawcus; the Bronze Medal was awarded to Bowman John Kerr, who also received the Maud Smith award; and Thanks on Vellums were accorded to the rest of the lifeboat's crew, Second Coxswain Samuel Crawford, Mechanic James Skinner, Assistant Mechanic William Henry and crew members J. Skinner Jnr, J. Henderson and C. Hurst.

Background information

The Blyth No.2 station was located at Cambois, to the north of the mouth of the River Blyth, where a lifeboat house was built on the foreshore. This house was demolished in the 1920s, but two stone memorial tablets from the building were saved and are now displayed outside the Dock Master's Office at Blyth, close to the lifeboat station.

The lifeboat house and slipway built in 1920 at the South Harbour, used until 1982 and since converted for the inshore lifeboat.

Cullercoats

Key dates

Opened	1852
RNLI	1853
Motor LB	1937-69
AWLB withdrawn	4.5.1969
Inshore LB	5.1965

Current lifeboat details

Inshore lifeboat

Type	Atlantic 21
Official Number	B-591
Name	Edmund and Joan White
Donor	Bequest of the late Edmund White, South Shields
Placed on station	1.10.1992
Launch	Tractor and do-do carriage

Location history

1852 The first lifeboat house was built; it was used until 1866.

1866 A new lifeboat house was built, located at the foot of the cliffs in the small bay at Cullercoats; this house was used until 1896.

1896 A new lifeboat house of an ornamental design with a turret was built on the site of the earlier houses; it was modified in 1963 for the 37ft Oakley class lifeboat.

1965 An inshore lifeboat station was established in May; the ILB was kept in the lifeboat house.

1992 The lifeboat house was converted to house an Atlantic 21 and launching tractor.

Medals and awards

Four medals have been awarded, all Silver.

Notable rescue

On 1 May 1991, while the relief Atlantic 21 inshore lifeboat B-514 *Guide Friendship I* was on exercise, it was called to help a windsurfer in trouble close to the entrance to the River Tyne in a force 6 wind with a 10-foot swell in the area. The windsurfer was found close to the pier clinging to his board. Despite heavy seas rebounding off the pier, the helmsman skilfully took the ILB into the broken water and saved the windsurfer.

Meanwhile, the Yacht Club rescue boat, which was also on hand, had capsized. Although it had been righted by its crew of two, they could not restart the engine. The ILB therefore took the disabled boat under tow to Tynemouth Haven, where all three survivors were landed.

For this rescue a letter of appreciation from the RNLI's Director, Lieut Commander Brian Miles, was sent to those involved. A letter of congratulations was also sent by the District Staff Officer of the Coastguard.

Background information

On 22 April 1939 the lifeboat *Richard Silver Oliver* capsized on exercise in a moderate north-easterly gale off Sharpeness Point. Of the ten people on board, four managed to struggle to shore but sadly the other six, including the Coxswain and Honorary Secretary, were drowned. There is a memorial window in the local Methodist Church to those lost.

All-weather lifeboats were stationed at Cullercoats between 1852 and 1969, during which time they were credited with 187 service launches and 354 lives saved.

Atlantic 21 *Edmund and Joan White* (B-591) being taken across the beach for an exercise launch.

Tynemouth

Location history

1932 The first lifeboat was kept in a boathouse at Prior's Haven, beneath the ruins of Tynemouth Priory.

1862 A new lifeboat house was built at Prior's Haven, on the same site; this house was used until 1905, has since been sold to the Tynemouth Sailing Club, and is still in existence.

1865 A No.2 station was established; a lifeboat house was built under the Spanish Battery, used until closure in August 1905.

1905 An experimental motor lifeboat was sent for trials, and kept afloat at moorings in the River Tyne until 1921.

1921 An existing boathouse was acquired at Clifford's Fort, in which the lifeboat was kept; a trolley-way was built for a trolley launch.

Key dates

Opened	1832
RNLI	1862
Motor LB	1905
Fast LB	1980
Inshore LB	4.1965

Current lifeboat details

All-weather lifeboat

Type	Arun
Official Number	1061
Operational Number	52-13
Year built	1979
Name	George and Olive Turner
Donor	Legacy from Mrs O. B. Turner, the Sir James Knott Trust, the Tyneside Lifeboat Appeal, and other gifts and legacies
Placed on station	22.2.1980
Launch	Afloat

Inshore lifeboat

Type	D class inflatable
Official Number	D-535
Name	Smugglers of Cromer
Donor	Cromer Smugglers
Placed on station	19.8.1998
Launch	Davit

1941 On 10 April the 1921 house and the lifeboat inside were destroyed during an air raid on Newcastle. Until 1947 the lifeboat was kept in the open on the trolley-way, which was repaired after the air raid.

1947 A new lifeboat house and roller slipway were built on the same site; the lifeboat was housed here until 1979, after which it was used for boarding boats and the station's inshore lifeboat until October 1997, when it was demolished and the slipway removed.

1965 An inshore lifeboat station was established in May; the ILB was kept in a small boathouse built in 1965 close to the Old Watch House.

1979 Moorings for a new fast afloat lifeboat were taken up at South Shields, and the lifeboat was reached by boarding-boat from North Shields.

1984 A pontoon berth was provided for the lifeboat at the Fish Quay, North Shields, outside the Harbour Commissioners Offices, with a crew room on the adjacent quayside; the lifeboat was kept here until 1998.

1998 A new lifeboat house, combining crew facilities, accommodation for the ILB with a launch davit, and an all-weather lifeboat mooring berth, was built at the eastern jetty of the Fish Quay, North Shields.

Medals and awards

Fifteen medals have been awarded, two Gold, nine Silver and four Bronze.

Eight medals have been awarded for shore-boat rescues, six Silver and two Bronze.

Notable rescue

The Tynemouth lifeboat undertook many difficult rescues during the First World War, including a very arduous service in November 1916. On 19 November, the steamship *Muristan* ran ashore at Blyth Bay when her steering gear broke during a strong gale and heavy sea. The lifeboat *Henry Vernon* was launched on 20 November and only managed to clear the harbour entrance with difficulty due to the severe conditions prevailing.

The lifeboat arrived off Blyth but could not approach or go alongside the wreck because of the large amount of debris surrounding it. As the lifeboat returned to her station, having seen no sign of life on board the casualty, she was hit by a huge wave that caused her engine to stop. She was then forced to put into Blyth overnight, where her engines were repaired by the mechanic.

On 21 November the lifeboat again went to the wreck, signs of life having been seen on board. The weather conditions had moderated slightly, so the lifeboat was taken alongside to find the 16 crew huddled together in the remains of the chart house. The lifeboat succeeded in rescuing all of them, and they were landed at Blyth.

For this outstanding rescue, the Silver medal was awarded to Coxswain Smith and Second Coxswain James Brownlee; additional monetary awards were given to the other lifeboatmen who took part.

Background information

The first purpose-built lifeboat was operated from South Shields at the mouth of the Tyne from 1790 under the auspices of the Tyne Lifeboat Institution. This organisation funded a second lifeboat for North Shields in 1798, and for more than 30 years they undertook many rescues in and around the estuary.

Another first for Tynemouth came in 1905, when the RNLI's first motor lifeboat, *J. McConnell Hussey*, a pulling and sailing lifeboat fitted with a motor, was placed on station.

Tynemouth's shore facility and ILB house built in 1998 adjacent to the mooring berth at the eastern jetty of the Fish Quay, North Shields.

Key dates

Opened	1800
RNLI	1865
Motor LB	1916
Fast LB	1990
Inshore LB	5.1966

Current lifeboat details

All-weather lifeboat

Type	Trent
Official Number	1225
Operational Number	14-21
Year built	1997
Name	MacQuarie
Donor	Bequest of Lieut Commander Hugh MacQuarie Stone MBE RD, together with bequest of Mrs Mary Noond
Placed on station	28.3.1997
Launch	Afloat

Inshore lifeboat

Type	D class inflatable
Official Number	D-470
Name	Landlubber
Donor	The landlubbers of Thirsk and district
Placed on station	7.9.1994
Launch	Trolley

Location history

1800 The first lifeboat at Sunderland was placed on the North Side of the River Weir, and a lifeboat house was built above the high-water mark; there was a station here until 1887.

1808 A second station was established on the South Side of the river, close to the South Pier; this was closed in 1900.

1850 A second station was established on the South Side by the Sunderland Shipowners Association, and was known as South Side No.2; this station was closed in 1864.

1858 A lifeboat house was built near the South Pier, at Polka Hole, for the lifeboat presented to the Sunderland Seamen's Association by Miss Burdett-Coutts; this house was used until the mid-1870s, and demolished in the 1960s.

1859 A station was established at Roker, to the north of the river mouth, where a lifeboat was in operation between 1859 and 1900; the RNLI took over the station in 1871 and a lifeboat house was built here with a pilot's room above.

1871 A lifeboat house was built at the South Outlet, and a station established there in 1872; on 25 July 1905 the house was destroyed by fire, and the station closed in 1912.

1900 A station was opened at the North Dock, where a lifeboat house and slipway were built; it closed in 1916 after a motor lifeboat had been permanently stationed at the South Side.

1902 A station at Hendon Beach, to the south of Sunderland, was opened and a lifeboat house constructed; this station was closed in 1912.

1911 Between 1911 and 1914 the motor lifeboat was kept afloat.

1916 A new lifeboat house with a lifting pontoon was completed at the Commissioner's Quay on the south side of the river; used until 1935, it has since been demolished.

1935 A new lifeboat house with a slipway was constructed at Greenwell's Quay, in the South Docks; used until 1990, it was demolished in 1996 after the station moved to the North Side.

1966 An inshore lifeboat station was established in May. The ILB was kept in a small house at Roker and launched across the beach; this house was used until 1998.

1990 Permanent moorings on the South Side of the river were taken up, close to the 1935 boathouse, which was used as a crew room.

1995 The moorings were moved to the North Side of the river; shore facilities were provided in the newly built Marina complex occupying the North Dock.

1998 A new ILB house was built at Roker beach, providing considerably improved crew facilities.

Medals and awards

Four medals have been awarded, all Silver.

Background information

The station has probably the most complex history of any in Britain. There were a number of different boats here at the same time during the 19th century, and the different stations were known by different names at different times. Stations were opened on both sides of the River Wear and in the docks to ensure that a lifeboat could be launched in any prevailing conditions.

14m Trent *MacQuarie* (ON.1225) moored in the North Dock Marina in 1997.

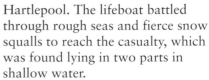

Key dates

Opened	1803
RNLI	1869
Motor LB	1923-6.1968 and 1977
Fast LB	1977
Inshore LB	5.1968

Current lifeboat details

All-weather lifeboat
Type	Tyne
Official Number	1131
Operational Number	47-023
Year built	1988
Name	*City of Sheffield*
Donor	City of Sheffield lifeboat appeal 1987-88, the bequest of Mrs Mary Mable Walker, and other gifts and legacies
Placed on station	24.7.1997
Launch	Afloat

Inshore lifeboat
Type	Atlantic 21
Official Number	B-568
Name	*Burton Brewer*
Donor	Appeal organised by Burton-on-Trent Branch
Placed on station	30.9.1986
Launch	Slipway

Location history

1803 The first lifeboat was kept in a house adjoining the Water Gate, near the North Pier; a station was operated from this site until 1923.

1841 A station was established at the North Sands; it was closed in 1915.

1854 The first lifeboat kept in the harbour was operated by the Seamen, and taken over by the RNLI in 1875.

1875 After taking over the station in the harbour, a new lifeboat house with a slipway was built; it was rebuilt on new site in 1885 following encroachment from the sea.

1907-8 A new double lifeboat house was built at Middleton for both the No 2 and No 3 lifeboats;

this was altered in 1938 for a larger motor lifeboat.

1965 The boathouse was demolished, as the lifeboat was kept afloat on moorings in the harbour.

1968 In May an inshore lifeboat was sent to the station, and on 20 June the offshore lifeboat was withdrawn.

1970 The lifeboat house at Middleton was demolished and rebuilt for the ILB, which was launched down the original slipway. In October an Atlantic 21 inshore lifeboat was sent to the station.

1977 The offshore lifeboat station was re-opened, and a fast afloat lifeboat was placed on station; it was kept moored in the docks, close to the Harbour Master's office.

1993 A new ILB house was built at Irvines Quay for the Atlantic 21, which was launched down a short slipway into the harbour.

Medals and awards

Eighteen medals have been awarded, one Gold, eight Silver and nine Bronze.

Notable rescue

On 26 January 1942 the lifeboat *The Princess Royal (Civil Service No.7)* was launched to the steamship *Hawkswood*, which had gone ashore in an easterly gale half a mile north of the Tees North Gare Jetty at

Hartlepool. The lifeboat battled through rough seas and fierce snow squalls to reach the casualty, which was found lying in two parts in shallow water.

Because it was impossible to approach the vessel in the depth of water, and as the crew on board were not in immediate danger, the lifeboat returned to her station to wait for high water, finally reaching the wreck in the early afternoon. There was more water in which to operate, but the gale was still blowing fiercely. With heavy seas breaking over the lifeboat, five men were taken off the fore part of the wreck and landed at Hartlepool. A third trip to the casualty was made to rescue men on the aft part, but despite several attempts this was unsuccessful. The remaining survivors were saved by the rocket apparatus later in the day.

For this rescue the Gold Medal was awarded to Coxswain Lieutenant William Bennison, the Silver Medal to Motor Mechanic Herbert Jefferson, and the Bronze Medal to each of the crew, Thomas Gilchrist, Robert Horsley, Edward Wallace, Richard Coulson, William Horsley and Herbert Pearson.

The Master of the *Hawkswood* said in a letter of thanks, 'We would like you to know that we will always remember the fearless and persistent determination displayed by the crew of the lifeboat under the command of Coxswain Bennison who showed such indomitable courage, initiative and superb seamanship.'

47ft Tyne *City of Sheffield* (ON.1131) at sea off Hartlepool. *Bob Williams*

Key dates

Opened	1829-c1854; ro1911
RNLI	1911
Motor LB	1911
Fast LB	1986

Current lifeboat details

All-weather lifeboat

Type	Tyne
Official Number	1110
Operational Number	47-008
Year built	1985
Name	Phil Mead
Donor	Trustees of the Phil Reed Charitable Trust, and local appeal
Placed on station	23.1.1986
Launch	Slipway

Location history

1829 The first lifeboat was placed at the mouth of the River Tees, and was on station until the 1840s.

1854 A lifeboat station to cover Tees Bay was established at Middlesbrough by the Tees Bay Lifeboat Society, and a lifeboat house was built on the Dock Cut; the station was taken over by the RNLI in 1858, but was closed in 1895.

1911 The Teesmouth station was re-opened and a motor lifeboat placed on station; it was kept afloat at the mouth of the Tees, moored off the South Gare Breakwater.

1914 A lifeboat house and slipway was built at Battery Hole, on the South Gare Breakwater, after the lifeboat had broken from her moorings and been damaged; this house was used until 1921.

1921 A new lifeboat house and deep-water roller slipway were built on the same site as the 1914 boathouse; this house is still in use albeit altered and modernised for subsequent lifeboats.

Launch of 47ft Tyne *Phil Mead*
(ON.1110) on an exercise in 1997.

Medals and awards

One medal has been awarded, a Bronze.

Notable rescue

On 1 June 1961 the lifeboat *Sarah Jane and James Season* was launched in a very rough sea and near gale to the yawl *Sybil Kathleen*, which was in difficulties during a passage north from Hamble to Norway. The yawl was running out of fuel and her engines were not powerful enough for her to make headway against the strong wind, so her crew dropped anchor in Skinningrove Bay.

Coxswain John Stonehouse found that approaching the casualty was almost impossible, so oil was thrown on to the waves to reduce their motion. The only hope of rescuing the yawl's crew was to tow her clear, but it took four attempts before a line was passed between the two vessels.

The casualty was then towed clear of the broken water and taken north to Hartlepool, as it was considered unsafe to enter Teesmouth with the yawl in tow. Once the casualty and her three crew had been safely landed, the lifeboat returned to her station.

For this rescue Coxswain Stonehouse was awarded the Bronze medal, the Thanks on Vellum was accorded to Mechanic Colin Coates, and the rest of the crew were issued with Medal service certificates.

Background information

On the afternoon of Sunday 28 February 1993 the Teesmouth lifeboat *Phil Mead* launched on service to the 97,000-ton Bahamian-registered tanker *Freja Svea*, which was dragging her anchor in storm force conditions in Tees Bay. While standing by the tanker in heavy seas the Teesmouth lifeboat was knocked down, losing one of her engines. The Hartlepool lifeboat *The Scout* was launched to escort the Teesmouth lifeboat back to station and then to take over stand-by duties at the scene.

While close to the tanker in about 8 fathoms of water *The Scout* was capsized twice by heavy seas and one crew member, Robbie Maiden, was washed overboard. The lifeboat performed exactly as she was designed to do and righted, and although some minor injuries were sustained none of the lifeboat crew on board were lost.

Later the Teesmouth lifeboat relaunched to escort the Hartlepool lifeboat back to the Tees, and Robbie Maiden was picked up by an RAF Sea King helicopter and taken to hospital, from where he was subsequently discharged.

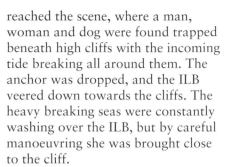

Key dates

Opened	1802
RNLI	1858
Motor LB	1931-86
AWLB withdrawn	22.3.1986
Inshore LB	10.1963; second 1986

Current lifeboat details

Inshore lifeboats

Type	Atlantic 21
Official Number	B-580
Name	*Leicester Challenge*
Donor	Leicester Branch of the RNLI
Placed on station	14.1.1990
Launch	Tractor and do-do carriage

Type	D class inflatable
Official Number	D-523
Name	*Peterborough Beer Festival 1*
Donor	Funded by visitors to the Peterborough Camra Beer Festivals in 1995 and 1996
Placed on station	23.7.1997
Launch	Trolley

Location history

1802 The first lifeboat was placed on station, funded by a local committee; it was kept in the town, and was taken over by the Tees Bay Lifeboat Society in 1825.

1859 The first RNLI lifeboat house was built on the sea front; it was demolished in 1972.

1877 An independent lifeboat, funded by the Free Gardners and named *Emma*, was placed on

station; to accommodate it, a boathouse was built on the Promenade with a Beachmen's Reading Room and accommodation for the Coxswain above. In 1936 this house was bought by Redcar Corporation to house the lifeboat *Zetland* as the centrepiece for a lifeboat museum, which came under the auspices of Langburgh District Council in 1969.

1963 An inshore lifeboat station was established in July; the ILB was kept in the boathouse.

1972 A new lifeboat house was built on the site of the 1859 boathouse; it is situated on the Promenade at the junction with Moore Street.

1986 The lifeboat house was converted to house an Atlantic 21 and its launching vehicle.

Medals and awards

Three medals have been awarded, two Silver and one Bronze.

Notable rescue

On 19 January 1992 the Atlantic 21 inshore lifeboat B-580 *Leicester Challenge* was launched to go to the aid of two persons who were cut off by the tide at Hunt Cliff, about 4 miles from the station. There was an onshore north-westerly wind, force 5, with a 5-foot swell.

In moderate seas the ILB quickly

reached the scene, where a man, woman and dog were found trapped beneath high cliffs with the incoming tide breaking all around them. The anchor was dropped, and the ILB veered down towards the cliffs. The heavy breaking seas were constantly washing over the ILB, but by careful manoeuvring she was brought close to the cliff.

Once in the shallow water, the engines were stopped and tilted clear to avoid damage from the rocks. One of the crew swam to the cliffs with a stern line and reached the two people who were sheltering. The seas were lifting the ILB and pounding her against the rocks, but she got close enough to the casualties to enable them to be helped on board.

Once the lifeboatman and the two rescued people were safely aboard, the ILB was hauled into deeper water and the engines were lowered. The ILB was then driven out through the surf, and immediately returned to Redcar. She was beached on the sand and the casualties were landed.

For this rescue Senior Helmsman Peter Hodge was awarded the Bronze Medal; the other crew members were presented with Medal service certificates.

Left The lifeboat house built in 1972 on the Promenade at the junction with Moore Street.

Right Atlantic 21 *Leicester Challenge* (B-580) inside the lifeboat house.

Current lifeboat details

Inshore lifeboat

Type	Atlantic 21
Official Number	B-576
Name	*Ellis Sinclair*
Donor	Gift of Messrs Sinclair, Roche & Temperley, named in honour of the firm's founder
Placed on station	18.5.89
Launch	Tractor and do-do carriage

Location history

Although the station is actually located in the small fishing village of Staithes, it is known as Staithes & Runswick to recognise the Runswick station closed in 1978. The following takes account of the location histories of both stations.

Runswick

1866 A lifeboat house was built when the station was first opened; it was moved and rebuilt on a more suitable site in 1875 and a slipway was added in 1876.

1910 A new lifeboat house was built on the same site; although altered extensively in 1970 for a new lifeboat, it was used until the station closed in 1978; it is now used as a store, and a private rescue boat is kept in the house that formerly accommodated the launching tractor.

Staithes

1875 A lifeboat house was built at Cowbar, on the west side of the small harbour; this house was altered several times between then and 1938, when the station was permanently closed; it was then converted into a cottage.

1978 The station was re-opened in January and an Atlantic 21 was sent for evaluation trials; the station became operational from 31 March 1978, and the 1875 boathouse was re-acquired and refitted to become operational again.

Medals and awards

Four medals have been awarded, one Gold, one Silver and two Bronze, all to lifeboatmen from Runswick.

Notable rescue

On 18 November 1893 the Runswick lifeboat *Cape of Good Hope* was launched to the brig *Carula*, which had been driven ashore in Runswick Bay in a severe gale and very heavy seas.

After a very difficult operation, the lifeboat managed to get alongside the casualty and took off the crew of six. The lifeboat then returned to the beach and safely hauled up.

For this rescue, as well as for giving long service to the station, Coxswain George Tose was awarded the Silver Medal.

Background information

On 8 February 1934 the lifeboat *The Always Ready* was launched to the salvage steamer *Disperser*, only to find that all but one of her crew had been taken off. In attempting to save the last man, Coxswain Robert Patton was crushed between the lifeboat and the casualty, but succeeded in saving the man's life. He subsequently died from his injuries and was posthumously awarded the Gold Medal; the lifeboat was renamed *Robert Patton – The Always Ready*. A relief of a Liverpool class lifeboat was carved on Patton's gravestone in Hinderwell Cemetery.

Recovery of Atlantic 21 *Ellis Sinclair* (B-576) after an exercise in 1992.
Steve Dutton

Location history

1802 The boathouse for the station's first lifeboat was situated on the west side of the harbour; it stood until 1847, when it was removed so that the 'Khyber Pass' could be built.

1823 A second lifeboat was provided for the town, and kept on the east side of the harbour suspended from two stanchions on the landward side of Tate Hill Pier; a boathouse was built on the Pier by the Piers & Harbour Board, and there was a lifeboat on Tate Hill Pier until the house was dismantled in May 1863.

Key dates

Opened	1802
RNLI	1861
Motor LB	1919
Fast LB	1974
Inshore LB	5.1966

Current lifeboat details

All-weather lifeboat

Type	Trent
Official Number	1212
Operational Number	14-14
Year built	1996
Name	George and Mary Webb
Donor	The Mary Webb Trust
Placed on station	10.4.1996
Launch	Afloat

Inshore lifeboat

Type	D class inflatable
Official Number	D-521
Name	OEM Stone II
Donor	Gift of Miss Olive Stone
Placed on station	23.7.1997
Launch	Slipway

1847 Following the demolition of the 1802 house, a new boathouse was built further up the quay on the west side; this house was renovated in 1861 after the RNLI had taken over of the station. The lifeboats were launched down a slipway and over the beach to the west of the West Pier.

1863 The Tate Hill Pier boathouse having been deemed beyond repair in 1862, a new boathouse was built on the West Quay, into which the No.2 lifeboat was moved.

1864 Between 1864 and 1889 there was a lifeboat operated by the Fishermen, and this was kept on the west side in a house adjacent to the RNLI's 1863 boathouse.

1894-5 A new double boathouse for both No.1 and No.2 lifeboats was built on Marine Parade, under the West Cliff, on the site of the 1863 RNLI boathouse and the Fishermen's boathouse; used until 1957, it has since become a Lifeboat Museum. The Yacht Club premises, built on top, were opened in November 1938.

1918 A new lifeboat house and slipway were built on the east side of the Harbour for the station's first motor lifeboat; this house, altered for subsequent motor lifeboats, was used for the offshore lifeboat until 1974 and has since been modified to house the D class inflatable.

1966 An inshore lifeboat station was established in May.

1974 A mooring pen was completed on the east side, near the 1918 boathouse, to enable a fast afloat lifeboat to be placed on station.

Medals and awards

Thirty-three medals have been awarded, five Gold, 12 Silver and 16 Bronze.

Two medals, both Silver, have been awarded for shore-boat rescues.

Notable rescue

On 9 April 1988 the D class inshore lifeboat D-260 *Gwynaeth* was launched to the yacht *Cymba*, which had capsized off Whitby Harbour, supported by the lifeboat *The White Rose of Yorkshire*. Both lifeboats had to negotiate heavy breaking seas at the harbour entrance.

The ILB approached the yacht in very rough, broken seas and picked one man out of the water, who was found to be dead. Meanwhile the lifeboat was taken inshore because the yacht was being driven inland with a survivor still on board and attached to the yacht by a line.

After being struck by two heavy seas during the first approach, the lifeboat was taken into very shallow water stern first to keep the bows towards the breaking rollers. On the third approach a line was thrown to the survivor, who unclipped his safety line and was dragged into the lifeboat.

Bronze Medals were subsequently awarded to Coxswain/Mechanic Peter Thomson and Helmsman Nicholas Botham in recognition of their courage and seamanship.

Background information

Housed in the 1895 double boathouse is the Whitby Lifeboat Museum, which was formally opened on 26 July 1958. The main exhibit is the station's last pulling lifeboat, the *Robert and Ellen Robson*, which was retained for display purposes in 1957 after it had been due to be removed.

In the Parish Church on the East Cliff is a large memorial to those who lost their lives when the lifeboat capsized during the 'fearful storm' on 9 February 1861, drowning 12 of the 13 on board. In Whitby Cemetery is a memorial to those lost when the troop ship *Rohilla* went aground and sank near Whitby on 30 October 1914. There were over 200 people on board, of whom 84 were lost; the Tynemouth motor lifeboat sailed 44 miles south from her station to assist.

14m Trent *George and Mary Webb* (ON.1212) moored on the east side of the Harbour near the 1918 lifeboat house.

Current lifeboat details

All-weather lifeboat

Type	Mersey
Official Number	1175
Operational Number	12-18
Year built	1991
Name	Fanny Victoria Wilkinson and Frank Stubbs
Donor	Legacy of the late Frank Stubbs, who died in 1957
Placed on station	27.9.1991
Launch	Carriage

Inshore lifeboat

Type	D class inflatable
Official Number	D-434
Name	John Wesley Hillard
Donor	The Gay and Peter Hartley Hillard's Charitable Trust
Placed on station	28.7.1992
Launch	Trolley

Location history

1801 A lifeboat house was built for the first lifeboat, near Mill Beck.

1821 The lifeboat house was moved to a site near the West Pier, on the sands adjoining the Coastguard watch-house close to the harbour.

1861 The lifeboat house was renovated when the RNLI took over.

1914 A new lifeboat house was built on the Promenade; used until 1940, it then became a store and a tractor house, and has since been converted into an amusement arcade.

1939 A new slipway was built on to the beach.

1940 A new lifeboat house was built at the head of the slipway; although altered to take subsequent lifeboats and the ILB, it is still in use.

1966 An inshore lifeboat station was established in April.

1987 A new tractor house was added to the boathouse.

Medals and awards

Nine medals have been awarded, five Silver and four Bronze.

Eight Silver Medals have been awarded for shore-boat rescues.

Notable rescue

On 23 November 1969 the lifeboat *J. G. Graves of Sheffield* was launched to the converted ship's lifeboat *Sheena*, which had capsized in the South Bay in a strong north-easterly wind and a very rough sea. The lifeboat reached the casualty within 5 minutes of being launched.

The casualty was found to be in a perilous position close inshore in very shallow water. Coxswain William Sheader skilfully manoeuvred the lifeboat through the heavy breakers and the lifeboatmen managed to pull one survivor out of the water. He was landed at the harbour, then the lifeboat returned to find another survivor.

Although the lifeboat was again in grave danger, touching the bottom at one point, another man was successfully pulled from the water; he was rushed to hospital but later died. After this outstanding service, the lifeboat then went out once more and escorted the coble *Eileen* and helped the coble *Faithful*.

For this service the Silver Medal was awarded to Coxswain William Sheader, and the Thanks on Vellum was accorded to each of the rest of the crew, Second Coxswain Thomas Rowley, Mechanic Allen Rennard, Assistant Mechanic Cecil Bean, Emergency Mechanic Robert Swalwell and crew members Jack Rowley and George Plumber. The Maud Smith Award was won jointly by Coxswain Sheader, for this rescue, and Coxswain Eric Offer of Dun Laoghaire.

Background information

When the RNLI took over the station in 1861, it supplied a new lifeboat, named *Amelia*. Sadly, this lifeboat was wrecked on 2 November 1861 on her first service launch with the loss of two of her crew, as well as three people who tried to effect a rescue.

On 8 December 1954, the lifeboat *E. C. J. R.* launched to stand by the local fishing cobles, and towed one fishing boat into the safety of the harbour. She put out again to escort the other fishing boats still at sea, by which time a severe gale was blowing. Once all the fishing boats were safe, some having made for Whitby, the lifeboat was recalled. However, as she approached the harbour she was capsized by a huge wave that smashed right over the boat. Although she righted herself successfully, three of the lifeboatmen on board were killed. A bronze plaque inside the lifeboat house commemorates the three.

12m Mersey *Fanny Victoria Wilkinson and Frank Stubbs* (ON.1175) and D class inflatable *John Wesley Hillard* (D-434) on exercise. *Steve Dutton*

Key dates

Opened	1804
RNLI	1852
Motor LB	1940
Fast LB	1991
Inshore LB	4.1966

Current lifeboat details

All-weather lifeboat

Type	Mersey
Official Number	1170
Operational Number	12-13
Year built	1990
Name	*Keep Fit Association*
Donor	Campaign by Keep Fit Association, various legacies, and an appeal in North and West Yorkshire
Placed on station	2.6.1991
Launch	Carriage

Inshore lifeboat

Type	D class inflatable
Official Number	D-446
Name	*Holme Team*
Donor	Landlord and regulars of Fleece Inn, Holmfirth
Placed on station	3.6.1993
Launch	Trolley

Location history

1804 The first lifeboat was kept in a house about 500 yards south-west of the town, on the sands.

1853 When the RNLI took over the station, the stone lifeboat house situated at the foot of Cargate Hill was repaired and continued in service.

1872 The lifeboat house was enlarged; it was used until 1889 and sold in 1890.

1889 A new lifeboat house was built on the coble landing; this was used until 1991 with various alterations and additions for larger lifeboats.

1966 An inshore lifeboat station was established in April; the ILB was kept in the boathouse.

1991 The 1889 boathouse was demolished and a new lifeboat house was built on the same site for the 12m Mersey lifeboat and inshore lifeboat; the facilities included a mechanic's store, drying room, galley, toilets and shower facilities, crew room and a souvenir sales outlet.

Medals and awards

One Silver Medal has been awarded, together with two Bronze Medals for a shore-boat rescue.

Notable rescue

On 20 December 1983 the lifeboat *Robert and Dorothy Hardcastle* was launched in a near gale force wind with heavy swell to the coaster *Rita*, which had struck a submerged object and lost the use of her engines 3 miles off Filey Brigg.

The lifeboat arrived on the scene as the coaster's crew were preparing to abandon ship. She circled the vessel to assess the best approach, using the searchlight to check for floating debris in the water. Hampered by heavy seas pushing the lifeboat towards the casualty, seven approaches were made before the first survivor could be taken off. The second was taken off after two more runs and the third after another five runs.

As the lifeboat approached again to take off the Captain, who was the last man on board, she was caught by a heavy breaking sea and struck the side of the coaster with some force. A second approach had to be made, and this time the Captain was safely taken off.

Once clear of the casualty, the lifeboat made for Scarborough, escorted by the Scarborough lifeboat, where all the survivors were landed. After a short rest, the Filey lifeboat returned to her station in the early hours of 21 December.

For this rescue Coxswain Frank Jenkinson was accorded the Thanks on Vellum, and Vellum service certificates were presented to the rest of the crew.

The lifeboat house on the coble landing, built in 1991 on the same site as the previous house.
Graham Taylor

Launching 12m Mersey *Keep Fit Association* (ON.1170) on exercise in 1996.

Key dates

Opened	1871
RNLI	1871
Motor LB	1934
AWLB withdrawn	15.8.1993
Inshore LB	1993

Current lifeboat details

Inshore lifeboat

Type	Atlantic 75
Official Number	B-703
Name	*Jason Logg*

Donor Memorial appeal organised by Graham Logg, of Harrogate, with kind support from family and friends

Placed on station	16.2.1994
Launch	Tractor and do-do carriage

Location history

1871 Two lifeboat stations were opened on Flamborough Head, both managed by one committee; the No.1 station was at North Landing and the No.2 station at South Landing. The house at South Landing was used until the station closed in 1938; it then became a store and was demolished in 1993 to make way for a new lifeboat house.

1890 At North Landing, a slipway from the boathouse over the steepest part of beach was constructed.

1934 The lifeboat house at North Landing was altered for the new motor lifeboat, and the slipway was rebuilt with a turntable added.

1981 Further modifications were made to the boathouse: a new winch house and winch were provided, together with a new tractor house. The house was used until 1993, when the lifeboat was withdrawn.

1993 A new ILB house was built at South Landing on the site of the 1871 boathouse for the Atlantic 75 and its launching tractor coupled in-line; it includes a store, toilets and shower, crew/instruction room, drying room and souvenir outlet.

Medals and awards

Eight medals have been awarded, six Silver and two Bronze.

Notable rescue

On the evening of 22 September 1971 the lifeboat *Friendly Forester* was launched to go to the aid of two men and their dog who were stranded under cliffs at Stapple Nook. There was poor visibility, but the wind was only force 2 or 3, with a moderate swell.

The lifeboat found the two men beneath the cliffs, and the only safe way out was by sea. To approach them, the lifeboat was required to work in a very confined area with the sea constantly breaking over her. Having dropped anchor, she veered down back into a narrow channel between submerged rocks. There was a 10-foot swell, and the lifeboat was working in very shallow water.

Once the lifeboat was close enough to the shore, lines were fired to the stranded men who were sheltering in a cave entrance. To assist with the rescue, crew member Alwyn Emmerson went ashore taking a life-jacket with him. Using the breeches buoy, the men were then hauled into the lifeboat, one after the other, followed by the lifeboatman.

Once all were safely on board, the lifeboat was gently eased through the broken water away from the rocks, the anchor was released, and she returned to her station late at night.

For this rescue the Bronze Medal was awarded to Coxswain George Pockley, and the Thanks on Vellum accorded to crew member Emmerson. The other members of the crew were presented with Medal service certificates.

Background information

One of the best known of Flamborough's lifeboats, *Friendly Forester*, is preserved and on display at the Blackgang Sawmill and St Catherine's Quay Museum on the Isle of Wight. She served at the station from 1953 until 1983, and is credited with saving 89 lives.

The ILB house built at South Landing in 1993, on the site of the first boathouse of 1871.

Launching Atlantic 75 *Jason Logg* (B-703) from the beach at South Landing in 1994.

Opened	1805
RNLI	1853
Motor LB	1931
Fast LB	1988
Inshore LB	4.1966

Current lifeboat details

All-weather lifeboat

Type	Mersey
Official Number	1169
Operational Number	12-12
Year built	1990
Name	Marine Engineer
Donor	Institute of Marine Engineers together with other gifts and legacies
Placed on station	13.8.1995
Launch	Carriage

Inshore lifeboat

Type	D class inflatable
Official Number	D-426
Name	Lord Feoffees II
Donor	The Lord Feoffees of the Manor of Bridlington
Placed on station	11.4.1992
Launch	Trolley

Location history

1806 The first lifeboat house was built on the corner of Chapel Street and the Promenade; it was still in use in 1853 when the RNLI took over the station, and was used until 1864.

1864 A new boathouse was built on a better site; used until 1904, it was then demolished as the council had acquired the site for a new road.

1903 A new lifeboat house was built, situated on the South Marine Drive, and the lifeboat was moved into it in April 1904; this house has been altered several times since for successive lifeboats and is still in use today.

1966 An inshore lifeboat station was established in April; the ILB was kept in a house on the South Promenade.

1978-9 A two-storey building

adjoining the 1904 boathouse was erected to provide a souvenir shop and crew room.

1988 The lifeboat house was adapted for a Mersey class lifeboat.

1993 A new ILB house was built on the Lower South Promenade to replace the previous building on the same site.

Medals and awards

Five medals have been awarded, two Silver and three Bronze.

Six Silver Medals have been awarded for shore-boat rescues, and two for shore rescues.

Notable rescue

On 2 April 1973 the lifeboat *William Henry and Mary King* was launched to go to the aid of the coble *Calaharis* in a NNE gale gusting to hurricane force and a very rough sea with heavy swell.

Once at sea, Coxswain John King learned that another motor fishing vessel, *White Knight*, of Grimsby, had broken down, so he set a course for her, leaving the Flamborough lifeboat to assist the *Calaharis*. As she progressed towards *White Knight*, the lifeboat was swept by very heavy seas with spray reducing visibility.

Three passes alongside the casualty were needed, in extremely

dangerous conditions, to save the crew of five. There were no injuries, and only minor damage to the lifeboat, but the passage back to station was slow and arduous. However, all of the rescued crew were safely landed at Bridlington harbour.

For this rescue the Silver Medal was awarded to Coxswain King, and the Thanks on Vellum was accorded to the rest of the crew, Second Coxswain George Traves, Bowman Denis Atkins, Mechanic Roderick Stott, Assistant Mechanic Anthony Ayre and crew members Fred Walkington and Kenneth Bentley.

Background information

Between circa 1860 and 1898 there were two lifeboats at Bridlington, one funded and operated by the RNLI, the other privately operated. On 10 February 1871 the East Coast was hit by a ferocious gale and at Bridlington both lifeboats were launched to a variety of vessels that had got into difficulty. While attempting to rescue the crew of one brig, the private lifeboat *Harbinger* was capsized, and six of those on board were lost. A memorial to those who lost their lives during this 'Great Gale', as it became known, including the six lost in the *Harbinger*, can be seen in the grounds of Bridlington Priory.

The lifeboat house built in 1903 on the South Marine Drive, extensively modified since, most recently in 1988 for the Mersey class lifeboat.

Key dates

Opened	1962-1913; ro1974
RNLI	1862
AWLB withdrawn	5.1913
Inshore LB	1974

Current lifeboat details

Inshore lifeboat

Type	D class inflatable
Official Number	D-541
Name	Brian and Margaret Wiggins
Donor	Legacy of Brian Wiggins
Placed on station	5.1.1999
Launch	Trolley

Location history

1862 A lifeboat house was built in Arthur Street near the lighthouse; it was used until 1881 and was then given to the Board of Trade for storing Rocket Apparatus. It is now used as the local Social Security Offices.

1881 A new lifeboat house was built in Seaside Road, opposite the Pier Hotel in the middle of the town; this house was used until the station was closed in 1913, and has since been used as an amusement arcade disguised by an extended frontage.

1974 An inshore lifeboat station was established. Until 1983 the ILB was kept in a small house at the south end of the town on the seafront, at the end of Southcliffe Road.

1983 A new purpose-built ILB house was constructed on the same site; used until 1998, it was demolished to make way for a new house.

1998 A new ILB house was built on the same site, providing greatly improved accommodation and crew facilities.

Medals and awards

Two medals has been awarded, both Bronze.

Notable rescue

On 15 May 1991 the D class inshore lifeboat D-394 *Banks' Staff II* was launched to the yacht *Frangipani*, which was in difficulties 2 miles offshore in gale force winds and heavy breaking seas. The conditions were at the limits of the ILB's operational capabilities, and launching was made difficult by the rough seas on the beach.

The yacht was reached despite poor visibility, and approached with skilled helmsmanship. One of the crew was taken on to the ILB, having breathed in engine fumes. The ILB then returned to Withernsea, safely negotiating the large seas, where the casualty was landed and taken to hospital.

The Bronze Medal was awarded to Helmsman John Hartland for showing fine seamanship and great courage during this service.

Background information

When the lifeboat was withdrawn from Withernsea it was transferred a few miles south to a new station at Easington, which was much nearer the area where the majority of wrecks occurred. However, this station was closed in 1933 and offshore lifeboat cover is now provided by the Humber lifeboat.

Right The opening of the ILB house built in 1998 on the sea front, on the site of the previous ILB houses.

Below D class inflatable *Banks' Staff II* (D-394, on station 1990-99) going through the surf off the beach at Withernsea.

Key dates

Opened	1810
RNLI	1.5.1911
Motor LB	1919
Fast LB	1977
Inshore LB	1964-65

Current lifeboat details

All-weather lifeboat

Type	Severn
Official Number	1216
Operational Number	17-05
Year built	1997
Name	*Pride of the Humber*
Donor Humber Lifeboat Appeal 1994 and 1995; fund-raising of North East region volunteers; and bequests of Miss Lucy Chandley, Miss Margery Ivory Hooton, Mrs Mary Self, together with other legacies	
Placed on station	8.3.1997
Launch	Afloat

Location history

1810 The station was established by Hull Trinity House at Spurn Point, the remote tip of the narrow Spurn peninsula at the mouth of the River Humber, and a lifeboat house was built for the first lifeboat and its launching carriage. Because of its remote location, the lifeboat crew and their families lived at the Point, and the RNLI's only full-time crew still man the boat.

1819 The first houses for the lifeboatmen and their families were built at Spurn.

1853 A new lifeboat house was built. At different times the lifeboat was kept in the house, or on the beach, or afloat; a boarding-boat was provided for the latter eventuality.

1858 A new series of cottages was built at Spurn Point for the crew; these remained in use until 1975. A look-out tower was also built, with a bell used to summon the lifeboatmen.

1908 The Humber Conservancy Board took over the running of the station until 1911.

1911 The RNLI took over the management of the station, and in 1912-3 a new lifeboat house and slipway were built; this was used until 1923.

1923 A new lifeboat house with roller slipway was built for the station's first motor lifeboat; it was used until 1977, when the lifeboat was placed on moorings, and was demolished in 1995.

1975 Seven new houses were built at Spurn for the lifeboatmen and their families to replace the 1858 cottages.

1977 The lifeboat was placed at moorings in the River Humber, just off the Pilot's Jetty; a davit-launched boarding-boat is kept at the end of the Jetty.

Medals and awards

Thirty-one medals have been awarded, three Gold, seven Silver and 21 Bronze.

Notable rescue

On 12 February 1940 the lifeboat *City of Bradford II* was launched to the steam trawler *Gurth*, of Grimsby, which had struck a sand bank in a strong westerly wind, with heavy and continuous snow. As two of the crew were ill there were only six men on the lifeboat and Coxswain Robert Cross could not spare any man to work the searchlight in the total darkness.

Despite this, the Coxswain took the lifeboat alongside the casualty in the pitch dark. The crew were repeatedly knocked down by seas, shaken and bruised and only saved from being washed overboard by clinging to the handrails. The sea was breaking continuously over the lifeboat, but with skilled use of the engines and helm, Coxswain Cross made 20 approaches alongside the trawler to rescue six survivors.

Then a rope, which was washed overboard, became entangled with one of the propellers, and the port engine stopped, but Coxswain Cross continued. It took a number of further attempts to get to the casualty, during which the lifeboat was badly damaged, but the last three men were eventually rescued.

Once all the survivors were on board, the lifeboat was taken into calmer water where the propeller was freed and the engine restarted. She then made for Grimsby where the rescued men were landed.

For this service, one of the outstanding rescues of the Second World War II, Coxswain Cross was awarded the Gold Medal, and the Bronze Medal was awarded to each of the crew, Mechanic John Major, Second Coxswain William Jenkinson, Bowman William Hood, and crew members Samuel Cross and Samuel Hoopell.

The houses built at Spurn Point in 1975 for the lifeboat crew.

Current lifeboat details

Inshore lifeboat

Type	D class inflatable
Official Number	D-454
Name	Blue Peter VI
Donor	Blue Peter TV Appeal (1993-4)
Placed on station	22.2.94
Launch	Trolley

Location history

1868 A lifeboat house was built when the station was first opened, and this was used until 1882 when the station was closed; it has since been demolished.

1965 An inshore lifeboat station was established at Cleethorpes in August, known as Humbermouth; a permanent house was never built, so the ILB was kept at the Humber Mouth Yacht Club until 1966, and from 1967 in a yard at the holiday camp; the station was closed on 27 March 1980 as the area was covered by the Humber lifeboat based at Spurn Point.

1987 An inshore lifeboat station was re-established at Cleethorpes on 29 June, and a purpose-built ILB house constructed on the southern end of the Promenade, at the Brighton Street Slipway.

Medals and awards

No medals have been awarded.

Notable rescue

On 19 May 1996 the D class inshore lifeboat D-454 *Blue Peter VI* was on exercise when it was alerted to a yacht that had lost its rudder and was in danger of hitting rocks around Bull Sand Fort.

The ILB found the yacht heading towards the rocks at speed, and tried to push it away. This failed, so lifeboatmen Steve Burton jumped on to the yacht just as its keel hit the rocks with some force. This threw those on board down on to the deck, but the yacht remained still on the rocks. The ILB stood by while the yacht's crew prepared the towing gear, despite the danger of it being smashed on the rocks by the force of the waves.

Eventually a tow line was rigged, and the ILB helmsman, Gary Barlow, managed to tow the yacht off the rocks and through a very small gap into deep water where, because of the conditions, the tow was handed over to the Humber lifeboat.

Background information

Cleethorpes operates one of the lifeboats funded by the Blue Peter Television Appeals; it was the sixth station to be adopted by Blue Peter.

Right D class inshore lifeboat *Blue Peter VI* (D-454) outside the ILB house built in 1987 at the southern end of the Promenade.

Below Blue Peter VI on exercise in 1997.

Current lifeboat details

Inshore lifeboat

Type	D class inflatable
Official Number	D-506
Name	*Patrick Rex Moren*
Donor	Legacy of Patrick Moren
Placed on station	9.7.1996
Launch	Land Rover and trolley

Location history

1882 A lifeboat house was built on the beach; it was used until 1900 and has since been demolished.

1900 A new lifeboat house was built in the town. It was used until 1920, when the station was closed; it is still standing and used as a store, now situated on the west side of the road out of Mablethorpe to Sutton.

1965 An inshore lifeboat station was established in May, and a wooden boathouse was built on the Promenade.

1976 A new ILB house was built to replace the previous one; an upper storey was added in 1986.

Medals and awards

One medal has been awarded, a Bronze.

Notable rescue

On 12 April 1998 the D class inshore lifeboat D-506 *Patrick Rex Moren* was launched in extreme conditions for this class of lifeboat to go to the assistance of the 17-foot fishing vessel *Lark*, which had broken down in the surf off the coast. There was a force 6 wind blowing, gusting to near gale force 7,

accompanied by wintry showers and a heavy swell.

The helmsman, Thomas Freeman, had considerable difficulty in negotiating the rough seas in order to reach the fishing boat, which was drifting helplessly towards the shore, having lost its anchor. He decided that it was too hazardous to take off the crew, so passed a line and towed her away from danger. In the huge seas this was a considerable feat for the ILB, which was smaller than the fishing boat and powered by one 40hp outboard engine.

For this rescue the Bronze Medal was awarded to Thomas Freeman, and Medal service certificates were presented to crew members Ian Finnis and Darren Worthington.

Background information

The station was first established in 1883 to replace one at Theddlethorpe, 3 miles to the north, where there were difficulties in obtaining both men and horses, used to help launch the boat.

However, on 27 November 1889 the lifeboat was taken by road to Theddlethorpe to launch. The barque *Elizabeth Argo* had requested assistance, but it was found that the lifeboat was not required. On this occasion great difficulty was experienced in hauling the carriage with horses through the snow, and it took 4 hours to travel as many miles.

On the return journey the Coxswain had the boat's sails set to relieve the strain on the horses, and the time was reduced to 2½ half hours.

Above The ILB house built in 1976 on the Promenade, opposite the launching ramp down on to the beach.

Right Launching D class inflatable *Patrick Rex Moren* (D-506) at the end of her Naming Ceremony in June 1997.

Key dates

Opened	1830
RNLI	1864
Motor LB	1932
Fast LB	1990
Inshore LB	1964

Current lifeboat details

All-weather lifeboat
Type	Mersey
Official Number	1166
Operational Number	12-008
Year built	1990
Name	*Lincolnshire Poacher*
Donor	Major donation to The Lincolnshire LB Appeal by the John & Lucille Van Geest Charitable Trust
Placed on station	7.8.1990
Launch	Carriage

Inshore lifeboat
Type	D class inflatable
Official Number	D-460
Name	*Leicester Fox*
Donor	Appeal by Leicester Branch
Placed on station	3.6.1994
Launch	Trolley

Location history

1830 The first lifeboat was provided by the Lincolnshire Coast Shipwreck Association; it was moved from Gibraltar Point and kept in a boathouse, also moved from Gibraltar Point, among the dunes at the back of what is now known as Lifeboat Avenue.

1864 The RNLI took over the station and had a new lifeboat house built, which was used until 1893; it is believed to have been incorporated into a private house, now known as 'The Old Lifeboat House', in Lifeboat Avenue.

1892 A new lifeboat house was built on the main Promenade, to the south of the Clock Tower; it had doors at both ends so that the boat could be taken out of either. This house was used until 1990 and has since been converted into a function room.

1964 An inshore lifeboat station was established in May; until 1990 the ILB was kept in a small house close to the beach.

1990 A new lifeboat house was built for a 12m Mersey class lifeboat, situated at the edge of the beach on Tower Esplanade; the ILB was also housed here and a souvenir shop was incorporated into the new building. It was the first new lifeboat house to be built for a Mersey.

Medals and awards

Four medals have been awarded, all Silver, the last for a service performed in December 1875.

Notable rescue

Early in the morning of 28 December 1965 the lifeboat *Charles Fred Grantham* was launched to assist with a search following the sinking of the oil rig *Sea Gem*, 47 miles north-west of Cromer, the previous day. Together with lifeboats from Wells, Cromer and Humber, she carried out an extensive search for survivors in gale force winds and heavy swell. The crew were at sea and standing by the casualty for 14 hours in severe weather conditions and intense cold in a lifeboat that had little shelter.

A Letter of Appreciation was received from the RNLI Committee of Management recognising the determination and high standard of seamanship shown throughout this arduous service.

Background information

The lifeboat station at Skegness is well known for its lifeboat families. There have been many Grunnills in the crew; Matthew Grunnill was Coxswain from 1908 to 1932, and his nephew Montague Grunnill was Second Coxswain from 1908 to 1934. Joel Grunnill served as Second Coxswain during the 1970s, and later became Honorary Secretary.

In the early years of the station Moodys held the senior posts in the lifeboat; Joseph Moody was Coxswain from 1877 to 1880 and John Smith Moody from 1900 to 1908. More recently the Perrin family have served the station; George Perrin was Coxswain of the station's first motor lifeboat in 1932, and his son Wilfred Perrin succeeded him as Coxswain in 1947.

The lifeboat house built in 1990 on Tower Esplanade for the 12m Mersey class lifeboat and D class inflatable.

The Naming Ceremony of 12m Mersey *Lincolnshire Poacher* (ON.1166) outside the lifeboat house on 30 September 1990, which was formally opened on the same day.

Key dates

Opened   1824-post 1843, 1867-1931;
                                    ro1979
RNLI   1867
AWLB withdrawn   1931
Inshore LB   6.1979

Current lifeboat details

Inshore lifeboat

Type	Atlantic 75
Official Number	B-749
Name	D. J. S. Haverhill
Donor	Bequest of David Sissons, a member of the Haverhill RNLI Guild
Placed on station	10.9.1998
Launch	Tractor and do-do carriage

Location history

1824 The station was established by the Norfolk Shipwreck Association who built a lifeboat house. The first lifeboat was out of use by 1851, although the house was still standing; it has since been demolished.

1867 A new lifeboat house was built at Old Hunstanton, to the north of the main town; it was used until 1900 and has since been converted into a beach shop.

1900 A new lifeboat house was built on a site adjacent to the first, and was used until the station closed in 1931; it was then used as a store.

1979 An inshore lifeboat station was established in June; the 1900 boathouse was re-acquired and is now used to house the Atlantic 21 and launching vehicle.

1996 A new fuel store was constructed adjacent to the lifeboat house.

Medals and awards

One medal has been awarded, a Bronze.

Notable rescue

On 31 March 1985 the Atlantic 21 inshore lifeboat B-556 *Spirit of America* was launched to an exhausted windsurfer who was in difficulties close to a wreck off Brancaster in a westerly gale and a rough broken sea. He was unable to reach the shore and the lifeboat crew were aware that only they could save the man's life.

The ILB grounded twice on the sandbanks in the dangerous shallows, spray reduced visibility almost to nothing and the rolling seas kept filling the boat. As the windsurfer was blown alongside, he was taken on board. He was found to be very weak and cold and was landed at the nearest beach where helpers were waiting.

The Bronze Medal was awarded to Helmsman Alan Clarke, who displayed great determination and skill throughout the operation.

Background information

At Hunstanton the first trials were held to assess the feasibility of using motorised tractors to launch lifeboats across beaches. The trials began on 26 March 1920 with a Clayton agricultural tractor powered by a 35hp motor, which had no difficulty in towing the lifeboat across the soft beach, and several days of trials proved to be a resounding success. A year later, following further trials at a number of different stations, the first motor tractor for service with the RNLI was delivered to Hunstanton.

Above Atlantic 75 *D. J. S. Haverhill* (B-749) and Talus tractor TW20H outside the lifeboat house built at Old Hunstanton in 1900.

Right *D. J. S. Haverhill* on an exercise to exchange Christmas gifts with the Skegness lifeboat in December 1998.

Key dates

Opened	1830
RNLI	1869
Motor LB	1936
Fast LB	1990
Inshore LB	6.1963

Current lifeboat details

All-weather lifeboat

Type	Mersey
Official Number	1161
Operational Number	12-003
Year built	1991
Name	Doris M. Mann of Ampthill
Donor	Legacy of Doris M. Mann, of Ampthill, Beds
Placed on station	3.7.1990
Launch	Carriage

Inshore lifeboat

Type	D class inflatable
Official Number	D-512
Name	Jane Ann II
Donor	Gift of Mrs Jan Bradford, Sudbury, Suffolk
Placed on station	13.11.1996
Launch	Trolley

Location history

1830 The first lifeboat was placed here by the Norfolk Shipwreck Association; a lifeboat house was built at the west side of the entrance to Wells Harbour.

1869 A new lifeboat house was built in the town, on The Quay, for the RNLI's first lifeboat. This house was used until 1895, and was later converted into a café; it is now split between the Harbour Office and a small Maritime Museum.

1895 A new lifeboat house was built at the far end of Beach Road, close to the entrance to the Harbour; it has been altered at various times and occasionally suffered flood damage.

1963 An inshore lifeboat station was established in June; the ILB was kept in a small house erected on the west side of the 1895 boathouse, at the entrance to the Harbour.

1983 The lifeboat house was modified to provide improved crew facilities.

1986 A new tractor house to accommodate a Talus MB-H tractor was constructed alongside the 1895 boathouse.

1990 The lifeboat house was extensively rebuilt and modified to house a 12m Mersey class lifeboat; a new main door was installed, and a new workshop, general store, souvenir sales outlet and concrete slipway were constructed.

Medals and awards

Three medals have been awarded, one Silver and two Bronze.

Notable rescue

On the morning of 15 February 1979, the lifeboat *Ernest Tom Neathercoat* was launched to the cargo vessel *Savinesti*, of Romania, which had broken down in a violent storm. The wind was strong gale force 9 to storm force 10, and there was continuous blizzard accompanied by very rough seas.

The lifeboat struggled to make headway through the appalling conditions, and was continually filling with water. However, she managed to reach the casualty, although the radar, MF radio and echo-sounder were all lost as the lifeboat was continually hit and filled by the seas. All of the crew had to shelter in the aft cockpit as the seas made the forward well untenable.

Despite having no radar and poor visibility, the lifeboat stood by for more than 2 hours in temperatures well below freezing, washed by huge waves. The Humber lifeboat arrived on the scene in the afternoon and the Wells lifeboat was released to return to her station. The passage back was made at half speed with the drogue streamed and snow blowing directly into the after cockpit.

The open lifeboat was at sea for more than 11 hours in these conditions, and Wells was cut off for three days by snow. For this service, the Silver Medal was awarded to Coxswain David Cox BEM, and Medal service certificates were given to the remainder of the crew.

Background information

At the west end of the quay at Wells-next-the Sea, close to the 1895 lifeboat house, is a memorial to the 11 lifeboatmen of the crew of 13 lost on 29 October 1880 when the lifeboat *Eliza Adams* capsized on service. She was returning to shore after launching to the brig *Ocean Queen*. The lost men left ten widows and 27 children.

The lifeboat house built in 1895 at the mouth of Wells Harbour, and extensively rebuilt and modified in 1990 to house a 12m Mersey lifeboat.

Key dates

Opened	1838
RNLI	1867
Motor LB	1936
AWLB withdrawn	18.4.1992
Inshore LB	1986 and 1992

Current lifeboat details

Inshore lifeboat

Type	Atlantic 75
Official Number	B-702
Name	Manchester Unity of Oddfellows
Donor	Gift from the Independent Order of Oddfellows Manchester Unity Friendly Society
Placed on station	29.1.1994
Launch	Tractor and do-do carriage

Location history

1838 The first lifeboat house was built in the village, about 30 yards from the high-water mark and 50 from the watch-house; it was used to house the station's first private lifeboat (see below).

1867 The first RNLI lifeboat house was built at the eastern end of the town. In 1870 and 1877 heavy gales destroyed the slipway. This house was used until 1900 and has since been converted into a craft centre.

1900 Following launching difficulties, the lifeboat was moved to the East roadway, where it was kept in the open until 1903.

1902 Owing to difficulties in launching across the beach, a new lifeboat house and timber launching slipway was built at Old Hythe, about a mile west of the town.

1904 A new corrugated lifeboat house and timber slipway were constructed at Old Hythe, from where the lifeboat was operated until 1936; all that remains of this house is a few concrete slabs.

1936 A new lifeboat house was built for the station's first motor lifeboat at the western end of the Promenade; this has been altered and modernised at various times since, and was used for the offshore lifeboats until 1992.

1962 A new tractor house was built to the west of the lifeboat house.

1994 The lifeboat house was upgraded and modernised to provide improved facilities for the Atlantic 75 and its launching tractor; the improved crew facilities included an enlarged crew room, kitchen, office, toilet, shower and watch-room.

Medals and awards

Three medals have been awarded, one Silver and two Bronze.

Notable rescue

On 31 October 1956 the Sheringham lifeboat *Forester's Centenary* was launched in very rough seas to go to the aid of the steam collier *Wimbledon*, which was taking in water off Blakeney. Sister ship the *Sydenham*, and another steamship, the *Eleanor Brook*, were standing by.

The lifeboat and casualty were being continually swept by heavy seas, and the latter's Master had been washed overboard. However, the lifeboat succeeded in taking off eight men who were transferred to another ship. The Master was picked up by the Eleanor Brook, but he could not be resuscitated.

After taking on more petrol from the Wells lifeboat *Cecil Paine*, the lifeboat made a further series of approaches despite the heavy seas, but each time the securing lines parted, forcing her to come round again. This required considerable skill on the part of the Coxswain, who had to work in exact unison with the mechanic.

The lifeboat house built in 1936 at the western end of the Promenade, and modernised in 1994.

Eventually the entire crew was taken off, despite the lifeboat being carried almost on to the *Wimbledon* by a heavy sea, damaging 6 feet of her fendering. Four survivors were transferred to the *Sydenham* and the others were landed at Wells, where beaching conditions were easier than at Sheringham. The lifeboat returned to her station on 4 November.

Coxswain Henry West was awarded the Silver Medal, and Mechanic Edward Craske, who had been up to his armpits in water at times, the Bronze Medal; the Thanks on Vellum was accorded to the rest of the crew, Acting Second Coxswain H. Bishop, Acting Bowman A. Scotter, Assistant Mechanic J. H. Bishop, and crew members D. Little, S. Little and R. West.

Background information

Between 1838 and 1935 two privately funded lifeboats were on station at Sheringham; the first, named *Augusta*, served from 1838 until 1894, and the second, *Henry Ramey Upcher*, from September 1894 until 1935. The boats were both funded by the Upcher family, and since the mid-1970s the latter has been displayed at Sheringham in her old boathouse on the Promenade.

Key dates

Opened	1805
RNLI	1857
Motor LB	1923
Fast LB	1985
Inshore LB	3.1967

Current lifeboat details

All-weather lifeboat

Type	Tyne
Official Number	1097
Operational Number	47-006
Year built	1985
Name	Ruby and Arthur Reed II
Donor	Bequest of Mrs R. M. Reed, with special local appeal, gifts and legacies
Placed on station	16.12.1985
Launch	Slipway

Inshore lifeboat

Type	D class inflatable
Official Number	D-436
Name	Chloe
Donor	Gift in memory of Chloe Long
Placed on station	12.8.1992
Launch	Trolley

Location history

1805 The first lifeboat was funded by local subscriptions, organised by a local committee, and was probably kept on the beach. The first lifeboat house, built some time after the station was founded, was situated near to the Coastguard cottages.

1857 In December the RNLI took control of the station from the Norfolk Shipwreck Association.

1868 A new lifeboat house was built at the foot of the East Gangway, a steep hill paved with granite blocks arranged with their corners sticking up to give a grip to horses' hooves pulling cargo up from the beach; this house was used until 1902.

1902 A new lifeboat house was built at the East Gangway to replace the smaller house of 1864 on the same site; it was used for the No.2 lifeboat from 1923, as in certain states of weather it was impossible to rehouse at the end of the pier. Since 1967 it has been converted into a lifeboat museum, with the former No.1 lifeboat *H. F. Bailey* (ON.777) on display inside.

1923 A new lifeboat house with a slipway 165 feet long was constructed at the end of the pier for the station's first motor lifeboat, and was used until 1996.

1967 An inshore lifeboat station was established in March and the No.2 lifeboat was withdrawn on 22 June. Initially the ILB was kept in the 1902 boathouse, and later in a small house to the west of the pier.

1984 A new ILB house was built on the Promenade, east of the Gangway.

1996 The 1923 lifeboat house was demolished and moved to Southwold, where it is used to house the former lifeboat *Alfred Corry*. Between 1996 and 1999, while the new house and slipway were being built, a carriage-launched lifeboat was operated from the beach close to the 1902 boathouse.

1998-9 A new larger house and slipway at the end of the pier were constructed. It became operational on 4 March 1999.

Medals and awards

Fifty-five medals have been awarded, three Gold, eight Silver and 44 Bronze.

One Silver Medal has been awarded for a shore rescue.

Notable rescue

On 26 October 1941 the lifeboat *H. F. Bailey* was launched to a ship that was reported to be aground on Hammond Knoll, a sandbank 25 miles away. There was a gale blowing and squalls of hail making conditions extremely cold, and when the lifeboat reached Hammond Knoll the steamship *English Trader* was seen aground on the sands with little more than her masts, funnel and chart-room above water.

After waiting for an opportunity to approach the ship, the lifeboat was hit by a huge wall of water that lifted the Coxswain, Second Coxswain, the Bowman and two of the crew out of the boat. The lifeboat keeled over so far that the watching men on the steamer could see her keel, but she did not capsize. As the water poured off the lifeboat, the Second Coxswain's son seized the wheel and steered towards those in the water.

After much effort all were gradually picked up, but the Signalman, who had been in the water nearly half an hour by the time he was hauled back on board, collapsed and was laid under the engine-room canopy. As the lifeboat had been at sea for 7 hours since leaving Cromer, and with ropes round one of the propellers making steering difficult, a course was set for Gorleston. When they arrived, the Signalman was found to be dead. However, the crew recovered a little, filled the petrol tanks, and readied themselves for another attempt.

The lifeboat set out again early the next morning. Although the gale was still blowing, the wind had changed direction. When the lifeboat reached Hammond Knoll, conditions had improved and the Coxswain was able to take the lifeboat straight alongside the steamer. In half an hour 44 men from the casualty had been rescued and were landed safely at Great Yarmouth.

For this truly remarkable rescue, one of the most famous in the RNLI's history, the Silver Medal was awarded to Coxswain Blogg, and Bronze Medals to Second Coxswain John Davies Snr, Mechanic Henry Davies, Assistant Mechanic James Davies, Bowman William Davies, Signalman Edward Allen, and crew members Henry Davies, James Davies, John Davies Jnr, Robert Davies, William Davies and Sidney Harrison.

Background information

The Cromer lifeboat is perhaps best known for the exploits of Henry Blogg, Coxswain between 1909 and 1947. During that time he became the most decorated lifeboatman in the history of the RNLI, winning three Gold and four Silver Medals for outstanding rescues, many of which took place during the two World Wars. His first award was a Gold Medal for the saving of 11 survivors from the steamship *Fernebo*, of Gothenburg, which was wrecked in January 1917. A bust of the former Coxswain is situated on top of the East Cliff outside the Old Watch House, overlooking the No.2 boathouse.

Top The lifeboat house built in 1902 at the East Gangway to replace the smaller house of 1864 on the same site; it has since been converted into a lifeboat museum.

Middle The lifeboat house and slipway built in 1998 at the end of Cromer pier.
Paul Russell

Bottom 47ft Tyne *Ruby and Arthur Reed II* (ON.1097) passes the end of Cromer pier.
Paul Russell

Below The bust of Coxswain Henry Blogg at the top of the East Cliff, outside the Old Watch House.

Location history

1866 A lifeboat house was built on the cliffs at Old Cart Gap, above the gap on to the beach. This house was used throughout the life of the station, and has since been demolished; its foundations can be seen near the front of the current ILB station.

1965 An inshore lifeboat station was established in June; the ILB was kept in a small house at the top of the cliffs, above the gap.

1987 A new ILB house was built on the same site; it includes a crew/instruction room, a drying room, toilet and washing facilities.

1998 The ILB house was extended to provide improved crew facilities.

Medals and awards

One Silver Medal has been awarded, for long service.

Notable rescue

On Christmas Day 1870, the brig *Minerva*, of Seaham, bound for Rochester with a cargo of coal, went ashore off Ostend, a village just north of Happisburgh (pronounced Haisborough). Although the beachmen were at church, four went off in a crab boat to the vessel and found her filling with water.

The Happisburgh lifeboat *Huddersfield* was taken by road on her carriage to Ostend, where she was launched. The brig's crew of seven had left in their own boat,

D class inflatable
Colin Martin
(D-468) outside the
lifeboat house
built in 1987.

from which they were picked up by the lifeboat. The lifeboat had to be landed at Palling, as returning to Happisburgh was impossible due to the state of the wind and tide.

Background information

Happisburgh is perhaps best known for the dangerous Haisborough Sands that run parallel to the coast for some 9 miles. Although both the sandbank and the village are pronounced the same way, the village is normally spelt Happisburgh and the sandbank Haisborough. This sandbank was a particular danger in the 18th and 19th centuries when vessels relied solely on wind power, and it was quite common for a ship on a passage along the East Coast to or from London to be stranded, often with fatal consequences.

Location history

1802 A lifeboat was first placed at Gorleston; it was kept on the beach and launched by carriage.

1866 The first RNLI lifeboat was sent to the station, and in 1868 a new house was built on the beach; launching was difficult due to a number of factors, including the encroachment of the sea, and the site was abandoned in 1881.

1881 A new lifeboat house and slipway were built on the west bank of the river.

1883 Another house was added to the north of the 1881 house to form a large double boathouse, from which the lifeboats were launched by slipway; it was used for the offshore lifeboat until 1967, and has been converted to house the ILB.

1891 A corrugated iron house and short slip on piles were built on the

east bank of the river for the small No.3 lifeboat; this station was closed in 1904, and the boathouse dismantled, ferried across the river and re-erected in Drudge Road, where it is still standing with its original wood-panelled ceiling.

1897 During 1897-98 and 1903-08 there was a steam lifeboat on station, moored at a berth in the river.

1967 A mooring pen was constructed upstream from the double

Key dates

Opened	1805
RNLI	1866
Motor LB	1924
Fast LB	1967
Inshore LB	5.1963

Current lifeboat details

All-weather lifeboat

Type	Trent
Official Number	1208
Operational Number	14-10
Year built	1995
Name	Samarbeta
Donor	Volvo Cars UK Limited and legacies of Elizabeth Longman and Constance Rogers
Placed on station	25.2.1996
Launch	Afloat

Inshore lifeboat

Type	Atlantic 21
Official Number	B-574
Name	Joseph B. Press
Donor	Bequests in memory of Captain Joseph B. Press, from the Manning Press family
Placed on station	12.11.1988
Launch	Davit

boathouse for the fast afloat lifeboat; this pen was used until 1993.

1993 A new mooring berth for the all-weather lifeboat was constructed adjacent to the double lifeboat house; the house itself was renovated and modernised so that one half houses the davit-launched Atlantic 21, and the other the former No.1 lifeboat *John and Mary Meiklam of Gladswood*, which is on display to visitors.

Medals and awards

Thirty-three medals have been awarded, one Gold, 15 Silver and 17 Bronze.

Six Gorleston men who went out on service in the Lowestoft lifeboat in 1922 were awarded Bronze Medals.

Three Silver Medals have been awarded for shore-boat rescues.

Notable rescue

On 19 October 1922 the Caister lifeboat attempted to launch to the steamship *Hopelyn*, whose steering had failed, but could not get clear of the beach because of the wind.

The Gorleston lifeboat, *Kentwell*, was launched, with Coxswain William Fleming, and was towed out by the tug *George Jewson*. She stayed at the wreck for 10 hours in the darkness; at daybreak the casualty's crew could not be seen, so they returned to station.

However, they learned that a 'flag' was being shown on the wreck, so the *Kentwell* went back. Despite a lack of water on the sandbank the lifeboat got close, but then heavy seas drove her against the *Hopelyn*, causing considerable damage. She was taken into deeper water to wait for a better opportunity.

Meanwhile the Lowestoft motor lifeboat *Agnes Cross* was launched, but it was now too dark and the sea too heavy for another attempt. Early on 21 October the *Agnes Cross* set out again. Despite having to avoid the broken plates sticking out from the casualty's hull, the extra power provided by the motor enabled her to come alongside long enough for the 24 crew to be rescued.

The lifeboat's anchor cable was fouled in the wreckage, so had to be cut before she could leave. She suffered a pounding out on the sandbank, but once clear reached Gorleston safely.

For this outstanding rescue both Coxswain Fleming, of Gorleston, and Coxswain Robert Swan, of Lowestoft, were awarded the Gold Medal. Silver Medals were awarded to Captain Carver, and R. Scott, Motor Mechanic on board the *Agnes Cross*, and Bronze Medals to each of the Gorleston crew.

Background information

As well as the RNLI vessels, a number of independently operated lifeboats have been operated by the various Beachmen Companies, common on the East Anglian coast. Several boathouses were built by these companies on the Quay next to the RNLI boathouse of 1881/3, including the Gorleston Volunteer Lifeboat House, which is now in a poor state of repair. The Rangers Boathouse, built next to this house, was demolished in 1993 to make way for the new lifeboat mooring pen.

Although the lifeboat is actually located at Gorleston, the station has been known as Great Yarmouth and Gorleston since 1926, reflecting the work done by the Great Yarmouth station, which had been closed in 1919.

In Gorleston Cemetery there is a small square memorial to the four lifeboatmen lost when the lifeboat *Refuge* capsized in November 1888. The tower of the Parish Church at Gorleston was restored in 1907-8 as a memorial to all the Gorleston lifeboatmen who have been lost at sea.

The double lifeboat house built in 1881/83 and extensively modernised in 1993, with the launch davit for the Atlantic 21 on the right.

Key dates

Opened	1801
RNLI	1855
Motor LB	1921
Fast LB	1987

Current lifeboat details

All-weather lifeboat

Type	Tyne
Official Number	1132
Operational Number	47-020
Year built	1987
Name	*Spirit of Lowestoft*
Donor The Lowestoft Lifeboat Appeal with other gifts and legacies	
Placed on station	16.11.1987
Launch	Afloat

Location history

1801 A lifeboat was first placed at Lowestoft, but was soon removed as the local boatmen refused to man it.

1807 A second boat was built specially for the station and a boathouse was built near the low lighthouse, beneath the town.

1858 After the RNLI had taken over the station, a new lifeboat house was built.

1870 A new boathouse was built alongside the 1858 boathouse. These two houses were used, with various alterations, until the lifeboats were moved to moorings in the harbour. They stood just to the north of the present Hamilton Dock, but were demolished in 1972.

1883 It was proposed that the large No 1 lifeboat should be kept afloat in the winter months, and the owners of the dock, the Great Eastern Railway Co, granted a mooring in the fork of two jetties at the inner end of North Pier.

1886 The mooring was used all year round.

1892 A gear-shed and store was built close to the moorings, which were used until 1955.

1955 A jetty to the seaward side of Hamilton Dock was used for the lifeboat's moorings from March 1955 until February 1969, when it was demolished.

1969 A temporary mooring was provided on the north side of Hamilton Dock, which was used until 1972.

1972 The lifeboat was moored in the Yacht Basin, with temporary shore facilities on the adjacent quay near the Yacht Club; these moorings were used until 1998.

1998 A new shore facility and workshop was built on the site of the former Pier Pavilion, and a new pontoon mooring in the south-eastern corner of the Basin was provided nearby as part of the development of a marina in the Yacht Basin.

Medals and awards

Thirty-six medals have been awarded, two Gold, 19 Silver and 15 Bronze.

Two Silver medals have been awarded for shore-boat rescues, the last one in 1990.

Notable rescue

On 21 November 1927 the lifeboat *Agnes Cross* went to the aid of the smack *Lily of Devon*, which had missed Lowestoft harbour entrance in an easterly gale and very heavy seas. She was being carried towards a concrete breakwater, heavy seas were breaking over her, and her crew of three were in the rigging.

Within 2 minutes the lifeboat was on the scene, anchored and veered down towards the casualty, but was swept by the heavy seas. She struck the bottom, but gradually edged nearer the casualty. She was thrown against the side of the smack, but managed to remain there long enough for the three men to be taken off and landed at Lowestoft. The engine starting handle was smashed when the lifeboat was driven against the casualty; luckily the engine kept going, for there would have been no way to restart it.

For this rescue the Silver Medal was awarded to Coxswain Albert Spurgeon, while the rest of the crew received additional monetary awards.

The pontoon berth installed in 1998 for 47ft Tyne *Spirit of Lowestoft* (ON.1132), close to the shore facility in the south-eastern corner of the Yacht Basin. *Gary Markham*

Key dates

Opened	1841-1940; ro1963
RNLI	1854
Motor LB	1925
AWLB withdrawn	1940
Inshore LB	7.1963

Current lifeboat details

Inshore lifeboat

Type	Atlantic 75
Official Number	B-750
Name	*Leslie Tranmere*
Donor	Annie Tranmere Trust
Placed on station	28.10.1998
Launch	Davit

Location history

1841 A lifeboat house was built, situated under the North Cliff. It was used until 1862 when it was undermined during a severe gale in which about a third of the house was destroyed.

1862 The lifeboat house was rebuilt in a more secure place on South Denes; enlarged in 1893, it was used until 1908, and has since been demolished.

1866 A new lifeboat house was built for the No.2 lifeboat; it was used until 1920 and has since been demolished.

1880 Both houses were repaired and the shingle floor cemented.

1904 Following erosion of the beach, sheet piling was built around the lifeboat houses to protect them.

1908 The No.1 lifeboat was moved to the harbour, where it was kept afloat and a boarding platform and store-house were constructed near the Ferry.

1925 A motor lifeboat was placed on station and was kept afloat in the harbour, formed by the estuary of the River Blythe.

1940 The station was closed because the boom placed across the harbour as an anti-invasion measure prevented the lifeboat putting to sea.

1963 An inshore lifeboat station, one of the first ten, was established in July; the ILB was kept in the store building of The Harbour Inn.

1966 A purpose-built wooden ILB house was constructed at Blackshore, some 100 yards from the first location; a combined Harbour Master's Office was added later. From this small house, the ILB was launched stern first down a short slipway into the river.

1993 A new ILB house was built on the Dock Wall, near the harbour entrance; the ILB is launched using a marine davit.

Medals and awards

Fourteen medals have been awarded, ten Silver one Bronze and, since the ILB has been on station, three further Bronze Medals.

Notable rescue

On the night of 16 January 1981 the Atlantic 21 inshore lifeboat B-518 *Solebay* was launched to the motor fishing vessel *Concord*, which had broken down in a SSE gale with continuous snow showers and a rough sea.

Helmsman Roger Trigg took the ILB alongside and put one of his crew on board. The casualty was then taken in tow by another fishing boat, the *Broadside*, and the ILB escorted both to Lowestoft. The tow parted four times, and each time the ILB helped to re-establish it, ensuring that the boats reached the harbour.

For this rescue the Bronze Medal was awarded to Helmsman Trigg, and the Thanks on Vellum was accorded to crew members J. P. A. Adnams and A. Chambers, as well as to the *Broadside*'s Skipper.

Launching Atlantic 75 *Leslie Tranmere* (B-750) on exercise in February 1999.

Atlantic 75 *Leslie Tranmere* (B-750) in the River Blyth on the same day.

Key dates

Opened	1851
RNLI	1855
Motor LB	1930
Fast LB	1993
Inshore LB	7.1977

Current lifeboat details

All-weather lifeboat

Type	Mersey
Official Number	1193
Operational Number	12-34
Year built	1993
Name	Freddie Cooper
Donor	Legacy of Mrs Winifred May Cooper, named in memory of a former director of East Midland Allied Press Limited
Placed on station	19.12.1993
Launch	Carriage

Inshore lifeboat

Type	D class inflatable
Official Number	D-520
Name	Bob Savage
Donor	Gift of Mr and Mrs Hugh Turner
Placed on station	30.6.1997
Launch	Trolley

Location history

1851 The station was established when the lifeboat from Sizewell was moved here. A wooden lifeboat house was built at Slaughden Quay, at the southern end of the town, and this was used until 1864 when it was demolished as the site was required for building purposes.

1864 A new brick lifeboat house was constructed; used until 1879, it was demolished in 1884.

1879 Due to encroachment of the boathouse, the boat was kept in the open under canvas at a site three-quarters of a mile to the north, just to the south of the Moot Hall. At many stations in East Anglia lifeboats were kept on the beach in the open.

1883 A store house was rented to provide a gear store.

1905 A smaller No.2 lifeboat was placed on station, also kept in the open and launched across the beach; it was withdrawn in 1959.

1930 A turntable was used for the No.1 lifeboat.

1959 A new turntable was built higher up the beach to give the lifeboat a better run down to the sea.

1963 Another new turntable was installed and a 62-foot launchway was built across the shingle to improve the launching arrangements.

1968 A new workshop and crew room was built on the beach close to the launching slipways.

1977 An inshore lifeboat station was established in July.

1978 The Old North Lookout on the promenade, previously used by the Fishermen's Guild, was adapted to house the ILB; it was extended in 1997 to accommodate the bladed tractor used for flattening the shingle.

1986 A new tractor house and workshop was constructed; this was used until 1993.

1993 A new lifeboat house was built on the beach, on the same site as the turntable and launchways, which were removed. A 'Penza' lifeboat house (see Lochinver entry), it consisted of two adjacent houses, one to accommodate the lifeboat and the other the launching tractor, linked by a single-storey section providing crew facilities.

The 'Penza' lifeboat and tractor houses built in 1993 on the beach at Aldeburgh.

Medals and awards

Eleven medals have been awarded, eight Silver and three Bronze.

Two medals have been awarded for shore-boat rescues, both Silver.

Notable rescue

During 1900 the Aldeburgh lifeboat performed two notable rescues, for which Coxswain James Cable was awarded the Silver Medal, his third. It also recognised his service in the lifeboat, as by this time he had assisted in the rescue of 269 lives.

The first took place on 15 February. The lifeboat *Reserve No.1* was launched at night in heavy seas and driving rain; Cable was swept overboard, but regained the lifeboat. Next morning the steamship *Hylton* was found with neither rudder nor propeller, and the lifeboat went to Lowestoft to arrange a tow.

On 4 October the same lifeboat was towed to the barque *Antares*. Three attempts had to be made to take off the crew of 11.

Background information

In the churchyard are the graves of the three lifeboatmen lost on 21 December 1859 when the lifeboat capsized on service, together with a memorial at the head of the graves of the seven men lost in the lifeboat *Aldeburgh*, which capsized on 7 December 1899, who also have a memorial plaque in the church itself.

There was a No.2 station in operation between 1905 and 1959.

Key dates

Opened	1821-26 and 1876-1917; ro1965
RNLI	1876
Motor LB	1967
AWLB withdrawn	1917
Fast LB	1967
Inshore LB	5.1965

Current lifeboat details

All-weather lifeboat

Type	Severn
Official Number	1202
Operational Number	17-03
Year built	1994
Name	Albert Brown
Donor	Bequest of Victoria Maisie Brown, London, in memory of her husband
Placed on station	2.10.1996
Launch	Afloat

Inshore lifeboat

Type	Atlantic 21
Official Number	B-571
Name	British Diver II
Donor	British Sub Aqua Club
Placed on station	31.10.1987
Launch	Davit

Location history

1821 The first lifeboat was placed on station by the Essex Lifeboat Association; it was used until 1826.

1876 The RNLI established a station, a lifeboat house was built on the East Beach, and the lifeboat was launched using a carriage. This house was used for the lifeboat until 1881, but was retained until the station closed in 1917; it has since been converted into a Museum and now houses the former Clacton-on-Sea lifeboat *Valentine Wyndham-Quin*.

1881 The lifeboats were moored afloat, near the Pier, and towed to wrecks by steam tugs. The sailing lifeboat was withdrawn in 1912.

1890 In addition to the pulling lifeboats, a steam lifeboat was placed on station and kept at moorings. In 1917 the station was closed when the steam lifeboat was bought by the Admiralty for use during the First World War.

1965 The station was re-opened and an inshore lifeboat was placed on station in May; the ILB was housed near the 1876 lifeboat house.

1967 A fast afloat motor lifeboat was placed on station and was kept afloat in The Pound, near Halfpenny Pier; moorings have since been taken up in the Navyard Wharf.

1977 A new ILB house was built on Halfpenny Pier, and a davit-launching facility for the Atlantic 21 installed; an extension was added in 1990, and a larger crew room provided in 1993.

Medals and awards

Three medals have been awarded, all Silver, while 14 medals have been awarded for shore or shore-boat rescues, also all Silver.

Four Bronze Medals were awarded for a rescue to two Trinity House officers.

Notable rescue

On 20 January 1881 the lifeboat *Springwell* was launched to the Dutch steamship *Ingerid*, wrecked off Clacton. The lifeboat crew had to break through ice and row for over 8 hours before being towed for 4 miles.

Seven men who had survived the freezing conditions were taken aboard the lifeboat with the help of a line. The tug *Dispatch* towed the lifeboat back to Harwich, where it arrived on 21 January.

Silver Medals were awarded to Second Coxswain William Britton and Captain St Vincent Nepean RN, the RNLI's District Inspector.

Background information

Harwich's current all-weather lifeboat, the *Albert Brown*, was the first 17m Severn class lifeboat to be placed on operational service.

17m Severn *Albert Brown* (ON.1202) and Atlantic 21 *British Diver II* (B-571).

The lifeboat house built in 1876 on the East Beach, now used as a Lifeboat Museum.

Current lifeboat details

All-weather lifeboat

Type	Tyne
Official Number	1154
Operational Number	47-036
Year built	1989
Name	Kenneth Thelwall II
Donor	Bequest of Kenneth Thelwall, Walkington, Yorks
Placed on station	15.5.1996
Launch	Afloat

Location history

1884 A lifeboat house and slipway, with a roadway between them, were built for the station's first lifeboat; this house was used until 1900, and since 1984 has been used for the Walton Maritime Museum, run by the Frinton & Walton Heritage Trust.

1900 When a larger lifeboat was supplied to the station, it was kept afloat at moorings off the pier, with the boarding-boat nearby; various improvements to the boarding stage at the pier have been made, although boarding the lifeboat in severe weather remains difficult as the moorings are very exposed. A crew room and souvenir outlet, on the outside of which are mounted the station's service boards, are situated in the centre of the town, overlooking the pier.

Medals and awards

Fifteen medals have been awarded, four Silver and 11 Bronze.

Notable rescue

On 14 September 1975 the lifeboat *Edian Courtauld* was launched following the sighting of a red flare off the Long Sand. The weather was overcast and the wind was NNE, force 7. To reach the casualty, the yacht *Tsunami*, the lifeboat was taken across the Long Sand despite confused and shallow seas that, at one point, completely washed over the lifeboat.

The yacht was found lying at anchor, flying a distress signal. The heavy seas were causing her to veer excessively, but the lifeboat was taken to within hailing distance to confirm that the crew would leave the yacht. With the lifeboat crew spaced along the side deck, three of the yacht's crew were taken off when the lifeboat was taken alongside.

However, as the other two on board refused to leave, towing the boat into deeper water was the only option. A line was got aboard, and in the strong gale and very rough sea the tow began. This proved to be a difficult operation as the yacht's rudder was jammed hard to starboard, and the keel was fractured. However, after 8 hours the lifeboat brought the yacht into the Walton River in the early hours of 15 September. All five members of the yacht's crew were then landed safely and taken home.

The Silver Medal was awarded to Coxswain Frank Bloom in recognition of his courage, good seamanship and determination throughout this service; the Thanks on Vellum was accorded to the other members of the lifeboat crew, Second Coxswain Dennis Finch, Mechanic Bryan Ward, Bowman Robert Kemp, Assistant Mechanic Keith Richardson and crew members Jack Barrett, Brian Oxley and Owen Bloom.

Background information

There were two private lifeboats operated at Walton, both named *True to the Core*. In service from 1894 until about 1911, they are credited with 35 launches in which 216 lives were saved. From 1901 to 1917 two private lifeboats, both named *Sailor's Friend*, were in service at nearby Frinton.

The Walton lifeboat *E. M. E. D.* was one of the 19 lifeboats of the Royal National Lifeboat Institution that took part in the evacuation from Dunkirk in May 1940, but she was manned by naval ratings and not by her own crew. She went over to Dunkirk in a little company of boats towed by a tug. Off Graveslines German aeroplanes attacked them three times; the blast broke the two ropes and threw men into the sea. One boat was sunk and others turned back, but the lifeboat went on. The officer in command was killed by a shell, and she returned to Dover with a rope round her propeller. A diver went down and cut it away, then she sailed again for Dunkirk. The lifeboat crew were bitterly disappointed that they were not allowed to sail with her.

47ft Tyne Kenneth Thelwall II (ON.1154) at moorings off the pier at Walton.

Key dates

Opened	1878
RNLI	1878
Motor LB	1912
AWLB withdrawn	10.8.1984
Inshore LB	7.1966; second 1984

Current lifeboat details

Inshore lifeboats

Type	Atlantic 75
Official Number	B-744
Name	Robert George Alexander
Donor	Legacy of Mr R. G. Alexander
Placed on station	10.10.1998
Launch	Slipway

Type	D class inflatable
Official Number	D-431
Name	Veronica
Donor	Bequest of Miss Doris Veronica Tudor-Williams
Placed on station	1.7.1995
Launch	Trolley

Location history

1878 A lifeboat house, with Masonic emblems incorporated into the structure to commemorate the donor, was built in Anglefield on the corner of Church Road; soon after its building a fence had to be placed around it to prevent cattle from causing damage. This house was used until 1901, and has since been converted into a public house.

1884 Two slipways were built on either side of the pier to improve launching, and the lifeboat was kept on the pier during the winter.

1901 The lifeboat was kept at moorings off the pier during the summer, and launched from the slipways on the pier in the winter; a boarding-boat was supplied to reach the lifeboat when it was on moorings, an arrangement that lasted until 1927.

1927 A new lifeboat house and roller slipway were built on the north side of the pier, and this house has remained in use ever since, with various alterations for subsequent lifeboats.

1966 An inshore lifeboat station was established in July; the ILB was kept in a small building on the promenade to the west of the pier.

1984 The pier lifeboat house was adapted to accommodate an Atlantic 21, and a launching cradle was installed.

1998 The lifeboat house was modified and extended for an Atlantic 75, incorporating improved crew facilities.

Medals and awards

Seventeen medals have been awarded, 15 Silver and two Bronze.

Five Silver medals have been awarded for shore-boat rescues.

Notable rescue

On 27 December 1917 the lifeboat *Albert Edward* was launched to a vessel that was reported to be aground on the Long Sands. The weather was bitterly cold with snow showers and a strong easterly gale.

The lifeboat located the casualty, the steamship *Iris*, which had several feet of water in her engine room. The Master initially refused to leave the ship, so the lifeboat stood by for several hours during which time the weather worsened. However, it was not until the seas were washing the vessel fore and aft that the Captain decided to leave.

The crew of 22, plus a pilot who was also on board, were rescued by the lifeboat with great difficulty and danger. As the lifeboat approached the stricken vessel, those on board jumped to safety one at a time. Both the rescuers and the rescued were numbed and almost frozen from their ordeal, having been exposed for over 24 hours in icy cold weather.

For this rescue the Silver Medal was awarded to Coxswain George Grigson and the Bronze Medal to Second Coxswain Jesse Salmon.

Background information

The Clacton station had an eventful time during the Second World War. The lifeboat *Edward Z. Dresden* was one of the 19 lifeboats that went to Dunkirk on 30 May 1940 to help in the evacuation of the British Expeditionary Force. Later, in August 1940, the lifeboat had to be kept moored at Brightlingsea in the River Colne, where she lay afloat, because she could no longer be operated from the pier lifeboat house at Clacton; the middle of the pier had been blown up to make it useless to invading forces, so reaching the lifeboat house was not possible.

The lifeboat house and slipway built in 1928 on the north side of the pier, and used for Atlantic rigid-inflatables since 1984.

Key dates

Opened	1963
RNLI	1963
Inshore LB	7.1963

Current lifeboat details

Inshore lifeboat

Type	Atlantic 21
Official Number	B-570
Name	*Himley Hall*
Donor	The Himley Hall Sailing Club, Dudley, and the Mersea Island Appeal
Placed on station	19.7.1987
Launch	Trolley

Location history

1963 An inshore lifeboat station was established in July, one of the first ten; the ILB was kept in the open until a house was acquired adjacent to the local Yacht Club, opposite 'The Hard'.

1981 The ILB house was enlarged and a crew room was added.

1991-2 A new timber-clad ILB house was built on a piled concrete platform 200 metres north-west of the previous house, with a slipway leading down to the tidal mud flats; it includes the Atlantic 21, a new launch and recovery winch, a crew room and galley, a souvenir outlet and toilet facilities.

Medals and awards

No medals have been awarded.

Notable rescue

On 26 May 1979 the Atlantic 21 inshore lifeboat B-529 *Alexander Duckham* was launched in a southerly storm force 9 gale and steep, breaking seas to go to an upturned sailing dinghy. Although the two occupants had swum ashore safely, crew member Jonathan French entered the wtaer to look under the dinghy to ensure that no one was trapped. Then for over 2 hours the ILB aided the many small boats in the area that had been caught out by the bad weather.

For this service the Thanks on Vellum was accorded to Helmsman James Clarke and Jonathan French.

The ILB house built in 1991-2 with a slipway leading down to the tidal mud flats and sheltered launching site.

Key dates

Opened	1966
RNLI	1966
Inshore LB	5.1966; second 1996

Current lifeboat details

Inshore lifeboats

Type	Atlantic 75
Official Number	B-733
Name	*Brandy Hole*
Donor	Fundraising activities by Brandy Hole Yacht Club
Placed on station	14.2.1997
Launch	Floating boathouse
Type	D class inflatable
Official Number	D-519
Name	*Ernest and Rose Chapman*
Donor	Gift from David and Barbara Chapman, Wickford, Essex, in memory of David's parents
Placed on station	12.5.1997
Launch	Trolley

Location history

1966 An inshore lifeboat station was established in May; it was to have closed at the end of the summer in 1968, but following the withdrawal of the rescue helicopters from RAF Manston this decision was reversed and the station remained operational. The ILB was housed in a Hardun building near the Yacht Club.

1988 A new brick ILB house was built to replace the previous house, close to the Yacht Club, to accommodate the station's D class inflatable.

1996 Following a decision to relocate the lifeboat station to the Yacht Harbour at Burnham-on-Crouch, a floating boathouse to house the Atlantic 75 was constructed, one of only three in the country (the others being at Poole and Brighton). At the same time a two-storey shore building next to the pontoon walkway leading to the floating boathouse was constructed to provide support facilities.

Medals and awards

No medals have been awarded.

Atlantic 75 *Brandy Hole* (B-733) passes the floating boathouse installed in 1996 in the Yacht Harbour at Burnham-on-Crouch.

Key dates

Opened	1879
RNLI	1879
Motor LB	1928
AWLB withdrawn	28.3.1976
Inshore LB	5.1965; second 1969; third 1987

Current lifeboat details

Inshore lifeboats

Type	Atlantic 21
Official Number	B-567
Name	Percy Garon II
Donor	Special local appeal
Placed on station	28.4.1986
Launch	Davit

Type	D class inflatable
Official Number	D-487
Name	Foresters London Pride
Donor	The Courts of London United District of the Ancient Order of Foresters Friendly Society
Placed on station	31.7.1995
Launch	Davit

Type	D class inflatable
Official Number	D-527
Name	Ethel Violet
Donor	Legacy of Peter Royal
Placed on station	27.10.1997
Launch	Trolley

Location history

1879 The station was established and, as a carriage launch was considered impractical, the lifeboat was placed near the end of the pier; between 1879 and 1891 it was kept on davits or moored at Pier.

1885 A No.2 station was established, and the lifeboat was launched from a carriage, often at Shoeburyness some 4 miles away. A lifeboat house was built in 1886 at the bottom of Hartington Road, and was demolished during the late 1970s.

1891 It was decided to keep the lifeboat afloat inside the head of the pier in the winter, and in the 1886 house during the summer.

1934 A new lifeboat house with a roller slipway was built at the east side of the seaward end of the pier; this was used for the lifeboat until 1976, and was then converted to house the station's Atlantic 21. Southend's pier, built in 1889 and 1.3 miles in length, is the longest such structure in Britain.

1965 An inshore lifeboat was sent to the station in May; it was housed in a boatshed on a jetty on the Promenade to the east of the Pier, and lowered into the water by davit.

1969 In April, in view of the withdrawal of the helicopters from Manston, a second inshore lifeboat was sent to the station; it was housed on the Promenade close to the pier.

1979 A new ILB house and slipway were built on the promenade just to the east of the Pier to replace the former ILB house, which was beyond economic repair.

1986 On 30 June the 1934 boathouse was severely damaged when a coaster smashed through the Pier, almost completely demolishing the lifeboat's slipway; the house was unusable and was subsequently demolished, and a temporary base was found for the pier ILBs.

1987 A new boathouse was constructed adjacent to the ILB accommodation on the Prince George extension of the Pier, and a new davit and winch was installed for launching and recovering the Atlantic 21 and D class.

1989 An extension was completed to provide permanent housing for one of the two D class ILBs and a souvenir outlet at the end of the pier.

1995 A Pier fire restricted access to the end of the Pier for two weeks, and damaged the RNLI building that houses the electric buggy used by the crew to reach the end of the pier.

Medals and awards

Nine medals have been awarded, one Silver and eight Bronze.

Two medals have been awarded for shore-boat rescues, both Silver.

Background information

The outstanding figure in the history of the station was Sidney H. B. Page. He was a member of the crew from 1911 until 1933, was Bowman from February to December 1933, Second Coxswain from January to June 1934 and Coxswain from July 1934 to December 1955. From 1911 until 1955 the Southend lifeboat rescued 431 lives. Page won the Silver Medal for gallantry, the Bronze Medal twice and the Thanks on Vellum four times. When he retired in 1955 he became honorary boathouse attendant. He died in 1962 aged 71.

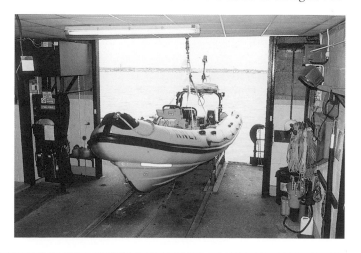

Relief Atlantic 21 *Wolverson X-Ray* (B-590) on the launching cradle inside the pier-end ILB house; the two ILBs at the end of the pier are launched by davit into the water.

Key dates

Opened	1969
RNLI	1969
Motor LB	1969
Fast LB	1974
Inshore LB	7.1972

Current lifeboat details

All-weather lifeboat

Type	Trent
Official Number	1211
Operational Number	14-13
Year built	1995
Name	George and Ivy Swanson
Donor	Bequests of Mrs Ivy Ethel Swanson, Miss Joan Dora May Bawden, Miss Joan Harris and Mrs Violet Wigington
Placed on station	16.3.1996
Launch	Afloat

Inshore lifeboat

Type	D class inflatable
Official Number	D-513
Name	Seahorse I
Donor	Proceeds of the Seahorse Ball, Surrey
Placed on station	31.10.96
Launch	Davit

Location history

1969 The station was established, initially on an evaluation basis until a satisfactory berth became available; the lifeboat was moored afloat in Berth 25 in a part of the old Docks.

1977 A new ILB house was constructed with crew facilities above; the ILB was kept on a trolley and lifted into the water by a davit.

1985 A new lifeboat berth was found as the old one was no longer tenable; after negotiations with Medway Ports Authority, berthing arrangements were provided at Gun Wharf Steps in Sheerness Docks.

1992 A new launching davit was installed on the quay.

Medals and awards

Four medals have been awarded, one Silver and three Bronze.

Notable rescue

On the night of 19 March 1980 the lifeboat *Helen Turnball* was launched to the radio ship *Mi Amigo* which was dragging her anchors in Black Deep near the Long Sand Bank, 24 miles from the station, in a strong easterly force 9 gale and a very rough sea. During the passage to the casualty the lifeboat had to reduce speed as she was shipping water and pounding heavily in the rough, short head seas.

Once on the scene, the lifeboat was manoeuvred alongside the *Mi Amigo* in confused seas, which caused the casualty to roll heavily. Getting the lifeboat alongside in between the extreme rise and fall of the sea was very hazardous as she was working in very shallow water. On 13 occasions the lifeboat was taken alongside, but many of the attempts had to be abandoned as the lifeboat was in danger of being landed on the casualty's deck.

During these approaches the four crew were successfully taken off one by one. During one approach the lifeboat was slammed against the side of the ship, but luckily nobody on board was injured. Once the last of the crew had been taken on

Launching D class inflatable *Kensington Rescuer* (D-362, on station 1988-96) into the dock in 1993.

board, the lifeboat was taken clear and into deeper water. She then set course for Sheerness, arriving in the early hours of 20 March.

For this service the Silver Medal was awarded to Coxswain/Mechanic Charles Henry Bowry; the Thanks on Vellum was accorded to the rest of the crew, Second Coxswain Arthur Lukey, Assistant Mechanic Roderick Underhill and crew members Malcolm Keen, Ian McCourt and William Edwards.

14m Trent *George and Ivy Swanson* (ON.1211) on exercise in the Thames Estuary in 1996.

Key dates

Opened	1963
RNLI	1963
Inshore LB	7.1963

Current lifeboat details

Inshore lifeboat

Type	Atlantic 21
Official Number	B-560
Name	British Diver
Donor	British Sub Aqua Club
Placed on station	10.7.1983
Launch	Tractor and do-do carriage

Location history

1963 An inshore lifeboat station, one of the first ten, was established in July; the ILB was kept at the East Quay.

1974 A new ILB house was built at the West Gate of the harbour for the Atlantic 21 lifeboat.

1980 A first floor was added to the boathouse, to improve the station's facilities.

1989 A single-storey extension to the side of the boathouse was constructed, providing improved crew facilities, a fuel store, turntable store, a general storeroom, drying room and a souvenir sales outlet with a display area.

Medals and awards

A Bronze Medal was awarded for a shore-boat rescue in 1956.

Notable rescue

On the evening of 19 April 1981 the Atlantic 21 inshore lifeboat B-516 was launched to the catamaran *Rumpleteazer*, which had broken steering gear and was making water in a north-easterly gale, very rough sea and poor visibility in darkness. The passage to the casualty had to be made at reduced speed, as the ILB headed into very short, heavy seas.

Once on the scene, the ILB was lashed alongside the casualty to provide power and steerage, by which time the wind had risen to gale force 8. The two boats headed downwind, on course for Herne Bay small boat anchorage. After waiting for a heavy squall to pass, the catamaran was anchored and the crew of three were taken off by the ILB.

The passage back to the station was made at two-thirds speed, despite one of the survivors suffering from hypothermia. Almost 2 hours after launching, the ILB was landed at Whitstable, where all three survivors were treated for fatigue and hypothermia.

For this service the Thanks on Vellum was accorded to Helmsman Michael Judge in recognition of the determination and seamanship he displayed throughout the rescue.

Background information

In anticipation of a new Atlantic 75 lifeboat being placed on station, plans have been produced for a completely new boathouse on the same site as the existing building; this should be completed in 1999.

The ILB house built in 1974 at the West Gate of the harbour and subsequently extended and enlarged.

Launching Atlantic 21 *British Diver* (B-560) on exercise in 1998.

British Diver leaving the harbour on exercise.

Key dates

Opened	1857
RNLI	1860
Motor LB	1925
Fast LB	1991
Inshore LB	5.1966

Current lifeboat details

All-weather lifeboat

Type	Mersey
Official Number	1177
Operational Number	12-20
Year built	1991
Name	*Leonard Kent*
Donor	Bequests of Mr Leonard Francis Kent, St Helier; Graeme Edward Godfrey, Ellen Agnes Houghton, Florence Evelyn Rodwell; Margate Branch Appeal
Placed on station	19.12.91
Launch	Carriage

Inshore lifeboat

Type	D class inflatable
Official Number	D-400
Name	*Tigger*
Donor	Gift of Mr John Davenport
Placed on station	17.12.89
Launch	Trolley

Location history

1857 The Margate Boatmen were presented with a lifeboat, which was taken over by the RNLI in 1860; this first lifeboat was kept on the stone pier in a house that was altered in 1861.

1866 A new lifeboat house, 'an ornate building on the lower promenade', was built on the site of the first house, which had been used by the Beachmen; the Town Council agreed that it could be built on the proviso that it had a flat roof upon which the Town Band could play during the season.

1897-8 Following difficulties with carriage launching, two slipways were constructed on either side of the wooden jetty to improve launching arrangements, and a No.2 lifeboat was placed on station; the lifeboats were kept in the open at the head of the slipways.

1923-5 A new lifeboat house for the station's first motor lifeboat was built on the eastern (No.2) slipway; this house was adapted at various times for subsequent lifeboats, and it also suffered damage at times during high tides and severe weather.

1928 The lifeboat on the western (No.1) slipway was withdrawn.

1966 An inshore lifeboat station was established in May; the ILB was housed in a small prefabricated building adjacent to the harbour.

1976-7 With the pier rapidly deteriorating and the cost of building a walkway to the boathouse prohibitive, the possibility of replacing the slipway launch with a carriage launch was investigated; tenders were issued in 1978.

1978 A new lifeboat house, situated at the Rendezvous, was constructed. Although the old house had been rendered inaccessible from the shore by gale damage, on 11-12 January 1978 the jetty was completely destroyed by severe gales, the house damaged beyond repair and much of the pier collapsed; after the storm the crew were lowered to the boathouse by helicopter and managed to launch the lifeboat.

1979 The lifeboat house and slipway on the pier was demolished.

1998 An extension to the lifeboat house was built, providing improved crew facilities and better ILB accommodation.

Medals and awards

Six medals have been awarded, five Silver and one Bronze.

Notable rescue

Early in the morning of 7 November 1952 the lifeboat *North Foreland (Civil Service No.11)* was launched to the barque *Vera*, which was ashore near the Mid-Barrow Lightvessel on the north side of the Thames Estuary. There was a north-westerly moderate gale gusting to a whole gale with squalls of rain and sleet, and continuous sheets of spray made visibility poor.

To reach the casualty the lifeboat had to travel 20 miles across the Thames estuary, reaching the scene just after 6.00am. After an extensive search of the sands in the locality, the casualty was spotted near the Maplin Spit Buoy with her crew of two in the rigging, which was visible above the water, holding on to the halliards.

In order to rescue the crew, the Coxswain had to take the lifeboat across the deck of the barque. The first attempt to do this failed, as the lifeboat was knocked back by a heavy sea, but the second was successful and one of the men was taken on board, having slid down the rigging to safety. Although the other survivor came down the rigging, he missed the lifeboat, so she was brought round again and at the third pass over the casualty took him on board.

Both men were suffering from exposure, and it was important to get them ashore as soon as possible, so they were landed at Brightlingsea. The lifeboat had been at sea for almost 7 hours, and had travelled a total of 43 miles during the rescue. She returned to her station in the afternoon, leaving just before midday and arriving 5 hours later.

For this rescue the Silver Medal was awarded to Coxswain Dennis Price, and the Thanks on Vellum was accorded to Second Coxswain Edward Parker and Mechanic Alfred Lacey.

Background information

A surfboat was operated by the local boatmen at Margate between 1857 and the 1930s. It was bought by public donation following the wreck of the *Northern Belle* in January 1857, from which many lives had been saved by similar boats operating from Broadstairs. Three of these surfboats were stationed consecutively at Margate, all named *Friend of all Nations*. They served until well into the 1930s, and the last one eventually became redundant when the RNLI motor lifeboat proved to be the most efficient means of life-saving.

The most famous incident involving the surfboats occurred in December 1897, when the second *Friend of all Nations* capsized on service with the loss of nine of her 13 crew. There are two monuments in memory of the men who were lost, one on the Promenade, depicting a lifeboatman looking out to sea, and another in Margate Cemetery.

Margate had a proud record of service during the Second World War. The lifeboat *The Lord Southborough (Civil Service No.1)* was one of the 19 that went to Dunkirk on 30 May 1940 to help in the evacuation of the British Expeditionary Force; under the command of Coxswain Edward Drake Parker she brought off some 600 men. Coxswain Parker was one of the two lifeboat coxswains who, for their services at Dunkirk, were awarded the Distinguished Service Medal. In addition to this rescue, the pilot of a British aircraft who was rescued on 3 September 1940, Officer Richard H. Hillary, turned out to be a descendant of Sir William Hillary, the Founder of the RNLI.

Top The lifeboat house built in 1978 at the Rendezvous, photographed in 1997 before it was extended and altered.

Middle 12m Mersey *Leonard Kent* (ON.1177) outside the altered lifeboat house in July 1998 prior to being launched on exercise.

Bottom Leonard Kent at sea off Margate.

Key dates

Opened	1802-? and 1851
RNLI	1865
Motor LB	1925
Fast LB	1976
Inshore LB	7.1969

Current lifeboat details

All-weather lifeboat

Type	Trent
Official Number	1197
Operational Number	14-02
Year built	1994
Name	Esme Anderson
Donor	Bequest of Mrs Esme Grace Anderson
Placed on station	24.8.1995
Launch	Afloat

Inshore lifeboat

Type	Atlantic 21
Official Number	B-558
Name	Ramsgate Enterprise
Donor	Ramsgate Station Branch Appeal
Placed on station	7.9.1984
Launch	Davit

Location history

1802 The first lifeboat was funded by the Trustees of Ramsgate Harbour; it had lapsed by 1824.

1851 The station was re-opened by the Harbour Trustees. The lifeboats were moored in the East Gully, Royal Harbour, and tugs were often available to assist with rescues. The crew's equipment and gear was housed on the ground floor of the Clockhouse, now the East Kent Maritime Museum, until 1993.

1969 An inshore lifeboat station was established; the ILBs were kept moored afloat until 1984.

1984 A wooden ILB house was built on the Western Crosswall for the Atlantic 21, with a launching davit on the adjacent quayside.

1993 The lifeboat was moved to pontoon moorings in the Yacht Marina to improve boarding arrangements.

1997 A new ILB house was built at the end of the Commercial Pier, incorporating improved crew facilities and a pontoon mooring berth for the all-weather lifeboat.

Medals and awards

Thirty-four medals have been awarded, two Gold, 31 Silver and one Bronze, including 11 medals awarded to the crews of the steam tugs that played an active part in rescues.

Six Silver Medals have been awarded for shore-boat rescues, and one Silver for a single-handed rescue.

Notable rescue

On 26 December 1985 the French trawler *Gloire a Marie II* went aground to the south of Ramsgate in a force 11 storm, darkness and violent seas. Getting on board the moored lifeboat *Ralph and Joy Swann* proved very difficult, but she left her moorings at 8.15pm and headed directly into the violent seas.

The lifeboatmen found the casualty aground off the entrance to the River Stour. Despite hazardous conditions in the shallows, Coxswain Ronald Cannon manoeuvred the lifeboat close to the casualty, and two lifeboatmen boarded her. They ascertained that the vessel was sound and seaworthy, that her main engines were working, and that neither the skipper nor his two sons were willing to leave their boat.

A line was passed and with great skill the Coxswain towed the trawler clear, despite huge 20-foot seas twice breaking the tow, keeping the lifeboat head-to-sea and turning the trawler's bows. Once clear of the shallows, the tow was dismantled and the trawler, with her seven-man crew, was escorted into Ramsgate under her own power.

For this service, which was carried out in appalling weather conditions, the Silver Medal was awarded to Coxswain Cannon for superb boat handling and seamanship, and Medal service certificates were presented to the other lifeboatmen involved.

Background information

The station was established by the Trustees of Ramsgate Harbour, and in 1863 was taken over by the Board of Trade. Between 1865 and 1922 the station was under the joint control of the RNLI and Board of Trade, with the RNLI providing the lifeboats; in 1922 the RNLI assumed sole responsibility.

Another aspect of the station during the 19th century was the use of the steam tugs for towing the lifeboat out to vessels in distress; they often also played a notable part in the rescues.

The ILB house and crew facility built in 1997 at the end of the Commercial Pier, with 14m Trent *Esme Anderson* (ON.1197) moored alongside the pontoon mooring berth.

Key dates

Opened	1856-1912 and 1927
RNLI	1856
Motor LB	1933-90
AWLB withdrawn	6.5.1990
Inshore LB	4.1964; second 1990

Current lifeboat details

Inshore lifeboats

Type	Atlantic 21
Official Number	B-589
Name	*James Burgess*
Donor	Gift of Mr and Mrs A. Burgess
Placed on station	28.5.92
Launch	Tractor and do-do carriage
Type	D class inflatable
Official Number	D-514
Name	*Lord Kitchener*
Donor	The Lord Kitchener public house, Welling, Kent
Placed on station	22.1.1997
Launch	Trolley

Location history

1856 The first lifeboat house, of wood, was built; it was used until 1871, then moved to North Deal.

1871 A new stone lifeboat house was built on the sea front, to the south of the old house, and was used until the station closed in 1912.

1927 The station was re-opened, and until 1990, when the all-weather lifeboat was withdrawn, the lifeboats were kept on a launching cradle at the head of the beach.

1964 An inshore lifeboat station was established in April; the ILB was kept in the 1871 boathouse.

1991-2 The lifeboat house of 1871, used to house the ILB since 1964, was lengthened to accommodate both the Atlantic 21 and its launching vehicle by the removal of the seaward gable wall, and a 6-metre extension was constructed; new facilities provided include a souvenir outlet, changing/drying room, work bench,

toilet, crew room, galley, office and storage areas. The D class inflatable ILB is kept in a container, situated on the beach in front of the boathouse, which has been given a wooden facade to blend in with the surrounding huts.

Medals and awards

Eleven medals have been awarded, three Gold, four Silver and four Bronze.

Notable rescue

On 2 January 1948 the steamship *Silvia Onorato* ran fast aground on the Goodwin Sands, and at 3.10pm the lifeboat *Charles Dibdin (Civil Service No.2)* was launched in appalling conditions. It took about an hour to reach the vessel, during which time the lifeboat had to go through mountainous seas.

The lifeboat attempted to go alongside the casualty, but in doing so was lifted by a huge sea and carried right over the steamer's deck. As the wave broke, the lifeboat was thrown straight at the wreck, but with engines full astern she managed to haul herself clear to safety.

Since there was not enough depth of water to pull the casualty off the sands, the lifeboat stood by during the night and following day waiting for the tide to turn, during which time several unsuccessful attempts were made to pull her off by tug.

The lifeboat house built in 1871, and extended in 1991-2, on the sea front at Walmer.

The lifeboat stood by throughout 4 January, but the steamer's Captain refused to abandon his ship. With the tide ebbing, the lack of water made it impossible for the lifeboat to remain alongside, so she returned to Walmer where the crew got some rest.

Later the same day the lifeboat returned. and eventually, with gales forecast, the Captain and Engineer were persuaded to leave the ship as their vessel could not now be saved. So in heavy seas the lifeboat was taken alongside and the crew of 28, plus two German stowaways, were taken off.

The lifeboat reached the shore at 6.15pm, 51 hours after first setting out. She had been at sea for 45 hours in weather that was deteriorating all the time, battling through heavy confused seas in bitterly cold weather.

For this service the Silver Medal was awarded to Coxswain Frederick Upton and the Bronze Medal to Mechanic Percy Cavell, and the Thanks on Vellum was accorded to each of the 11 lifeboatmen involved.

Background information

Walmer is one of three stations established to cover the treacherous Goodwin Sands. The other two, North Deal and Kingsdown, were closed in 1932 and 1927 respectively as a motor lifeboat was stationed at Walmer in 1933.

Key dates

Opened	1837-1914, 1919-22, 1930-41 and 1947
RNLI	1855
Motor LB	1930-40 and 5.1947
Fast LB	1967

Current lifeboat details

All-weather lifeboat

Type	Severn
Official Number	1220
Operational Number	17-09
Year built	1996
Name	City of London II
Donor	City of London Centenary Appeal, with bequests of Mrs Edna Horsfield, Dover, Mrs Gertrude Koss, and other gifts and legacies
Placed on station	15.3.1997
Launch	Afloat

Location history.

1837 The first lifeboat house was built by the Dover Humane Society; it was situated on the sea front, at Townsend.

1853 The lifeboat was kept beneath and launched by davits, which were situated on the east side of the Royal Pier; after the lifeboat had been swept from these davits during a storm in December 1855, the 1837 boathouse was put into use again.

1865 The RNLI built a lifeboat house close to the Clock Tower at the western end of the harbour; this was rebuilt in 1878 and used until the lifeboat was withdrawn in September 1914 due to problems of manning caused by the War.

1919 The lifeboat was kept afloat at moorings at The Camber, at the eastern end of the harbour, until 1922 when the station was closed.

1930 The station was re-established and the lifeboat was kept afloat at moorings at The Camber, until in 1941 it was again closed.

1947 The station was re-established and the lifeboat was moored in a former submarine pen in the Eastern Docks; this berth was used until 1984.

1984 Due to harbour development, a new afloat berth in the Western Docks was provided, with shore facilities on the adjacent key.

Medals and awards

Twenty medals have been awarded, seven Silver and 13 Bronze.

Notable rescue

On 1 December 1975 the lifeboat *Faithful Forester* was launched to the coaster *Primrose*, which had suffered steering failure in force 10 gale conditions. The weather was so bad that no tug or pilot vessel could get out of the harbour to assist the crippled vessel.

The lifeboat struggled out of the harbour, with the wind increasing in strength all the time, then battled through the appalling conditions to the casualty, reaching it in the early hours of 2 December. The mountainous seas were reported to be in excess of 25 feet high, but the coaster's crew had managed to rig temporary steering gear and the vessel was thus able to maintain her position.

While standing by the coaster, at one point the lifeboat was hit by 100mph winds, which heeled her over for fully half a minute until the

Above 17m Severn *City of London II* (ON.1220) at sea after her Naming Ceremony on 28 May 1998, with the white cliffs and Dover Castle in the background.

Right The lifeboat house built in 1865 close to the Clock Tower at the western end of the harbour.

wind eased. She then successfully righted herself, fortunately with no injuries to the crew on board, and continued with the service.

The Master of the casualty then steered a course for Dover, escorted by the lifeboat. The coaster slowly reached Dover harbour and, as no pilot boat could get out in the conditions, the lifeboat took up position ahead and guided the casualty through the harbour entrance to safety.

For this rescue the Silver Medal was awarded to Coxswain Arthur Lidden and the Bronze Medal to Second Coxswain Anthony Hawkins, and the Thanks on Vellum was accorded to the rest of the crew, Second Assistant Mechanic Richard Hawkins and lifeboatmen John Smith and Gordon Davis.

Background information

The lifeboat station at Dover has not been operated continuously: it was closed 1914-19 and 1922-30 because of the impositions placed on Dover by the two World Wars, and 1941-47 after the lifeboat, *Sir William Hillary*, had been taken over by the Admiralty for use as an air-sea rescue launch during the War.

Key dates

Opened	1966
RNLI	1966
Inshore LB	5.1966

Current lifeboat details

Inshore lifeboat

Type	Atlantic 21
Official Number	B-573
Name	*The Lady Dart and Long Life II*
Donor	RNLI Ladies Darts League Appeal and the Long Life Beer Promotion
Placed on station	1.6.1988
Launch	Tractor and do-do carriage

Location history

Although the original lifeboat station was situated at Littlestone, it was known as New Romney, a town that stood by the sea when it was one of the Cinque Ports.

1861 A lifeboat was first placed here in August 1861 and the lifeboat house built at Dungeness, to the south, was moved north to New Romney.

1871 A new lifeboat house was built on ground rented from the Corporation of New Romney, and in 1883 a slipway was built to improve launching. This house was used until the station closed in 1928, and was demolished in 1940 under Military Defence Orders during the building of wartime coastal defences. There is a plaque on Littlestone seafront marking the site.

1966 An inshore lifeboat station was established; it was known as Littlestone and the ILB was kept in an ILB house built on the beach.

1973 A new ILB house was built, and used until 1977.

1977 Another new ILB house, financed from local resources, was built on the beach on the same site; visible from the coast road, it was refurbished and extended in 1993 with major improvements to create better crew facilities.

Medals and awards

Five medals have been awarded for rescues off New Romney, four Silver and one Gold. Two of the Silver medals were for shore-boat rescues.

Atlantic 21
The Lady Dart and Long Life II (B-573)
on the do-do
carriage outside the
lifeboat house.

Notable rescue

On 10 April 1876 the New Romney lifeboat *Dr Hatton* was launched over the soft sands of Romney Bay to the schooner *Tobina*, which was dragging her anchors in a strong gale and heavy sea. She had struck the Roar Bank, off Littlestone, and her crew had taken to the rigging as the masts had remained above the water.

The launch was accomplished with extreme difficulty, and once afloat the lifeboat reached the wreck to find that two of her crew had been drowned. The remaining five men on board were rescued just as the casualty completely sank.

For this rescue, and to recognise long service, the Silver Medal was awarded to Coxswain Michael Murphy, who was also the Chief Boatman of HM Coastguard at Littlestone. The lifeboat crew was made up of coastguardmen.

Key dates

Opened	1874
RNLI	1874
Motor LB	1933
Fast LB	1992

Current lifeboat details

All-weather lifeboat

Type	Mersey
Official Number	1186
Operational Number	12-27
Year built	1992
Name	*Pride and Spirit*
Donor	Gift of Mr Eric and Mrs Jean Cass, of Virginia Water, Surrey, and named after two Seabourn Cruise Line ships *Pride* and *Spirit*
Placed on station	24.9.1992
Launch	Carriage

Location history

1854   A lifeboat house was built close to the Coastguard station at No.1 Battery to cover the dangerous spit on which vessels were frequently wrecked.

1861   Due to launching problems the lifeboat was moved north to the new station at Littlestone, known as New Romney.

1874   The station at Dungeness was re-established; although said to be at Lydd, and sometimes so titled, this village was some distance inland and the lifeboat was over 2 miles away on the soft shingle at Dungeness.

1892   As it was considered impossible to launch a large boat over the shingle, when a second, larger lifeboat arrived in December 1892 she was kept afloat near the Point. After 1894 she was kept on a carriage in the open.

1905   Although the No.2 boat was at first kept afloat, a new house was built for her, which was used until 1938 and has since been demolished.

1933   The first motor lifeboat was placed on station and was launched over the beach using skids.

1938   A new boathouse and launchway was built, and in 1939 the original No.1 station was closed, leaving only one lifeboat on station.

Throughout its existence, much has been spent to improve the launching arrangements necessitated by the ever-changing shingle, as the Point has grown through the force of the sea. In 1947 the slipway was extended, and in 1953 the boathouse and slip were resited. In 1966 and 1967 the slipway was resited yet again, undermined by severe gales.

1974   Experiments with a tractor and carriage launch were undertaken in September; the best launch site was to the north of the Point, towards Littlestone.

1976-7   A new lifeboat house was built to house the carriage-launched lifeboat to the north of the slipway site; carriage launching has helped to alleviate the problems caused by the shifting beach. This house remains in operation today, with some additions.

1979-80   A new house was built for the bulldozer used to flatten the shingle and ease launching.

1989   The boathouse was extended to provide improved crew facilities.

1994-5   A new crew room was added to the boathouse, which was enlarged and extended.

Medals and awards

Sixteen medals have been awarded, 13 Silver and three Bronze.

One Silver medal has been awarded for a shore-boat rescue.

Background information

In the 1890s the crew at Dungeness requested a lighter type of lifeboat, which would be easier to launch over the shingle than the SR designs then in service. Felix Rubie, the RNLI's Chief Surveyor of Lifeboats, designed a new type of self-righting lifeboat specifically for the station, which became known as the Rubie self-righter. The new design was 34 feet long and had 10 oars to give it sufficient power to get off the beach in severe weather. However, although it was of similar dimensions to the standard self-righter, by using treated canvas instead of wood for the bulkheads and the air cases in the double bottom, a considerable weight saving was achieved.

The prototype of the new design was sent to Dungeness in December 1894, and it weighed only 1 ton 17 cwt without gear, whereas the standard boat of this size weighed between 3½ and 4 tons according to the amount of fixed ballast. The type became known as the 'Dungeness' class; in total 18 were built, the last in 1918, and all were operated from stations where carriage launching was practised. A slightly larger version of the design was built in the 1900s, 35 feet in length, of which 15 were built by the RNLI.

12m Mersey *Pride and Spirit* (ON.1186) outside the lifeboat house built in 1977.

Key dates

Opened	1832-1928; ro1966
RNLI	1832 (RNIPLS)
AWLB withdrawn	1928
Inshore LB	6.1966

Current lifeboat details

Inshore lifeboat

Type	Atlantic 75
Official Number	B-727
Name	Commander and Mrs Rodney Wells
Donor	Bequest of Mrs Eva Lilian Wells in memory of Commander Rodney Wells
Placed on station	17.7.1996
Launch	Tractor and do-do carriage

Location history

1803 A lifeboat built by Greathead was placed at Rye, but little is known of the station until the RNIPLS took over.

1832 The station was re-established by the RNIPLS, and a lifeboat house was built at Rye.

1856 A new lifeboat house was built, and used until 1862. A new station was established at Camber, known as Rye, on the east side of Rye Bay; a lifeboat house was built here in 1857, and used until 1876.

1862 The station at Rye was transferred to Winchelsea and a new lifeboat house built on the beach, halfway between Rye Harbour and Winchelsea; this station was renamed Rye Harbour in 1910, and remained operational until 1928 when it was closed following the lifeboat disaster (see below). The 1862 boathouse remains unaltered externally in use as a store, with an information board on one wall detailing its history.

1876 A new brick lifeboat house was built at Camber; this house was used until 1901, when the station was closed, and it has since been demolished.

1966 An inshore lifeboat station was established in June; the ILB was kept in a small house on the west bank of the River Rother. This house was used until 1984.

1984 A new brick ILB house was built on the same site.

1994 The ILB house was enlarged and extended to accommodate an Atlantic 75 and its launch tractor, and provide improved crew facilities including changing/drying room, workshop, toilets, self-contained office for the National Rivers Authority, a crew room, galley and office. A new timber slipway and an elevated walkway leading to the boathouse were also constructed.

Medals and awards

Six medals have been awarded, two Gold and four Silver.

Two medals have been awarded for shore-boat rescues, one Gold and one Silver.

Notable rescue

On 24 May 1981 the D class inshore lifeboat D-241 was launched to the 24ft ketch *Midley Belle*, which had lost her main sheet and whose engine had failed while returning to harbour in an increasing fresh westerly wind with seas 8 feet high over the bar.

The ILB ran alongside the yacht three times to rescue three of the seven people on board, who were landed at the mouth of Rye Harbour. The ketch was then sailed by her crew into open seas, escorted by the ILB in force 8 winds, and was eventually taken in tow by the Dungeness lifeboat.

For this service a framed letter of appreciation signed by the Chairman was awarded to Helmsman Keith Downey.

The memorial in the churchyard on the road from Rye to Rye Harbour to the lifeboatmen lost in November 1928.

Background information

The lifeboat station at Rye was closed in 1928 following a dreadful tragedy on 15 November when the lifeboat *Mary Stanford* capsized on service with the loss of the whole crew of 17, which represented practically the whole male fishing population of the village. The lifeboat was launched in a south-westerly gale with heavy rain squalls and heavy seas to the vessel *Alice*. News was received that the crew of the *Alice* had been rescued by another vessel, and the recall signal was fired three times, but apparently the crew of the lifeboat had not seen it, and as they came into harbour the boat capsized. A local fund was established for the relief of the dependants of the men lost and this raised over £35,000.

A memorial tablet made of Manx stone was presented to Rye Harbour by the people of the Isle of Man, and this can be seen in the churchyard on the road from Rye to Rye Harbour. A memorial stained glass window was placed in Winchelsea Church, depicting a lifeboat putting out to a ship in distress while figures on the shore watch it as it passes.

Key dates

Opened	c1835-post 1852 and 1858
RNLI	1858
Motor LB	1931
Fast LB	1989
Inshore LB	1964

Current lifeboat details

All-weather lifeboat

Type	Mersey
Official Number	1125
Operational Number	12-002
Year built	1988
Name	Sealink Endeavour
Donor	Sealink British Ferries Ltd promotion, with bequests from Dr William R. H. Murphy, Mrs Dorothy M. Kellett and other gifts and legacies
Placed on station	13.3.1989
Launch	Carriage

Inshore lifeboat

Type	D class inflatable
Official Number	D-540
Name	Cecile Rampton II
Donor	Gift of Miss Yolande Rampton
Placed on station	4.10.1998
Launch	Trolley

Location history

1858 A lifeboat house was built at the east end of the town. It was used until 1882.

1881-2 A new ornamental boathouse was built at the eastern end of Marine Parade; used until 1949, it has since been demolished.

1949 A new lifeboat house was built on the beach for the station's second motor lifeboat.

1963 A new tractor house was built adjacent to the boathouse.

1964 An inshore lifeboat station was established in April; the ILB was kept in a small house built on the beach next to the 1949 boathouse.

1981 A new crew room and souvenir shop was built in the boathouse.

1988 The lifeboat house was adapted for a Mersey class lifeboat; the house was used until 1995, when it was demolished.

1995 A new lifeboat house was constructed on the site of the 1949 house; it includes housing for the Mersey class lifeboat and launching tractor, the D class ILB, a garage for the bulldozer, changing room, workshop, souvenir sales outlet, a presentation/training room, public viewing galley and operations room.

Medals and awards

Nine medals have been awarded, two Gold, three Silver and four Bronze.

Notable rescue

On 27 September 1974 the reserve lifeboat *Jane Hay* was launched in a strong force 9 gale, very rough sea and heavy rain to search for the fishing vessel *Simon Peter* in distress off Rye Harbour.

After a difficult launch and prolonged search, a rescue helicopter found the casualty 9 miles off Hastings, with the wheelhouse stove in. The lifeboat was guided to the vessel, after which the helicopter returned to base.

On the lifeboat's first approach the survivors were too exhausted to move and she was forced to move away. On the second approach, despite 40-foot seas breaking over the fishing vessel, the crew of three were taken off, two being dragged bodily into the lifeboat.

The lifeboat then returned to her station through heavy following seas, and the survivors, all exhausted from their ordeal, were safely landed.

The Silver Medal was awarded to Coxswain/Mechanic John Martin and the Bronze Medal to Second Coxswain George White; the Thanks on Vellum was accorded to the remainder of the lifeboat crew, Assistant Mechanic Harry Benton, Second Assistant Mechanic Robert Shoesmith and crew members Richard Adams, Michael Barrow, Albert White and Richard Read. A framed latter of thanks was presented to the head launcher.

Background information

In 1948 a stained glass window was dedicated at St Clements Church, one pane showing a fisherman in lifeboat oilskins and a kneeling woman beside a sailing boat; the fisherman depicted is former Coxswain Ned Adams.

The station has historically served as a destination for school visits from London as well as receiving many other group and individual visitors. When the new lifeboat house was built in 1995, a presentation room, which doubles as a crew training room and is fully accessible to the disabled, was incorporated to give a view over the deck of the Mersey and provide space for information displays.

12m Mersey *Sealink Endeavour* (ON.1125) being launched at the end of her Naming Ceremony on 21 September 1989. *Paul Russell*

Part 2
South Coast of England:
Eastbourne to Weston-super-Mare

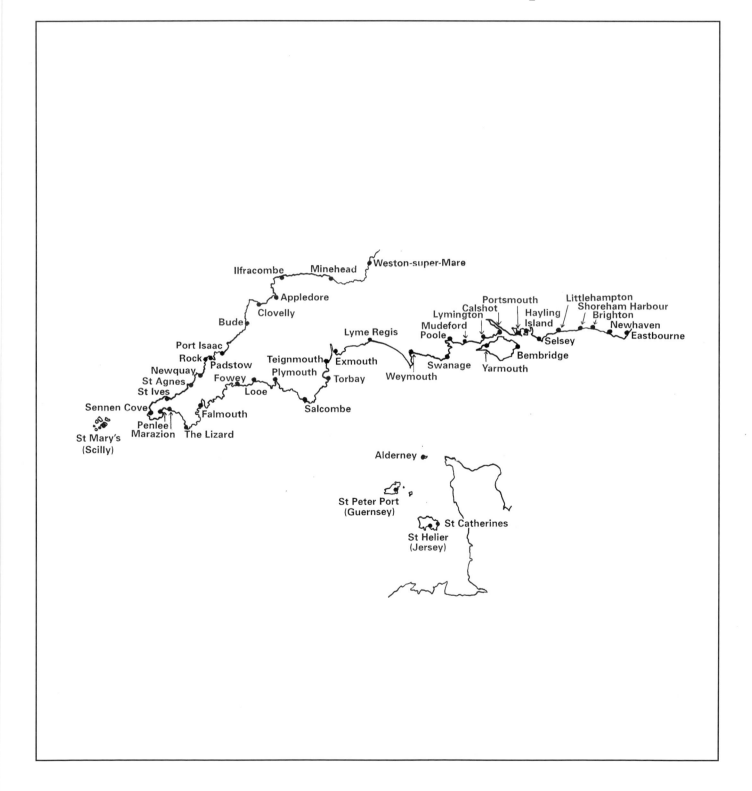

Key dates

Opened	1809-post 1816, 1825-37, 1858-1931; ro1965
RNLI	1825-37 (RNIPLS); 1858
AWLB withdrawn	7.7.1931
Inshore LB	4.1965

Current lifeboat details

Inshore lifeboat

Type	Atlantic 75
Official Number	B-737
Name	Thelma Glossop
Donor	Gift of Mr and Mrs Roy Glossop
Placed on station	1.7.1997
Launch	Floating boathouse

Location history

1825 The RNIPLS supplied a lifeboat, and a cave in the cliffs near the Chain Pier, found in 1824, was adapted for use as a boathouse. This arrangement was maintained until 1837, when the lifeboat was transferred from the station.

1858 The RNLI station was re-opened and the Town Council gave a site for a boathouse on the beach, opposite the Bedford Hotel and near the new West Pier; this house was only used for ten years before demolition.

1868 A new lifeboat house was built on the beach near the new West Pier, opposite the Bedford Hotel.

1886 Following alterations to the beach, including the building of new groynes, it became necessary to move the lifeboat to a site between the two piers. The RNLI took over two roomy arches being constructed under the Western Esplanade opposite Cannon Place, and surrendered the 1868 lifeboat house to Brighton Corporation. No 109 Arch was used for the RNLI lifeboat, No 110 for the lifeboat's equipment, and No 111 for the Town Council Lifeboat; these arches were used until the RNLI lifeboat was withdrawn in 1931, by which time the Shoreham motor lifeboat served the area. A plaque mounted outside the arches records their use.

1965 An inshore lifeboat station was established in April; the ILB was kept in an arch under the Promenade to the east of the Palace Pier. On 30 October 1974 the ILB was withdrawn for the winter, and in 1975 the station closed temporarily until Marina facilities became available; the arch was subsequently used by lifeguards operating their own dinghy in the 1980s.

1975 The station was non-operational until 1977, when crew training began in preparation for the re-opening of the station.

1978 The station was re-opened and the lifeboat was kept afloat, then on a pontoon, in Brighton Marina.

1979 The station became fully operational in April after a pontoon berth was installed in the Marina; the Atlantic 21 inshore lifeboat was launched from the pontoon down a small tipping slipway. A temporary shelter for the boat was constructed over the pontoon in 1980, and in 1981 this was replaced by a permanent shelter; crew facilities were provided in a temporary Portacabin on the adjacent quayside. This was the first floating boathouse built by the RNLI for an Atlantic ILB.

Medals and awards

Ten medals have been awarded, one Gold, seven Silver and two Bronze.

Background information

A number of independent lifeboats were operated at Brighton throughout the 19th century. The first was provided through the efforts of John Godlee, who succeeded in getting the lifeboat from Newhaven transferred to Brighton, where it was considered of more use. The Brighton Humane Society provided two lifeboats that were operated from 1837 until the 1850s. Brighton Corporation also funded lifeboats, the first of which entered service in 1840 and saved at least 15 lives. The second was built in 1879 and remained at Brighton until 1932, when she was sold.

Atlantic 75 *Thelma Glossop* (B-737) launching from the floating boathouse in Brighton Marina.

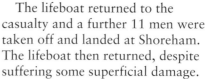
Key dates

Opened	1865-1924 and 1929
RNLI	1865
Motor LB	1929
Fast LB	1990
Inshore LB	7.1967

Current lifeboat details

All-weather lifeboat

Type	Tyne
Official Number	1158
Operational Number	47-040
Year built	1990
Name	Hermione Lady Colwyn
Donor	Shoreham Lifeboat Appeal, and bequest of Lady Colwyn
Placed on station	30.9.1990
Launch	Slipway

Inshore lifeboat

Type	D class inflatable
Official Number	D-501
Name	Forest Row Choir
Donor	Forest Row Choir Appeal
Placed on station	14.5.1996
Launch	Trolley

Location history

1865 A lifeboat house was built of brick on Kingston Beach; used until 1892, it has since been demolished.

1870 A slipway was built, at the expense of the Harbour Board, to improve launching.

1892 A new lifeboat house of timber was constructed, with a watch-room, after the station was moved from the inner side of the Harbour to a site close to the Coastguard Station on Shoreham Beach, on the west side of the Harbour.

1903 The lifeboat house was moved back a safe distance from the sea; it used until 1924 and has since been demolished.

1924 In October the station was closed owing to siltation of the Harbour entrance, not re-opening until October 1929 when the bar had been dispersed.

1933 A new lifeboat house and slipway was built on Kingston Beach, directly opposite Shoreham Harbour, and has since been altered to accommodate successive lifeboats.

1967 An inshore lifeboat station was established in July; the ILB is housed beneath the main boathouse in its own garage.

1990 The lifeboat house and the slipway were refurbished to accommodate a Tyne class lifeboat.

Medals and awards

Eight medals have been awarded, five Silver and three Bronze.

Notable rescue

On 21 January 1980 the lifeboat *Dorothy and Philip Constant* was launched to the motor vessel *Athina B*, which was in difficulties 1½ miles off Shoreham with violent seas breaking over her. A strong gale, force 9, was blowing from the southeast, but the lifeboat was able to make full speed for the casualty.

With some difficulty the Captain's wife and two children were taken off. Another woman was rescued after two further approaches, during one of which the lifeboat was overwhelmed. It was decided to land the women at Shoreham, as they needed medical attention.

47ft Tyne *Hermione Lady Colwyn* (ON.1158) launching down the slipway for the first time after arriving on station in September 1990.

The lifeboat returned to the casualty and a further 11 men were taken off and landed at Shoreham. The lifeboat then returned, despite suffering some superficial damage.

By this time *Athena B* had floated clear, but was driven aground again in heavy surf off Brighton, so both Shoreham and Newhaven lifeboats put out once more. By this time it was dark, and the Shoreham lifeboat was further damaged along the side of the casualty, but managed to save ten men. Another jumped to the lifeboat but missed and had to be pulled from the water.

In all, 26 people were saved, the service having taken from 8 in the morning to nearly midnight. The Silver Medal was awarded to Coxswain Kenneth Voice, and the Thanks on Vellum was accorded to the other members of the crew, Second Coxswain Kenneth Everard, Mechanic Jack Silverson, Assistant Mechanic Michael Fox, Emergency Mechanics Geoff Tugwell and John Landale, and crew member Peter Huxtable.

Background information

The first lifeboat stationed at Shoreham was provided by the Shoreham Harbour Commissioners in 1845; it was 30 feet long, cost £100, and was credited with saving two lives.

Key dates

Opened	1884-1921; ro1967
RNLI	1884
AWLB withdrawn	5.12.1921
Inshore LB	4.1967

Current lifeboat details

Inshore lifeboat

Type	Atlantic 21
Official Number	B-564
Name	*Blue Peter I*
Donor	Blue Peter TV Appeal
Placed on station	7.9.1985
Launch	Trolley

Location history

1884 A lifeboat house was built on the east bank of the River Arun.

1903 The lifeboat house was moved to a new site close to the lighthouse; it was used until 1921 when the station was closed as no suitable men were available and a motor lifeboat was due to be placed at Selsey. The house later became a café until it was demolished.

1967 An inshore lifeboat station was established. Until 1979 the ILB was kept in a small garage situated on the east bank of the river.

1979 A new ILB house was built near the Fishermen's Quay, from which the ILB was launched down a short ramp into the river.

Medals and awards

Two medals were awarded for a rescue in 1840, one Gold and one Silver.

Notable rescue

On 19 September 1981 the Atlantic 21 inshore lifeboat B-523 *Blue Peter I* was launched to help dinghies that had been caught out by a sudden deterioration in the weather; a force 8 gale was blowing and heavy rain was reducing visibility.

It was found that all the dinghies were safe except the trimaran *Lara of Bosham*, which had a dinghy in tow and was in difficulties. The ILB was taken alongside, but a heavy sea drove her against the vessel's hull, causing some damage. The two people in the dinghy, suffering from exposure, were taken on board the lifeboat and placed in survivor bags.

The ILB then returned to Littlehampton, a passage that

The ILB house on the east bank of the River Arun near the Fishermen's Quay, with Atlantic 21 *Blue Peter I* (B-564) outside.

required considerable skill on the part of the Helmsman due to the adverse conditions. After landing the survivors, it was taken back out, encountering heavy confused seas up to 12 feet high. Two of the trimaran's crew, who were suffering from seasickness, were taken off and landed at Littlehampton, then the lifeboat returned for a third time to escort the vessel safely across the bar.

The Thanks on Vellum was accorded to Helmsman David Woollven for his expert boat-handling and fine leadership. Framed Letters of Thanks, signed by the RNLI Chairman, were presented to crew members Geoff Warminger and Michael McCartain.

Background information

Littlehampton was the first station at which one of the Blue Peter-funded lifeboats was stationed. There are proposals for a new ILB house to be built on the site of the current one.

Location history

1860-1 A lifeboat house was built at Selsey Point, the boat being launched over the beach on skids.

1894 A second, larger lifeboat was placed on station, which was kept afloat until 1896, when the smaller boat, intended for work inshore, was withdrawn. This boat was also launched over the beach on skids.

1913 In order to ease launching difficulties, a new wooden slipway was constructed to the west of the boathouse, but this did not prove to be a satisfactory long-term solution.

1920-1 A new concrete slipway was built, leading from the boathouse; the lifeboat was launched from a trolley on rails, which was hauled by ropes until it reached a slipway some 75 yards out to sea. The trolley would then be tipped up to form the top portion of the slipway, down which the boat would be launched.

Key dates

Opened	1861
RNLI	1861
Motor LB	1922
Fast LB	1983
Inshore LB	3.1968

Current lifeboat details

All-weather lifeboat

Type	Tyne
Official Number	1074
Operational Number	47-001
Year built	1981
Name	City of London
Donor	City of London Appeal
Placed on station	21.11.1983
Launch	Slipway

Inshore lifeboat

Type	D class inflatable
Official Number	D-533
Name	Peter Cornish
Donor	The Peter Cornish Memorial Appeal; donations from family, friends and colleagues
Placed on station	26.5.1998
Launch	Trolley

1925 Work began on the construction of a new lifeboat house on piles, across the approach gangway, with a trolley track.

1927 A new lifeboat house was built, to house the station's first motor lifeboat. In 1952-3 the substructure was strengthened and the slipway lengthened.

1958 Work began on another new lifeboat house, completed in 1960, needed as the old boathouse and slipway had become unserviceable as a consequence of coast erosion. The new boathouse had a reinforced concrete deep-water roller slipway with a gradient of 1:5, and a new steel approach gangway.

1968 An inshore lifeboat station was established in March; the ILB was kept in a house by the approach gangway to the main boathouse and launched down a path laid on the shingle to the east of the main slip.

1987 A new ILB house was built to replace the old Hardun timber building; it had a crew room, store and souvenir shop.

Medals and awards

Eight medals have been awarded, five Silver and three Bronze.

Notable rescue

On the night of 9 September 1983 the lifeboat *Charles Henry* was launched to the yacht *Enchantress of Hamble*, aground off Selsey Bill in a southerly gale and a very rough sea. The casualty's location was uncertain, but after further communication her position was established.

At night, and in the heavy seas, Coxswain Michael Grant had to rely solely on radar information and his own knowledge to safely negotiate a passage through the sandbanks to where the casualty was lying. The yacht was found in an area known as The Streets, but approaching it was very difficult due to the surrounding rocks. However, a passage amongst the rocks was found, although there were continuous heavy and irregular breaking seas and the lifeboat was hitting the bottom regularly.

The first run alongside the casualty failed as the lifeboat was struck by a heavy sea, knocking her off course. On the second run, however, four people were taken off as the lifeboat was pinned alongside the yacht by constant use of the engines. A line was then passed to the two remaining men on board who secured the yacht, and they were then taken off.

Leaving the scene was difficult because of the rocks and the Hook Sands, on which the lifeboat could be grounded. On her return it was too rough to rehouse the lifeboat so she was taken to Portsmouth, entering the harbour just after midnight on 10 September with the casualty in tow.

For this rescue, in which both the yacht and its crew of six were saved, the Silver Medal was awarded to Coxswain Grant in recognition of the courage, determination and seamanship he displayed; Medal service certificates were presented to the rest of the crew.

The lifeboat house and slipway built in 1960; the reinforced concrete slipway has a gradient of 1 in 5.

47ft Tyne *City of London* (ON.1074) launching for the station's annual Lifeboat Day in August 1991.

Key dates

Opened   1865-1924; ro1975
RNLI   1865
AWLB withdrawn   29.9.1924
Inshore LB   3.1975; second 1995

Current lifeboat details

Inshore lifeboats

Type	Atlantic 75
Official Number	B-712
Name	*Betty Battle*
Donor	Gift of Mr and Mrs Derrick Battle, Ashtead, Surrey
Placed on station	21.6.1995
Launch	Tractor and do-do carriage

Type	D class inflatable
Official Number	D-496
Name	*Leonard Stedman*
Donor	Farnham Branch RNLI
Placed on station	12.3.1996
Launch	Trolley

Location history

1865 A lifeboat house was built on the south shore of Hayling Island, at its western end; it was used until 1914, and was heavily converted during the late 1980s to become the 'Inn on the Beach'.

1913-4 A new house for a larger lifeboat was built, with doors at both ends, about 2 miles east of the previous house. This building was used until the station closed in 1924, after motor lifeboats had been stationed at Bembridge and Selsey; it has since been used as the village hall, and was a store in the 1990s.

1975 An inshore lifeboat station was established in March, in conjunction with the Hayling Island Research & Rescue Organisation, and a new ILB house was built at Sandy Point, at the south-eastern tip of the island.

1980 A new ramp was built over the beach to improve launching arrangements.

1994-5 A new ILB house was built on the same site to accommodate both Atlantic and D class ILBs, the station having been up-graded to operate two lifeboats. The new house also featured a crew room, drying/changing room, workshop and display/museum area.

Medals and awards

Three medals have been awarded, one Silver and two Bronze.

Four medals have been awarded for shore-boat rescues, all Silver.

Notable rescue

On 25 October 1992 the 75ft ketch yacht *Donald Searle*, with 17 crew on board, got into difficulties at the edge of the East Pole Sands at the eastern end of Chichester Bar. The yacht's engines had failed and her sails had been blown out in the strong gale, with rough seas and a heavy swell.

As the station's Atlantic 21 inshore lifeboat B-548 *Aldershot* was already out on service, Frank Dunster launched his own 28ft rigid-inflatable *Hayling Island* and headed for the casualty, which was by now

in very shallow water. He took the boat alongside the ketch and took off two people, whom he landed back at Hayling Island knowing that the Bembridge lifeboat and a helicopter were on the way.

Meanwhile the ILB was also on its way and, after battling through very steep seas, reached the casualty. The ILB was taken alongside five times and succeeded in taking off seven people, who were landed at the lifeboat station. The remaining people on board the casualty were taken off by helicopter.

For this rescue Silver Medals were awarded to Roderick James, Helmsman of the ILB, and Frank Dunster, and the Thanks on Vellum was accorded to ILB crew members Christopher Reed, Warren Hayles, Evan Lamperd and Damien Taylor.

Background information

The current ILB station has its origins in the Hayling Island Rescue & Research Organisation (HIRRO), founded in 1971 by Frank Martin. This organisation provided a rescue service and also carried out research into rescue methods using divers.

The ILB house built for Atlantic and D class inshore lifeboats in 1994-5 at Sandy Point, at the south-eastern tip of the island.

Atlantic 75 *Betty Battle* (B-712) on exercise off Hayling Island in 1996.

After talks during 1973 between the HIRRO and the RNLI, it was announced in October that the two bodies were to join forces. An Atlantic 21 was allocated to the station in Spring 1974, and became operational on 25 March 1975; the new station was formally opened by Frank Judd MP on 2 August 1975. In March 1978 it was announced that, by mutual consent, the two organisations had decided to discontinue the joint operation and the RNLI assumed sole responsibility for the station.

Key dates

Opened	5.1965
RNLI	1965
Inshore LB	1965; second 1967

Current lifeboat details

Inshore lifeboats

Type	Atlantic 75
Official Number	B-730
Name	*CSMA Frizzell*
Donor	Members of the Civil Service Motoring Association Ltd and Frizzell Financial Services
Placed on station	26.11.1996
Launch	Trolley

Type	D class inflatable
Official Number	D-421
Name	*Lord Raglan*
Donor	Appeal by the Lord Raglan public house, Wokingham
Placed on station	2.4.1992
Launch	Trolley

Location history

1965 An inshore lifeboat station was established in May; an ILB house was built at Eastney Point, facing Langstone Harbour.

1967 The rigid-hulled inshore lifeboats, on station between 1967 and 1975, were kept at moorings in the harbour at Eastney.

1975 A new ILB house was built on the same site for both Atlantic and D class inshore lifeboats, and the afloat ILBs were withdrawn.

1991 Another new ILB house was built on the same site, providing a changing/drying room, a shower, toilet, first-aid reception area, workshop, crew training/briefing room and an office.

Medals and awards

Four medals have been awarded, all Bronze.

Notable rescue

In the early hours of 7 September 1974 the D class inshore lifeboat D-184 was launched to the motor cruiser *Valon*, which was in difficulty in the Cockle Rythe area off Langstone Channel. The casualty was being illuminated from the shore by the Coastguard mobile patrol, but the wind was force 9, gusting to force 10, with very poor visibility.

The run to the casualty was made at full speed directly down wind, and with accurate positions from the Coastguard the casualty was quickly reached. In absolutely appalling conditions, the ILB was taken alongside the *Valon* and two people were found to be on board. They were both lashed to the boat, so getting them on board the ILB was only achieved with some difficulty.

As the ILB left the casualty the wind was gusting to storm force 11, well beyond its the operating limit, and the return passage to station took over an hour. Visibility was zero due to driving rain, spindrift and solid water, but the two casualties were safely landed at Eastney and taken to hospital.

For this rescue Bronze Medals were awarded to both Helmsman Sydney Thayers and William Hawkins, and a Bronze Second-Service Clasp was awarded to Dennis Faro in recognition of their gallantry, dedication to duty, judgement and expert seamanship.

Background information

There was a lifeboat station at Portsmouth between 1886 and 1918, situated at Southsea, which is credited with saving six lives during the 32 years of its existence.

When the ILB station was established in 1965 it was known as Eastney; in 1978 it was renamed and became known as Portsmouth (Langstone Harbour), then from 1 September 1995 its name was again amended, this time to Portsmouth.

The ILB house built in 1993 at Eastney for Atlantic and D class inflatables.

Key dates

Opened	1963
RNLI	1963
Inshore LB	6.1963

Current lifeboat details

Inshore lifeboat

Type	Atlantic 21
Official Number	B-583
Name	Ken Derham
Donor	Mudeford Lifeboat Appeal
Placed on station	24.11.1990
Launch	Trolley

Location history

1963 An inshore lifeboat station was established in June; the ILB was kept in a small house which was built at Mudeford Quay.

1981 A new ILB house was constructed at Mudeford Quay, near the entrance to Mudeford Harbour.

1988 A crew room was constructed in the ILB house to provide improved crew facilities.

Medals and awards

No medals have been awarded, although one Gold and five Silver medals have been awarded for shore or shore-boat rescues.

Notable rescue

On 30 October 1994 the Atlantic 21 inshore lifeboat B-583 *Ken Derham*

was launched to go to the aid of a boy clinging to a pole on a rock groyne off Barton Cliff. He was being constantly washed by large waves in force 6 winds, very rough seas and driving rain.

When the ILB arrived on the scene, Helmsman Ian Parker realised that he would not be able to get close enough to reach the boy, so Stuart Ward went into the water to try to get him off the pole. Battered by the waves, Ward was constantly swept past the casualty and on to the rock groyne. The teenager was too scared to release his grip on the pole, and eventually Ward became too exhausted to continue and was hauled to safety by the Coastguard.

Crew member Toby Abbott then entered the water with a rope tied round him, and managed to reach the teenager and break his grip on the pole. Helmsman Parker single-handedly kept the ILB head to sea as

The ILB house built in 1988 near the entrance to Mudeford Harbour.

he struggled to haul Abbott and the casualty back on board the ILB. For this service the Thanks on Vellum was accorded to Helmsman Parker and crew members Ward and Abbott.

Background information

Before the ILB station was established, the late Ken Derham operated a single-handed rescue service from Avon Beach at Friars Cliff with an 11-foot rowing dinghy. He was awarded the RNLI's Silver Medal in recognition of his great courage, skill and determination when, single-handed, he put out in this rowing-boat to rescue two people from a motor fishing boat in a heavy breaking ground sea on 30 March 1959. Mr Derham became the first Honorary Secretary of the lifeboat station when it was established in 1963, and held the post until 1976.

Poole

Dorset

Location history

1865 A lifeboat house was built at Sandbanks, at the northern entrance to the harbour. To reach it for a launch, the crew were usually taken by coach the few miles from the town's High Street.

1882 A new lifeboat house was built at the north end of Poole Quay on a site at the Fisherman's Dock leased from the Corporation.

1897 A slipway was constructed in line with the lifeboat house, as the Corporation slipway used by the lifeboat was often blocked by boats;

this house was used for the lifeboat itself until 1962, then became the crew room until 1974.

1962 The lifeboats were kept moored afloat in the Fishermen's Dock, just off the lifeboat house, until 1974.

Key dates

Opened	1865
RNLI	1865
Motor LB	1939
Fast LB	1974
Inshore LB	1964

Current lifeboat details

All-weather lifeboat

Type	Brede
Official Number	1089
Operational Number	33-07
Year built	1983
Name	Inner Wheel
Donor	Gift of Inner Wheel Clubs of Great Britain and Ireland, plus other gifts
Placed on station	16.10.1983
Launch	Afloat

Inshore lifeboat

Type	Atlantic 75
Official Number	B-710
Name	Friendly Forester II
Donor	Gift of the Ancient Order of Foresters Friendly Society in memory of Nora Gladys Green
Placed on station	26.4.1995
Launch	Floating boathouse

1964 An inshore lifeboat station was established in March; the standard D class inflatable was withdrawn in January 1970.

1967 A Hatch class ILB, the first of several rigid-hulled ILBs to serve at the station, was placed on service, but was withdrawn the following year. In June 1969 a Dell Quay Dory was sent to the station; these ILBs were moored afloat, first in the Fishermen's Dock close to the 1882 boathouse, and later at Lilliput Marina and the Town Quay, until replaced in November 1994.

1974 The station was moved to Poole Harbour Yacht Club, at Lilliput Marina, and an alongside berth was established for both lifeboat and ILB, with a workshop and store on the quayside; the lifeboats operated from this location until 1989.

1989 The station was resited at the Town Quay, adjacent to Poole Bridge, and a pontoon mooring was installed.

1990 A two-story extension to the police services building on Poole Quay was constructed to provide crew facilities including a changing room, shower room and toilet, fuel and oil stores, an office and kitchen.

1994 A floating boathouse was constructed alongside the lifeboat berth at Poole Bridge for housing an Atlantic 75 inshore lifeboat.

1996 A piled walkway with a hinged gangway was built to give direct access to the lifeboat.

Medals and awards

One Silver Medal has been awarded.

Seven medals have been awarded for shore-boat rescues, one Gold and six Silver.

Notable rescue

On the night of 1 July 1986 the lifeboat *Inner Wheel* and the Relief D class inshore lifeboat D-180 were launched to a boy and a girl who had got lost in the darkness in marshland in Poole Harbour. The ILB was driven on to the mud after negotiating very shallow water, and one of the crew waded through mud waist deep to reach the two children.

Another crew member assisted while the third got the mattress out of the ILB to support the casualties over the mud, in which they were all frequently sinking. The boy, who was suffering from hypothermia, was taken over the mud and ashore, then the girl was similarly rescued, and it was not until 4.00am on 2 July that the ILB was back at her station.

The Thanks on Vellum was accorded to crew members David Coles, Steven Vince and Raymond Collin in recognition of their physical exertions, determination and ingenuity.

Background information

In 1975 the lifeboat house on Poole Quay became a Lifeboat Museum, housing the former Poole lifeboat *Thomas Kirk Wright*, on station between 1939 and 1962. It was given to the National Maritime Museum for display purposes, after being sold to a private owner in 1962. In 1991 the building was surrendered to the Council, but the lifeboat is still inside and on display.

33ft Brede *Inner Wheel* (ON.1089) moored in the berth at Poole Bridge adjacent to the floating boathouse, which was installed in 1994.

Key dates

Opened	1875
RNLI	1875
Motor LB	1928
Fast LB	1992
Inshore LB	4.1993

Current lifeboat details

All-weather lifeboat

Type	Mersey
Official Number	1182
Operational Number	12-23
Year built	1992
Name	*Robert Charles Brown*
Donor	The J. Reginald Corah Foundation Fund, The Maud Elkington Charitable Trust, The Florence Turner Charitable Trust, and other gifts and legacies
Placed on station	12.6.1992
Launch	Slipway

Inshore lifeboat

Type	D class inflatable
Official Number	D-475
Name	*Phyl Clare 2*
Donor	Gift of Mrs Phyl Cleare, Bournemouth
Placed on station	8.4.1995
Launch	Trolley

Location history

1875 A lifeboat house and stone launchway were built; this house is still in use today, albeit much altered.

1890 The slipway was lengthened and the house enlarged for a new lifeboat.

1927-8 The lifeboat house was altered for the station's first motor lifeboat, and in 1975 it was extensively altered to accommodate a Rother class lifeboat.

1991-2 There was a major renovation of the house as the station was adapted for a 12m Mersey class lifeboat; the slipway was dismantled and completely rebuilt.

1993 An inshore lifeboat was sent to station in April for one season's operational evaluation. To accommodate it a 'lean-to' building with a dedicated ILB slipway was constructed in 1994 on one side of the main boathouse; the ILB station was permanently established from 8 April 1995.

Medals and awards

Ten Medals have been awarded, five Silver and five Bronze.

Notable rescue

On the night of 28 October 1996 the relief lifeboat *Lifetime Care* was launched to the 90ft yacht *Be Happy*, which was in difficulties 20 miles south of St Albans Head. The yacht had lost one engine and her sails, and was taking in water through a broken window. The wind was gusting to hurricane force, there were very rough seas and it was pitch dark.

During the difficult passage to the yacht, the lifeboat lost power in one of her engines due to cooling problems, and it had to be shut down; the radar and Decca Navigator were also not functioning, but guided by a helicopter searchlight the yacht was reached. The rough sea and driving rain made a tow impossible, so the lifeboat went alongside.

The force of the sea drove the yacht against the lifeboat, injuring four lifeboatmen, one of whom sustained a broken arm. The yacht's crew of five, three men and two women, were all safely rescued, and landed back at Swanage just after midnight on 29 October.

For this rescue the Bronze Medal was awarded to Coxswain Christopher Haw, and Medal service certificates were presented to the rest of the crew.

Background information

Before the RNLI established lifeboat stations at Weymouth and Swanage, the Portlanders, with their small lerrets, were active in saving lives around Portland, the Isle of Purbeck and Chesil Beach. The lerret was a six-oared boat without a rudder, and it was normally used without a sail. It had been evolved as the most effective boat for launching from a steep and pebbled shore and was quite well suited to life-saving as it could be launched in very difficult conditions.

12m Mersey *Robert Charles Brown* (ON.1182) and D class inflatable *Phyl Clare 2* (D-475) on exercise in August 1997.

Key dates

Opened	1869
RNLI	1869
Motor LB	1924
Fast LB	1976
Inshore LB	1995

Current lifeboat details

All-weather lifeboat

Type	Arun
Official Number	1049
Operational Number	54-04
Year built	1976
Name	Tony Vandervell
Donor	The Vandervell Foundation
Placed on station	3.1976
Launch	Afloat

Inshore lifeboat

Type	Atlantic 21
Official Number	B-746
Name	Phyl Clare 3
Donor	Jack and Phyl Cleare
Placed on station	18.5.1998
Launch	Trolley

Location history

1869 The first lifeboat house was constructed and a slipway was built through the quay for launching into the river.

1897 Arrangements were made locally for a tug to tow the lifeboat out of the harbour on service.

1924 The lifeboat house was rebuilt to enable a motor lifeboat to be housed.

1930 Moorings in the river next to the lifeboat house on the south side of the harbour were taken up, and the lifeboat has been moored there ever since. The boathouse was altered and the quay built up to suit the new launching arrangements.

1996 The old Ferryman's Hut and Mast Store at Hooker's Dock was demolished to make way for a new ILB house to accommodate the Atlantic 75 on the south side of the harbour, facing the harbour

entrance, near the Yacht Club; the main boathouse was altered to provide improved crew facilities.

Medals and awards

Fourteen Medals have been awarded, nine Silver and five Bronze.

Notable rescue

On 14 October 1976 the lifeboat *Tony Vandervell* was launched to the yacht *Latifa*, which was in difficulties 1½ miles south of the East Shambles buoy in a WSW hurricane and phenomenal seas. She had damaged sails, a shattered main boom and split mast.

The lifeboat reached the yacht successfully despite being thrown on to her beam ends several times in the dreadful conditions. The wind was force 12 and the waves were estimated to be between 40 and 50 feet in height.

Once on the scene, the Acting Coxswain decided to tow the yacht to safety as the only way to save those on board. An unsuccessful attempt was made to fire a line across the casualty; the second attempt was lost, but at the third attempt a line was successfully got across the yacht.

Once a nylon tow line had been secured, the passage to Weymouth began, and despite the conditions it was possible to make about 4 knots. No navigational buoys were sighted

during the return passage due to the severity of the seas, but they got in to Weymouth harbour just before 9.00pm. The yacht and her crew of eight had been saved in conditions that were worse than any of the participants could remember, and the worst to which the lifeboat, the first to be built from glass reinforced plastic, had been subjected; it was felt that she had proved herself completely.

For this rescue the Silver Medal was awarded to Second Coxswain Victor James Pitman in recognition of his courage, determination and seamanship on only his second service in command; the Thanks on Vellum was accorded to the other members of the crew, whose average age was 50, Mechanic Derek Sargent, Emergency Mechanic Eric L. Pavey and crew members Bertie Legge, Lionel Hellier, Bernard Wills and John Kellegher.

Background information

Weymouth lifeboat station was established to cover the area around Portland, where fast-running tides meet a mile or so off Portland Bill to produce the Portland Race and confused waters off the Shambles Bank. The first lifeboat in the area was at Portland, where the RNIPLS sent a lifeboat in February 1826. The boat was never used for life-saving, however, and by 1850 was reported as useless and rotten.

The south side of the busy harbour at Weymouth, with 54ft Arun *Tony Vandervell* (ON.1049) at moorings.

Key dates

Opened	1853-1932; ro1967
RNLI	1853
AWLB withdrawn	11.1932
Inshore LB	5.1967

Current lifeboat details

Inshore lifeboat

Type	Atlantic 75
Official Number	B-741
Name	*Pearl of Dorset*
Donor	Local appeal
Placed on station	29.9.1997
Launch	Tractor and do-do carriage

Location history

1853 A lifeboat house was built, situated among other houses to the east of Cobb Road.

1867 The 1853 site was inconvenient so a new lifeboat house was built on West Beach, facing the seafront road to the west of the Cobb; this house was used until 1884, after which it was given to the owner of the site who had sold a new site to the RNLI.

1884 A new lifeboat house was built on the lower part of Cobb Hill, facing the sea; this house was in use until 1932 when the station was closed, and has since been converted into a public convenience.

1967 An inshore lifeboat station was established in May; the ILB was kept in a small house at the head of the harbour, into which the ILB was launched.

1982 The ILB house was refurbished and modernised to create an operations room, shower and crew room; this house was used until 1997, and has been demolished.

1997 A new masonry ILB house was built on the Cobb for an Atlantic 75 and launching vehicle.

Medals and awards

Ten medals have been awarded, one Gold, six Silver and three Bronze.

Notable rescue

On 13 August 1979 the Atlantic 21 inshore lifeboat B-512 was launched to the yacht *White Kitten*, which was dragging her anchor in broken water off Beer Head in a south-westerly storm and a rough sea. The yacht's crew were exhausted and had been without sleep for more than two days. An extra crew member was taken by the ILB because of the severity of the weather.

Once on scene the ILB was taken alongside the yacht and two women and a boy were safely taken off. A crew member who was then a sailing instructor, Colin Jones, was transferred on to the casualty and he managed to sail the yacht with two men on board to Lyme Regis, despite the difficult conditions. The rescued women and boy were landed at Lyme Regis, after which the lifeboat proceeded to sea again to meet the yacht and escorted her to safety.

For this service Bronze Medals were awarded to Helmsman John Hodder and crew member Colin Jones in recognition of their courage and skill in effecting a rescue.

Background information

The earliest attempt to set up a lifeboat to cover Lyme Bay was made in 1825 when Captain Spence, of the Coastguard at Lyme Regis, had a shore-boat specially converted for life-saving purposes. Airtight cases were fitted under the thwarts and lashed outside each gunwale. Although this boat was found to be satisfactory by the Dorset Branch Association of the embryonic RNIPLS, there is no record of whether it was ever used for life-saving.

The official opening in April 1998 of the ILB house built on the Cobb the previous year.

Atlantic 75 *Pearl of Dorset* (B-741) in Lyme Bay at the end of her Naming Ceremony, 4 April 1998.

Key dates

Opened	1803-? and 1859
RNLI	1859
Motor LB	1933
Fast LB	1983
Inshore LB	5.1966

Current lifeboat details

All-weather lifeboat

Type	Trent
Official Number	1210
Operational Number	14-12
Year built	1995
Name	*Forward Birmingham*
Donor	Forward Birmingham Lifeboat Campaign, together with other gifts and legacies
Placed on station	6.7.1996
Launch	Afloat

Inshore lifeboat

Type	D class inflatable
Official Number	D-516
Name	*Spirit of the Exe*
Donor	The River Exe Combined Water Sports Clubs
Placed on station	27.5.1997
Launch	Trolley

Location history

1803 The first lifeboat house was situated near Passage House, but it was washed away by the tide during a storm in 1814 and the station lapsed until 1859.

1859 A lifeboat house was built on the beach; this house was used until 1903 and was then demolished.

1903 A new lifeboat house was built on the same site and was used until 1961; in 1962 it was converted into a Lifeboat Display Centre and now houses the inshore lifeboat.

1961 The lifeboat was placed on moorings in the estuary off Exmouth Docks; a wooden boarding-boat was used to reach her, and crew facilities were constructed on the quayside. The current inflatable boarding-boat is launched by davit.

1966 An inshore lifeboat was sent to the station in May; the ILB is kept in the 1903 boathouse and launched across the beach.

Medals and awards

Six medals have been awarded, five Silver and one Bronze, all for rescues carried out from Exmouth but none with the lifeboat.

Notable rescue

On 7 April 1985 the lifeboat *Caroline Finch* was launched to a speedboat that had sunk 1½ miles east by south of Exmouth, leaving those on board in the water with no life-jackets. Very heavy seas were encountered as the lifeboat crossed the bar at the mouth of the River Exe, and after a search of the area the three people were spotted in the water.

Because of the height of the waves, it was too dangerous to get close enough to lift them out, so lifeboatman Geoffrey Ingram volunteered to enter the water and assist the casualties. With his life-jacket fully inflated, he was able to give support to two girls who were in considerable difficulty, while the man managed to swim to the lifeboat. All were eventually pulled on board and landed at Exmouth suffering from shock and hypothermia.

For this service the Thanks on Vellum was accorded to crew member Geoffrey Ingram in recognition of his meritorious action.

Above The lifeboat house built in 1903, and now used for the station's inshore lifeboat.

Right 14m Trent *Forward Birmingham* (ON.1210) arriving on station for the first time in June 1996.

Key dates

Opened	1869-1925; ro1931
RNLI	1869
Motor LB	1931
Fast LB	1988

Current lifeboat details

All-weather lifeboat

Type	Tyne
Official Number	1130
Operational Number	47-022
Year built	1988
Name	*The Baltic Exchange II*
Donor	The Baltic Exchange with other gifts and legacies
Placed on station	30.8.1988
Launch	Afloat

Location history

1869 A lifeboat house and slipway was built at South Sands, and was used until the station was closed in 1925; the house is still standing and remains largely unaltered externally.

1930 The station was re-opened, and the lifeboat was placed on moorings in the middle of the estuary, reached from the quay by boarding-boat. A crew gear store was established at Customs Quay.

1992 The building on the quayside used as a crew room was modified and modernised to provide a larger wet clothing storage area, a new museum and display area, a meeting room, toilet, shower and a reception area.

Medals and awards

Ten medals have been awarded, one Silver and nine Bronze.

Three Silver medals have been awarded for shore-boat rescues.

Notable rescue

In the early hours of 8 January 1992 the lifeboat *Baltic Exchange II* launched to the 1,200-ton coaster *Janet C*, which had suffered total power failure in south-westerly gale force winds and heavy seas. Attempts had been made to contact a tug, but without success.

On reaching the scene, several attempts were made to attach a line between the lifeboat and coaster, and eventually a tow was connected. The coaster had been drifting relentlessly towards the rocks, but once the tow was established the casualty was slowly pulled clear and held for 3 hours until the arrival of a tug. Despite the considerable difference in size, the lifeboat was actually able to pull the coaster away from Start Point.

For this service the Bronze Medal was awarded to Coxswain/Mechanic Frank Smith in recognition of his courage, seamanship, leadership and determination during the rescue. A framed letter of appreciation signed by the Chairman of the Institution was presented to Staff Coxswain John Marjoram for the support he gave to Coxswain/Mechanic Smith, who was officially on leave but had made himself available for this service because of the prevailing conditions and his knowledge of the Start Point area.

Background information

Two lifeboats from Salcombe have capsized while on service. The first capsize occurred on 27 October 1916 after the lifeboat *William and Emma* had been launched to the assistance of the schooner *Western Lass*, which had gone ashore on the east side of Prawle Point in a furious gale. The crew of the vessel were rescued by the Coastguard using rocket apparatus before the arrival of the lifeboat. When the lifeboat was returning to harbour, she capsized just outside the bar at the entrance to the estuary and 13 of her crew of 15 were drowned. A memorial table to those lost in this disaster is set into the face of the local War Memorial, which overlooks the harbour.

The second capsize occurred more recently, on 10 April 1983, and fortunately with no loss of life. The lifeboat *The Baltic Exchange* was on service to an upturned inflatable dinghy in a gale force 9, gusting to force 11. As the casualty was approached, the lifeboat was hit by a huge wall of water, causing her to turn over while travelling at full speed. The emergency air-bag inflated automatically and the lifeboat righted, exactly as intended. All members of the crew were immersed during the capsize, and one was washed overboard, but he was quickly recovered once the boat was upright. The lifeboat was not damaged, and was able to proceed to Brixham after the casualty had been saved by a helicopter. A framed letter of appreciation signed by the Chairman, The Duke of Atholl, was presented to Coxswain Graham Griffiths and the crew in recognition of their fortitude and determination following the capsize of the lifeboat.

47ft Tyne The Baltic Exchange II (ON.1130) moored in the middle of Salcombe harbour.

Key dates

Opened	1803-?, 1825-40 and 1862
RNLI	1825-38 (RNIPLS); 1862
Motor LB	1926
Fast LB	1974
Inshore LB	5.1967-12.1983

Current lifeboat details

All-weather lifeboat

Type	Arun
Official Number	1136
Operational Number	52-40
Year built	1987
Name	*City of Plymouth*
Donor	The City of Plymouth Appeal with other gifts and legacies
Placed on station	26.1.1988
Launch	Afloat

Location history

1803 The first lifeboat was supplied by a local committee, but it was never used for life-saving.

1825 The RNIPLS established a lifeboat at Cawsand; this was removed in 1838 having never been used.

1862 The station was re-established by the RNLI, and a lifeboat house was built on the western side of Mill Bay; it was used until 1898 and has since been demolished.

1898 A new lifeboat house and launchway were constructed at the Camber, near the West Pier, in Millbay Docks; this house was used until 1926 and has since been used as a store by the army.

1926 The lifeboat was placed on permanent moorings in Millbay Harbour; the lifeboat was kept here until 1988.

1967 An inshore lifeboat station was established in May, but the ILB was withdrawn in July 1968 and replaced by a rigid-hulled ILB; these ILBs, of which there were several different types, were kept at moorings in the harbour close to the offshore lifeboat. On 31 December 1983 the McLachlan ILB was permanently withdrawn.

1976 A new crew facility was built on the Princess Pier at Millbay Docks; this was used until 1988 and has since been demolished.

1979 Mooring piles were provided for an ex-HM Dockyard pontoon, which enabled the lifeboat to be kept moored alongside, thus improving boarding arrangements.

1988 Due to the redevelopment of Millbay Docks, the station was relocated to Sutton Harbour where a berth was obtained.

1992 A new berth was found in Millbay Marina, and the old three-storey Customs House, at the end of Millbay Pier, was restored and refurbished to provide crew facilities including a wet clothing drying area, a souvenir sales area, a training room, storeroom, showers and toilets, and a crew room. In 1994 a small extension was constructed to provide a mechanic's workshop.

Medals and awards

Sixteen medals have been awarded, 12 Silver and four Bronze.

Three Silver medals have been awarded for shore-boat rescues.

Background information

In March 1943 Plymouth's lifeboat, *Robert and Marcella Beck*, was requisitioned by the Admiralty and stationed in Iceland with the Fleet Salvage Officer for life-saving service on the most hazardous of the convoy routes, the northern route to Russia. In July 1945 she was sent back to Scotland and used on the Clyde; she then went to Blyth and Grimsby, returning to Plymouth in February 1946, but not released by the Navy until April 1946. She was then sent for overhaul and refit and did not return to her station until February 1947. While she was away her place was taken by a Belgian lifeboat, the *Minister Anseele*, which was picked up derelict in the English Channel early in the war, repaired and lent by the Belgian Government to the British lifeboat fleet.

52ft Arun *City of Plymouth* (ON.1136) moored in Millbay Marina.

Key dates

Opened	1830-post 1880 and 1884
RNLI	1884
Motor LB	1937
Fast LB	1975
Inshore LB	1968-9

Current lifeboat details

All-weather lifeboat

Type	Tyne
Official Number	1157
Operational Number	47-039
Year built	1989
Name	*Alexander Coutanche*
Donor	The Jersey Lifeboat Appeal together with a donation from the States of Jersey
Placed on station	13.12.1989
Launch	Afloat

Location history

1830 The first lifeboat, funded by the States of Jersey, was kept in a boathouse near the shore at Havre des Pas.

1884 The RNLI established a station after that on Alderney had been closed due to difficulty in obtaining a crew; a new lifeboat house was built near the Picket House, People's Park, on a site granted by the Corporation.

1896 The lifeboat house was moved and rebuilt in London Bay, St Helier Harbour, with doors at each end, and a short slipway was constructed; the lifeboat was launched by carriage.

1913 The launching slipway was extended and, in 1921, strengthened.

1936 The lifeboat house was lengthened at the landward end to accommodate the new motor lifeboat; the rear door was abolished, and a new slipway was built. This house was then used until 1948. In August 1968 it was used for the inshore lifeboat that was stationed here until October 1969.

1948 The lifeboat was placed on moorings in the harbour; a German-built concrete bunker on Albert Pier was taken over and converted for use as a gear store and crew rest room.

1993 New shore facilities were constructed on Albert Pier close to the lifeboat moorings opposite the 1948 crew facilities, incorporating a souvenir sales outlet, engineer's workshop, drying room, store, shower and toilets, and a crew room.

Medals and awards

Thirteen medals have been awarded, one Gold, three Silver and nine Bronze.

Four Gold Medals were awarded in 1825 and three Silver Medals in 1872 for shore-boat rescues.

The lifeboat house in London Bay, at St Helier Harbour, rebuilt in 1896 and used until 1948.

The shore facilities constructed in 1993 on Albert Pier, adjacent to the lifeboat moorings.

47ft Tyne *Alexander Coutanche* (ON.1157). *Rick Tomlinson*

Notable rescue

On the evening of 18 September 1973 the lifeboat *Elizabeth Rippon* was launched to the yacht *Bacchus* in a force 7-8 winds with a very rough sea and heavy swell. The yacht had been damaged extensively and was holed on the starboard side three cables east of La Sambue Rock.

To reach her the Coxswain had to navigate through many dangerous rock outcrops, but after a rough passage reached the yacht, which was found lying at anchor. Despite the dangers of the locality, the lifeboat was slowly taken towards the casualty and was grounded four times on submerged rocks.

Once alongside, six survivors, four men and two girls, were taken off at the first attempt, leaving the partly submerged yacht at anchor. The lifeboat was then taken back through the narrow channel into the open sea, and returned to station under reduced speed.

For this rescue the Silver Medal was awarded to Coxswain Michael Berry; the Thanks on Vellum was accorded to the remainder of the crew, Assistant Mechanic Dennis Aubert and crew members Alan Alexandre, David Aubert, Robin Stevens and David Mills.

Background information

Between June 1940 and May 1945, during the German occupation of the Channel Islands, the station was not under the RNLI's control. When the Chief Inspector visited in June 1945 he found that the lifeboat *Howard D* had been used by the Germans and that she had also gone out on service as a lifeboat with her crew under German guards and rescued 35 lives.

Key dates

Opened	10.1969
RNLI	1969
Inshore LB	10.1969

Current lifeboat details

Inshore lifeboat

Type	Atlantic 21
Official Number	B-587
Name	*Jessie Eliza*
Donor	Bequest of Lawrence Allan Davey
Placed on station	28.9.1991
Launch	Tractor and do-do carriage

Location history

1969 An inshore lifeboat station was established in October; the ILB was housed in an old wartime bunker in the cliff.

1984 A new ILB house was built on the harbour-quay for a C class inshore lifeboat; this house was used until 1991 and has since been used by the Jersey Canoe Club.

1991 An old farm building, found to be suitable to accommodate an Atlantic 21, was altered to provide crew facilities. The previous boathouse was of insufficient size to house the Atlantic 21 and launching tractor.

Medals and awards

No medals have been awarded.

Notable rescue

On the night of 1 January 1994 the Atlantic 21 inshore lifeboat B-587 *Jessie Eliza* was launched into breaking seas to a person reported to be in distress off Plemont. The 12-mile passage was undertaken in large confused seas, a SSW 30-knot wind and driving rain.

The ILB reached the scene late at night, and in total darkness a search for the missing person was begun. The casualty, a surfer clinging to his board, was soon located and recovered on to the ILB at the first attempt. He was suffering from hypothermia and shock, so was taken to the nearest landing place where an ambulance was waiting. The passage back to station was equally difficult, and the ILB arrived at St Catherines in the early hours of 2 January after a night in severe conditions.

For this rescue the Thanks on Vellum was accorded to Helmsman Nigel Sean Sweeney in recognition of his perseverance, skill and seamanship; framed letters of appreciation signed by the Chairman, Michael Vernon, were presented to crew members Paul Richardson and John Heyes for their valuable contribution to this service.

Atlantic 21
Jessie Eliza (B-587)
on exercise.
Rick Tomlinson

Key dates

Opened	1866-1930; ro1992
RNLI	1866
AWLB withdrawn	7.1930
Inshore LB	6.1992

Current lifeboat details

Inshore lifeboat

Type	D class inflatable
Official Number	D-461
Name	*Spirit of the RAOC*
Donor	Donation from 12 Supply Regiment, the Royal Logistic Corps
Placed on station	12.8.1994
Launch	Trolley

Location history

1866 A lifeboat house was built on the beach at East Looe, near the harbour entrance, with a reading and assembly room for the use of the pilots and fishermen on the first floor; it was used until 1930, when the station was closed, and is still standing, little altered externally, having had a variety of uses since.

1992 An inshore lifeboat station was established in June; until 1998 the ILB was housed in a boathouse provided by East Looe Town Trust, situated on the beach adjacent to the 1866 boathouse.

1998 A new ILB house was opened at Middleton's Corner, East Looe Quay, converted from one of the oldest stone buildings in Looe.

Medals and awards

One Silver Medal has been awarded.

Notable rescue

On 7 December 1901 the lifeboat *Boy's Own No.1* was launched to the ship *Gipsy*, which had gone aground on the rocks opposite Downderry Coastguard Station. Only after a considerable effort and with the help of extra launchers did the lifeboat get away.

Once on the scene the lifeboat stood by the casualty while attempts were made to refloat her, none of which were successful. The lifeboat then took off 14 of the crew, the rest leaving on the ship's boat, and returned to Looe with the aid of a tug, reaching the station in the early hours of 8 December.

The French Government awarded a Gold Medal (Second Class) to Coxswain Edward Toms, and Silver Medals (Second Class) to all the other lifeboatmen involved.

Background information

The station's last offshore lifeboat, *Ryder*, was restored at Polruan in 1998 and is on display at the Polperro Heritage & Smuggling Museum. The service boards from the station can be seen in the Guildhall Museum in Looe.

Above The lifeboat house of 1866 on the beach at East Looe (left), and the council store used to house the ILB between 1992 and 1998 (right).

Below The ILB house opened in 1998 at Middleton's Corner, East Looe Quay, formed by converting an old stone building. *Paul Richards*

Key dates

Opened	1922
RNLI	1922
Motor LB	1928
Fast LB	1982
Inshore LB	8.1996

Current lifeboat details

All-weather lifeboat

Type	Trent
Official Number	1222
Operational Number	14-18
Year built	1997
Name	Maurice and Joyce Hardy
Donor	Gift and bequest from Maurice G. Hardy CBE CEng, Twyford, Hants, and USA
Placed on station	10.10.1996
Launch	Afloat

Inshore lifeboat

Type	D class inflatable
Official Number	D-526
Name	Olive Herbert
Donor	Gift from the Olive Herbert Charitable Trust
Placed on station	30.9.1997
Launch	Davit

Location history

1859 A lifeboat station was established at Polkerris; closely linked to Fowey, it was in fact known as Fowey at various times during its existence.

1922 The lifeboat was moved to Fowey and the Polkerris station was closed; the lifeboat was kept moored afloat.

1928 A motor lifeboat was sent to the station, kept moored afloat just off the town quay. No boathouse was built here, but a building was found for the crew's gear close to the Town Quay; the service boards are displayed on the outside walls of the Royal British Legion Club, facing the Quay.

1995 New moorings were found for the lifeboat, upstream from the Quay, opposite Berrills Yard.

1996 An inshore lifeboat station was established in August on a summer-only basis; the ILB was kept in a temporary wooden container on the quayside beneath the launch davit, close to the lifeboat moorings.

1997 A new purpose-built shore facility and ILB house were completed in Berrills Yard, opposite the lifeboat moorings, on the landward side of the road through the town.

Medals and awards

One Bronze Medal has been awarded.

Notable rescue

Early in the morning of 23 March 1947 the reserve lifeboat *The Brothers* was launched in a gale and heavy seas to the auxiliary motor vessel *Empire Contamar*. The vessel had run on to rocks in Par Bay, and the lifeboat had to search the bay to find her.

The casualty was found to be stuck fast on the rocks, with only the bow and poop showing. Attempts were made to get alongside and under her bow, which afforded some shelter, but the seas were too heavy. With some difficulty the lifeboat approached again and after two attempts managed to get a line on board.

The line was made fast by the casualty's crew and seven men were hauled through the sea on to the lifeboat. They were all extremely cold, so were put in the lifeboat's cabin while she made good speed back to Fowey.

For this rescue Coxswain John Watters was awarded the Bronze Medal, while the crew received extra monetary awards.

Background information

The lifeboat station and lifeboats currently operated were all dedicated together at a unique triple ceremony. On 4 October 1997 both the all-weather lifeboat and inshore lifeboat were named and dedicated, and the ILB house was formally opened.

The shore facility built in 1997 in Berrills Yard, opposite the lifeboat moorings, which also houses the D class ILB.

14m Trent *Maurice and Joyce Hardy* (ON.1222) on exercise.
Paul Richards

Key dates

Opened	1867
RNLI	1867
Motor LB	1931
Fast LB	1979
Inshore LB	1967 and 27.3.1980

Current lifeboat details

All-weather lifeboat

Type	Severn
Official Number	1201
Operational Number	17-02
Year built	1994
Name	*The Will*
Donor	The Will Charitable Trust
Placed on station	11.3.1997
Launch	Afloat

Inshore lifeboat

Type	Atlantic 21
Official Number	B-595
Name	*Falmouth Round Table*
Donor	Falmouth Round Table
Placed on station	9.3.1994
Launch	Trolley

Location history

1867 A lifeboat house was built near the Dry Docks.

1885 The boathouse was moved to a new site; it was used until 1918 and has since been demolished.

1918 Moorings were taken up for the lifeboat in the middle of the large natural harbour; in 1931 the first motor lifeboat was placed on station.

1956 A new store and workshop were constructed at the edge of the harbour.

1980 On 27 March a rigid-hulled McLachlan ILB, which was being used as a boarding-boat, was redesignated as an inshore lifeboat and kept moored afloat in the harbour.

1981-2 A new crew room and store house were constructed at Customs House Quay.

1993 A new ILB house was built at Tinners Walk, Port Pendennis, to accommodate the trolley-launched Atlantic 21; the building includes a workshop, drying and changing room, toilet and shower, fuel store and souvenir sales outlet. It is jointly occupied by the RNLI and HM Coastguard, but the two halves of the building are totally independent. The station's service boards are displayed on the wall of an adjacent building.

1995 A new pontoon berth and refuelling facility was constructed for the all-weather lifeboat adjacent to the Tinners Walk lifeboat slipway.

Medals and awards

Seven medals have been awarded, two Gold, two Silver and three Bronze.

Three Silver Medals have been awarded for shore-boat rescues.

Notable rescue

On 19 January 1940, in a south-easterly gale and heavy seas, the steamship *Kirkpool*, of West Hartlepool, started dragging her anchors in Falmouth Bay. She struck the beach and lay broadside on with seas breaking against her. The lifeboat *Crawford and Constance Conybeare* was launched to go to her aid as tugs were unable to get close enough.

Despite heavy seas, Coxswain John Snell took the lifeboat through the heavy surf and round the bows of the steamer to get between the casualty and the shore. Once in position, the Coxswain placed the lifeboat alongside and took off an injured man, who was on a stretcher, and 13 firemen, all of whom were safely landed at Falmouth.

The lifeboat then returned to the steamer and, with seas breaking right over both vessels, repeated the manoeuvre to rescue the other 21 on board. By the afternoon all had been safely landed, although the injured man died the following day.

For this rescue the Silver Medal was awarded to Coxswain Snell for his great skill in handling the lifeboat, and the Bronze Medal to Mechanic Charles Williams; the Thanks on Vellum was accorded to the rest of the crew, Second Coxswain L. Morrison, Bowman H. Tonkin, Assistant Mechanic C. Brown, and crew members R. Tonkin, N. Morrison and T. Soult.

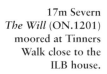

The ILB house built in 1993 at Tinners Walk, Port Pendennis, to accommodate the Atlantic 21; it is jointly occupied by the RNLI and HM Coastguard.

17m Severn *The Will* (ON.1201) moored at Tinners Walk close to the ILB house.

Key dates

Opened	1859
RNLI	1859
Motor LB	1918
Fast LB	1988

Current lifeboat details

All-weather lifeboat

Type	Tyne
Official Number	1145
Operational Number	47-030
Year built	1988
Name	David Robinson
Donor	Legacy of Sir David Robinson
Placed on station	7.8.1988
Launch	Slipway

Location history

1859 The first Lizard station was established; a lifeboat house was built near the top of the roadway leading down into Polpeor Cove, the southernmost tip of the Lizard headland; this was used until 1892.

1885 A No.2 station was established at Church Cove, on the east side of Lizard Point, where a lifeboat house was built; the station was closed in 1899. The boathouse still exists, and has been little altered externally; the two enamel roundels either side of the main door can still be seen, as can the stone plaque commemorating the donor.

1892 A new lifeboat house was built closer to the beach at Polpeor Cove; this was used until 1915, then became a winch house.

1914 A new lifeboat house with a deep-water slipway was built at Polpeor Cove for the station's first motor lifeboat; this was used until 1961. Both the 1892 and 1914 boathouses are still standing, albeit in a rather poor condition.

1961 A new lifeboat house with a roller slipway was built at Kilcobben Cove, situated on a tongue of rock at the foot of a cliff 140 feet high; the

Cove lies half way between the villages of Lizard and Cadgwith, and 1¼ miles east of The Lizard lighthouse. An access road nearly a quarter of a mile long was built to the top of the cliff. The new station replaced the old Lizard station, and eventually that at Cadgwith.

Medals and awards

Four medals have been awarded, three Silver and one Bronze.

Notable rescue

On 3 September 1984 the lifeboat *James and Catherine Macfarlane* was launched to two yachts that were caught in a south-westerly near gale about half a mile off Prah Sands, west of Porthleven. The wind was force 6 when the lifeboat launched, but once past Lizard Point the full force was felt and the sea was very rough.

On reaching the scene, one of the yachts, *Bass*, which had lost its rudder, was being towed by the other yacht, *Alto*. The lifeboat passed a heaving line then a tow rope to the first yacht, which was sheering considerably and shipping water, and took over the tow. In the difficult conditions the line parted once, but was successfully reattached. Throughout the tow the yacht was

sheering out of control due to the loss of the rudder.

Meanwhile, the other yacht got into difficulty and requested assistance, so the lifeboat had to check on it. However, because it was not advisable to tow both vessels, the Penlee lifeboat *Mabel Alice* was launched. She reached the scene, rigged a tow, and brought the yacht to safety at Newlyn. The first yacht and her crew of three were also eventually brought to Newlyn by the Lizard lifeboat after an arduous tow.

For this rescue the Bronze Medal was awarded to Coxswain/Mechanic Peter Mitchell in recognition of the courage and high standard of seamanship displayed; Medal service certificates were presented to the remainder of the crew.

Background information

There were lifeboats at The Lizard from 1859 to 1961 and at Cadgwith from 1867 to 1963. However, The Lizard station was extremely exposed and in certain conditions launching lifeboats here and at Cadgwith was a difficult operation. When the station was moved to the new lifeboat house and slipway at Kilcobben Cove in 1961, it was initially known as the Lizard-Cadgwith station, but since July 1987 has been known as The Lizard.

47ft Tyne David Robinson (ON.1145) outside the lifeboat house at Kilcobben Cove in 1989.

Marazion

Key dates

Opened	4.1990
RNLI	1990
Inshore LB	1990

Current lifeboat details

Inshore lifeboat

Type	D class inflatable
Official Number	D-411
Name	None
Donor	Appeal by the South West Federation of Sea Anglers
Placed on station	23.3.1991
Launch	Trolley

The small house in one of the quayside buildings on St Michael's Mount in which the station's ILB is kept.

Location history

1990 An inshore lifeboat station was established, becoming operational on 28 April; the ILB is kept in one of the quayside buildings on St Michael's Mount, and launched into the small harbour beneath the Mount, which faces the village of Marazion.

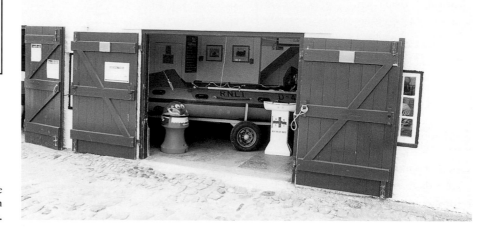

1991 On 1 October Marazion became an independent station, having initially been a satellite station to Penlee.

Medals and awards

No medals have been awarded.

Penlee

Key dates

Opened	1913
RNLI	1913
Motor LB	1922
Fast LB	1983

Current lifeboat details

All-weather lifeboat

Type	Arun
Official Number	1085
Operational Number	52-24
Year built	1983
Name	Mabel Alice
Donor	Gift of Mr David Robinson in honour of his wife, and as a tribute to Penlee
Placed on station	8.5.1983
Launch	Afloat

Location history

1803 The forerunner of the Penlee station is that at Penzance, where the first lifeboat to cover Mount's Bay was stationed; the first lifeboat was sold in 1812 having never been used.

1855-6 A new lifeboat house was built of wood, in the vicinity of the present railway station; in 1862-3 it was moved to Wherrytown adjacent to the Coastguard station and was used until 1884.

1884 A new brick lifeboat house was built at Penzance, at the foot of Jennings Street, facing the tidal harbour; this house was used until 1917, and was then sold to Penzance Town Council. During the 1980s and 1990s it was used to house an RNLI souvenir stall, and remains unaltered.

1908 A station was opened at Newlyn, and the lifeboat was kept in the open on her carriage at the edge of the harbour; in 1913 the lifeboat was transferred to Penlee.

1913 A new lifeboat house and steep concrete roller slipway was built at Penlee Point; this was altered several times for successive lifeboats, and was used until 1983.

1983 A mooring berth was dredged in Newlyn Harbour for the afloat lifeboat, the moorings being taken up on 8 May. An access gangway and assembly room were built, providing a crew room, workshop, store, toilet and shower facilities.

Medals and awards

Thirteen medals were awarded to lifeboatmen from Penzance, two Gold and 12 Silver.

Thirteen medals have been awarded to lifeboatmen from Penlee, one Gold, one Silver and 11 Bronze.

Notable rescue

On 25 January 1975 the lifeboat *Solomon Browne* was launched in a strong gale gusting to hurricane force, a very rough sea and heavy rain squalls, to the assistance of the crew of the motor vessel *Lovat*, who had abandoned ship 18½ miles south of Mousehole Island. Despite the severity of the weather, the lifeboat made full speed because of the extreme urgency of the situation.

On arriving at the scene the lifeboat joined two helicopters in the search for bodies. Despite the boat rolling considerably, making the operation particularly hazardous, the lifeboat crew eventually managed to recover five bodies. The helicopters picked up others, and once all the crew of the *Lovat* had been accounted for, the lifeboat returned to Newlyn harbour.

For this rescue the Bronze Medal was awarded to Coxswain William Richards in recognition of the courage, determination and skill he displayed.

Background information

On 19 December 1981 the lifeboat *Solomon Browne* was launched in hurricane conditions to go to the aid of the Coaster *Union Star*, which had engine failure and was being swept towards the southern coast of Cornwall. The Coxswain repeatedly took the lifeboat alongside the coaster to try and rescue the eight people on board, eventually managing to take four people off. A helicopter was unable to get a line to those on the coaster, so the lifeboat made a further attempt to rescue the remaining four and radio contact with her was lost.

It was subsequently discovered that the lifeboat had been completely wrecked with the loss of her crew of eight. The coaster was also lost and there were no survivors.

Coxswain William Trevelyan Richards was awarded the Institution's Gold Medal for the manner in which four people were taken off the coaster. The remainder of the crew, Second Coxswain/Mechanic James Stephen Madron,

Assistant Mechanic Nigel Brockman, Emergency Mechanic John Robert Blewett, crew members Charles Thomas Greenhaugh, Kevin Smith, Barrie Robertson Torrie and Gary Lee Wallis were awarded Bronze Medals. The Institution paid pensions to the dependants of the lifeboat crew in accordance with its usual practice and a local appeal raised over £3 million.

Several memorials have been erected to remember the eight lifeboatmen who gave their lives in the *Solomon Browne*. In 1985 Penzance Town Council decided to create a Memorial Garden in their memory; the land adjacent to the boathouse at Penlee Point was generously given to the Town Council and the materials used were given by local people and builders. The centrepiece of the garden was the splendid stainless steel memorial plaque in colour given by the Port Talbot Branch of the RNLI. In Paul Church, near Mousehole, is a stone memorial with a plaque on the front.

52ft Arun *Mabel Alice* (ON.1085) moored in Newlyn Harbour, with the access gangway and the shore facility built in 1983.

The memorial garden to the eight lifeboatmen of the *Solomon Browne* lost in December 1981; it is situated adjacent to the lifeboat house at Penlee Point.

The memorial to the lost crew members of the *Solomon Browne*.

SERVICE NOT SELF
IN MEMORY OF THE CREW OF THE PENLEE LIFEBOAT
SOLOMON BROWNE,
WILLIAM TREVELYAN RICHARDS, COXSWAIN.
JAMES STEPHEN MADRON, 2ND COXSWAIN MECHANIC.
NIGEL BROCKMAN, ASSISTANT MECHANIC.
JOHN ROBERT BLEWETT, EMERGENCY MECHANIC.
BARRY ROBERTSON TORRIE, CREWMAN.
CHARLES THOMAS GREENHAUGH, CREWMAN.
KEVIN BRIAN SMITH, CREWMAN.
GARY LEE WALLIS, CREWMAN.
WHO GAVE THEIR LIVES IN SERVICE
19TH DECEMBER 1981.

Key dates

Opened	1869-1933; ro1967
RNLI	1869
AWLB withdrawn	1933
Inshore LB	28.6.1967

Current lifeboat details

Inshore lifeboat

Type	D class inflatable
Official Number	D-366
Name	Peter and Mollie Tabor
Donor	Mr & Mrs P. R. Tabor
Placed on station	23.11.1998
Launch	Trolley

Location history

1869 A lifeboat house was built, situated quite far up the hill leading down to the east side of the small bay (see below); this was the only site available at the time for a boathouse, which was used until 1927 and has since been converted into a shop and Post Office.

1927 A new lifeboat house was built, more conveniently located at the head of the beach; it was used until the station closed in 1933, then became a garage for the Slipway House Hotel.

1967 An inshore lifeboat station was established in July 1967; the ILB was kept in part of a stone building on the beach, which was the property of Port Isaac Fishermen Ltd.

1993-4 The 1927 boathouse was re-acquired, and the ground floor was converted to house the ILB and provide improved crew facilities.

Medals and awards

One Silver Medal has been awarded, together with two Silver Medals for shore-boat rescues.

Notable rescue

On 4 May 1977 the D class inshore lifeboat D-139 was launched in light winds and fine weather to a seriously injured man who had fallen from the cliffs at Jackets Point, 3 miles north-east of Port Isaac. At the first approach to the Point, the lifeboat crew could not see the casualty, but after approaching from the north-east a narrow entrance became apparent in which the casualty could be seen.

The ILB was taken ashore through the swell that was creating heavy breaking surf, avoiding the submerged rocks at the entrance to the cave, and was beached on the rocks close to the casualty. First-aid was administered to the injured man who had fallen while climbing. Two other crew members then climbed down the cliff, and helped to strap the casualty firmly to the stretcher that the Coastguard had lowered down to them.

With two extra crew members providing additional ballast, the ILB was relaunched into the surf with the casualty stretcher on board and was successfully taken back through the heavy surf and away from the rocks, causing no undue discomfort to the casualty. It returned to Port Isaac where the injured man was landed safely and taken straight to hospital.

For this rescue the Thanks on Vellum was accorded to Helmsman Clive Martin and Vellum service certificates were presented to the other four members of the crew.

Background information

The first station, high up the hill on the eastern side of the village, made launching the boat a difficult business and involved taking it down the steep slope and through the narrow streets on its carriage. These remarkable launching arrangements became well known from the many oft-published photographs taken of the lifeboat negotiating the streets.

The lifeboat house built in 1869 on the hill leading down to the east side of the small bay; this house was used until 1927 and has since been converted into a shop and Post Office.

The lifeboat house built in 1927 and used since 1994 to house the D class inflatable, with the ill-fated D class ILB *Spirit of the PCS RE* (D-517) outside on her launching trolley. Shortly after this photograph was taken in August 1998 she was wrecked on service.

Key dates

Opened	1837-1923; ro1966
RNLI	1853
AWLB withdrawn	1923
Inshore LB	5.1966

Current lifeboat details

Inshore lifeboat

Type	D class inflatable
Official Number	D-495
Name	*Elsie Francs II*
Donor	Gift of Mr Stuart Underdown
Placed on station	30.3.1996
Launch	Trolley

Location history

1837 A local committee established a lifeboat station, with a lifeboat funded by King William IV, and had a lifeboat house built; however, the design of the boat was disliked by the local boatmen and by the early 1850s it had been neglected and was in a bad state of repair.

1853 The RNLI took over the station and supplied a new lifeboat.

1863 A new lifeboat house was built on the west side of the canal, above the Falcon Swing Bridge; at suitable states of tide the boat could be launched from the back of the boathouse directly into the canal, from where it would pass through the locks and proceed to sea.

1923 The station was closed owing to the severe decline of the local coasting trade, and because a large motor lifeboat had entered service at Padstow. The house of 1863 is now used as holiday flats; the inscription stone over the door commemorating the donor can still be seen.

1966 An inshore lifeboat station was established in May; an ILB house was built on the South Pier of the locks, at the harbour end of the canal-side road, and the ILB was launched over the beach; the house was modernised in 1991.

Medals and awards

Two medals have been awarded, both Silver.

Nine Silver Medals have been awarded for shore rescues.

Notable rescue

On the evening of 21 April 1993 the D class inshore lifeboat D-343 was launched to five climbers who were stranded at the base of a cliff inside Gull Rock, on the north side of Marsland Point, in danger of being cut off by the rising tide. Three were fit and willing to climb the cliff, but the fourth was suffering from shock and the other from lacerations, a suspected broken foot and back pains after a 30-foot fall.

On arriving at the scene, Helmsman Michael Sims assessed the situation and decided to put crew

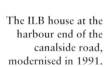

The lifeboat house built in 1863 on the west side of the canal, above the Falcon Swing Bridge; used until 1923, it was later converted into holiday flats.

The ILB house at the harbour end of the canalside road, modernised in 1991.

member James Wade ashore; Wade entered the surf and swam some 20 feet to reach the ledge. The Helmsman then took the ILB stern first through the surf and on to the ledge. The two casualties were wrapped in survivor sheets and placed on board.

The ILB was then relaunched and proceeded through surf to Welcome Mouth beach, where the casualties were landed to an ambulance. The ILB launched once more through 8-10-foot surf for the return passage to Bude, which was reached in darkness.

For this rescue the Thanks on Vellum was accorded to Helmsman Michael Sims in recognition of his leadership, skill and courage. Framed letters of appreciation signed by the Chairman, Mr Michael Vernon, were presented to James Wade and Keith West.

Key dates

Opened	1870-1988; ro1998
RNLI	1870
Motor LB	1936
AWLB withdrawn	15.8.1988
Inshore LB	5.1998

Current lifeboat details

Inshore lifeboat

Type	Atlantic 21
Official Number	B-531
Name	Waveney Forester
Donor	Court Waveney, Independent Order of Foresters Friendly Society St Peters Huntingdon, and legacies of Mr A. R. Godwin and Mrs Ethel Burton
Placed on station	14.3.1998
Launch	Tractor and do-do carriage

Location history

1870 A lifeboat house was built on the harbour shore.

1892 The lifeboat house was rebuilt on the same site, and a stone slipway was constructed on the foreshore to improve launching in the harbour; the house was altered at various times until 1968 when the lifeboat ceased to be shore-based. It is now a Grade II listed building.

1968 A cruising lifeboat, one of the 70ft Clyde class (see below), was kept at moorings off the harbour.

1988 The station was closed on 15 August and the lifeboat was withdrawn; the lifeboat house was used for a private lifeboat (see below).

1998 The station was re-opened; an Atlantic 21 was placed on temporary station duty on 14 May, following crew training in 1997, operating from the original lifeboat house; in November the station was declared permanent.

Medals and awards

Six medals have been awarded, two Silver and four Bronze.

Two Silver Medals have been awarded for shore-boat rescues.

Notable rescue

On 28 July 1954 the lifeboat *William Cantrell Ashley* was launched into a very rough sea to the motor ketch *Progress*, which had suffered engine failure under the lee of Lundy Island.

The previous day the lifeboat had been called out to the same vessel, helped her to anchor safely and returned to her station. However, the casualty had got into difficulties again and the lifeboat arrived on scene to find her rolling heavily.

Approaching her to take off the occupants was difficult as runs alongside had to be timed to coincide with the rolling. In all, ten runs were made before all on board were safely taken off – not only the owner's family but also a variety of domestic animals, including a cat and its kittens!

Once the lifeboat had completed the rescue, which took about an hour, it returned to Clovelly where the casualties were landed. For this rescue, the Bronze Medal was awarded to Coxswain George Lamey.

Background information

The recent history of the station is somewhat unusual. Between 1968 and 1988 large 70ft Clyde class cruising lifeboats were operated, and Clovelly was one of only two stations that operated such boats (the other was Kirkwall). When this lifeboat was withdrawn in August 1988, the RNLI closed the station. However, between 1990 and 1997 an independent inshore lifeboat, an 18ft rigid-inflatable named *Pride of Clovelly*, was operated by the Clovelly Trust. The original lifeboat house was used as a base for this boat.

The lifeboat house built in 1870 on the harbour shore, rebuilt in 1892 and used for the RNLI's lifeboat until 1968. Between 1988 and 1998 it housed the ILB operated independently of the RNLI by the Clovelly Trust, as depicted in this 1996 view.

Location history

1825 The first lifeboat was kept in a barn near King's Watch House at Badsteps, in Appledore, and launched over skids into the river.

1829 The lifeboat was moved into the King's Watch House itself, where it was kept until 1831; this building still stands, albeit much altered, at the top of the slope leading down to the present station at Badsteps.

1831 A new boathouse was built on a new site at Winterdown, and a second lifeboat was acquired; the lifeboats were launched by carriage into the river or over the burrows.

Key dates

Opened	1825
RNLI	1855
Motor LB	1922
Fast LB	1988
Inshore LB	1972

Current lifeboat details

All-weather lifeboat

Type	Tyne
Official Number	1140
Operational Number	47-027
Year built	1988
Name	George Gibson
Donor	Mr George C. Gibson OBE, through the Gibson Charitable Trust
Placed on station	19.6.1988
Launch	Afloat

Inshore lifeboat

Type	Atlantic 75
Official Number	B-742
Name	Douglas Paley
Donor	Gift from Mrs Evelyn Anne Paley, Sussex, in memory of her late husband Air Commodore Douglas Paley
Placed on station	11.12.1997
Launch	Trolley

1848 A new lifeboat station was established on the north side of the river at Braunton Burrows, and a boathouse was built to the north of the lighthouse at Airy Point; the crew were ferried across the estuary to the station as its location was very remote. The station at Braunton Burrows was temporarily closed in 1918 as many of the launchers had been called to serve in the War; it was permanently closed the following year.

1852 A substantial new stone lifeboat house was built on Northam Burrows, on the south side of the estuary, close to the Pebbleridge, and the station was moved here from Appledore.

1856 A new house was built on Northam Burrows adjoining the 1852 house; these two houses were used until 1897, when the station here was closed; they were pulled down in 1913 after becoming derelict, although a few remains can still be seen close to the 7th green of the Royal North Devon Golf Course.

1889 The station was moved back to Appledore, where the crew lived, and a lifeboat house was built at Badsteps with a stone slipway over the river foreshore for a launch into the river.

1922 The lifeboat house was altered for the station's first motor lifeboat. Rails were laid and the boat was launched from a bogie; separate slips for launching and rehousing were built.

1938 The heavier motor lifeboat that was sent to the station was kept afloat at moorings in the river, off Badsteps; the boarding-boat was kept on a carriage in the boathouse.

1972 An inshore lifeboat was sent to the station; the ILB was kept in the 1889 boathouse.

1980 The crew built and funded a first-floor crew room within the boathouse.

1989 Improvements were carried out to the boathouse yard over which a roof was constructed.

Medals and awards

Twenty-nine medals have been awarded, 23 Silver and six Bronze.

Background information

The stations located around the Taw and Torridge bar and estuary at Appledore, Northam and Braunton have a somewhat complicated history. Stationing lifeboats at both north and south sides of the river mouth enabled a casualty to be reached by the boat most suitably placed, depending upon the wind and tide.

The lifeboats stationed at Appledore between 1825 and 1856 were superseded by the station at Northam Burrows, which was operational between 1852 and 1897. There were two lifeboats at Northam Burrows during the periods 1856-61 and 1870-89, so a numbering system was adopted, and the stations were known as Appledore No.1 and No.2.

The power of sailing lifeboats, and subsequently motor lifeboats, meant that the station at Appledore, which was re-opened in 1889, was the easiest location from which to operate. Between 1889 and 1897, when there was also a lifeboat at Northam Burrows, this station was known as Appledore No.2.

The remotely sited station at Braunton Burrows, on the north side of the estuary, was operational from 1848 to 1919. It was known as Appledore No.3 from 1848-62 and 1894-97; between 1862 and 1894 it was controlled by a Barnstaple Committee and known as Braunton; then from 1897 to 1919 it was known as Appledore No.2.

The lifeboat house built in 1889 at Badsteps with a stone slipway over the river foreshore; it was subsequently altered and extended to accommodate both Atlantic 75 and boarding boats.

Key dates

Opened	1861-1905; ro1980
RNLI	1861
AWLB withdrawn	1905
Inshore LB	17.6.1980; second 1995

Current lifeboat details

Inshore lifeboats

Type	Atlantic 75
Official Number	B-725
Name	*Spirit of Penarth*
Donor	Penarth Lifeboat Appeal
Placed on station	15.5.1996
Launch	Tractor and do-do carriage
Type	D class inflatable
Official Number	D-534
Name	*Severn Rescuer*
Donor	Appeals in the Wales and West Mercia Region
Placed on station	22.6.1998
Launch	Trolley

Location history

1860 A lifeboat house was built on the Esplanade, facing the sea at the foot of the cliff below the Coastguard station, on the western side of Penarth Head; it was used until 1884 when the Esplanade was built in front of it, thus preventing the lifeboat being launched. The house was later converted into a café and is now a restaurant.

1884 A new lifeboat house and short concrete slipway, down which the lifeboat was launched over skids, was built on Penarth beach just to the west of the entrance to Penarth Dock; it was used until the station was closed in 1905, and has since been demolished.

1980 An inshore lifeboat station was established, and became operational on 17 June; an old deck-chair store on the Esplanade, to the east of the 1860 boathouse, was converted to house the ILB, and was used until 1995; the ILB was launched over the beach.

1995 A new ILB house was constructed for the Atlantic 75 and launching tractor, D class ILB, workshop, souvenir sales outlet, crew changing room, oil and petrol stores, crew room and shower and toilet facilities.

Medals and awards

Three medals have been awarded for shore-boat rescues, one Gold and two Silver.

Notable rescue

On 17 November 1867 the lifeboat was launched to the brig *Marie*, of Grieffswald, from which she saved 11. The lifeboat was at sea for over 10 hours and all the lifeboatmen returned totally exhausted from their efforts.

Above The ILB house built in 1995 on the Esplanade for Atlantic 75 and D class inshore lifeboats.

Right Atlantic 75 *Spirit of Penarth* (B-725) and Talus 4WH tractor TW27H on the launchway opposite the boathouse prior to the Naming Ceremony of B-725 in June 1996.

Right Spirit of Penarth afloat after the ceremony.

Key dates

Opened	1901
RNLI	1901
Motor LB	1922
Fast LB	1968

Current lifeboat details

All-weather lifeboat

Type	Arun
Official Number	1082
Operational Number	52-23
Year built	1982
Name	Margaret Frances Love
Donor	Bequests of Mr Frank Love and Lady Frances Murphy, with other gifts and legacies
Placed on station	11.5.1997
Launch	Afloat

Location history

1901 A lifeboat house and slipway were constructed on the shore in the tidal entrance basin of the Docks between the West Breakwater and the passenger landing pontoon; this house was used until 1979 with various alterations.

1920 The lifeboat house and slipway were adapted for a new lifeboat.

1937 An annex was built at the rear of the house.

1968 A permanent mooring was taken up in the tidal entrance basin, with the boarding-boat moored nearby.

1973 A second lifeboat was placed on station, and was slipway-launched from the 1901 boathouse.

1979 The No 2 lifeboat was withdrawn on 11 July and the No.2 station was closed; the house was left unused, and both it and the slipway remain largely unaltered.

1985 New shore facilities were constructed on the dockside, comprising a fuel store and storehouse.

1991 An ex-show bungalow was donated to the RNLI by Associated British Ports for use as a crew room. The old crew room was some 6 years old and in a bad condition.

1995 A timber-framed building was constructed to provide a changing/drying room, workshop, toilet facilities and a diesel fuel store.

Medals and awards

Twelve medals have been awarded, one Gold, three Silver and eight Bronze.

Notable rescue

On 17 September 1935 the lifeboat *Prince David* was launched to the French schooner *Goeland*, which had been driven on to Friar's Point on Barry Island after drifting with a heavy list in a WNW gale.

Once on scene the lifeboat crew saw that there was no time to lose as the vessel was in danger of being smashed on the rocky foreshore. At risk of damaging the lifeboat, the Coxswain quickly took her close to the vessel, picking one of the crew out of the water where he had jumped in his anxiety to be rescued. The lifeboat then went alongside the casualty and the five other crew slid down ropes on to the rescue vessel.

The actual rescue was quickly accomplished, enabling the lifeboat to return to her station. Less than a minute after the last of the crew had been rescued, the schooner went on the rocks where the heavy seas broke her up

For this rescue the Silver Medal was awarded to the Honorary Secretary/Acting Coxswain Archibald Jones, and Bronze Medals to each of the crew, Second Coxswain Henry Hobbs, Mechanic Hewitt Swarts, Stanley Alexander, Thomas Alexander, William Cook, Henry Housdon and Frederick Searle.

The lifeboat house and slipway built in 1901 in the tidal entrance basin of the Docks, and used until 1979.

52ft Arun *Margaret Frances Love* (ON.1082) moored at Barry Dock.

Key dates

Opened	1963
RNLI	1963
Inshore LB	1963

Current lifeboat details

Inshore lifeboat

Type	Atlantic 21
Official Number	B-554
Name	American Ambassador
Donor	American-British Lifeboat Appeal
Placed on station	28.10.1982
Launch	Tractor and do-do carriage

Location history

1963 An inshore lifeboat station was established at the United World College of the Atlantic at St Donat's Castle in October; it was one of the nine inshore rescue boat stations established experimentally by the RNLI, and one of three kept open through the winter of 1963/4. The rescue boats, manned by the members of the staff and pupils of the College, were the college's own boats with expenses paid by the RNLI; several boats were operated at the same time.

1973 The RNLI sent its first official lifeboat, an Atlantic 21; a small house was built in a compound near the launchway through the Castle walls.

1993 The concrete slipway was found to be deteriorating so repair work was carried out.

1994 The slipway was extended to improve launch and recovery, and a tractor was supplied in September.

1996 The previous boathouse was extended to house an Atlantic 75 and launching vehicle; the area previously used by the College as a workshop and engine shop was taken over to increase the room available for lifeboat and launching vehicle, and improved crew facilities were provided.

Medals and awards

No medals have been awarded.

Notable rescue

On 11 November 1968 the inshore lifeboat was launched to help four men who were marooned on the wreck of the dredger *Steepholm* on the Tuskar Rock. Three rescue boats, *X7*, *X5* and *X4*, were launched in a light south-easterly wind.

X7 arrived on the scene to find that the men had been stranded when their dinghy had broken away. The ILB was taken alongside the wreck and the crew had to pick the right moment to effect the rescue of the men as the waves were 6-8 feet high at times. *X7* landed the men at Ogmore while *X4* salvaged the dinghy.

For this rescue letters of appreciation, signed by the Secretary, were sent to the ILB's crew, G. Unger, W. de Vogel and P. Allen.

Background information

Atlantic College is notable in the history of the RNLI for two reasons. First, it was here that the rigid-inflatable Atlantic 21 inshore lifeboat was designed and developed.

Experimental work on the development of a fast rescue boat for the RNLI, larger than the standard inshore lifeboat and capable of night operation, was carried out during the 1960s under the supervision of Rear Admiral Desmond Hoare, the Headmaster. The boat developed had a rigid wooden hull with an inflatable sponson attached to it, and had twin outboard engines fitted, which enabled a speed of over 30 knots, while the sponsons gave the boat great stability. This design was improved by the RNLI and entered service in the early 1970s as the Atlantic 21. As a result of this pioneering work, the design was named after the college.

Second, Atlantic College was the first station at which a female helm was accepted as qualified, 18-year-old Elizabeth Hostvedt from Norway, and the first at which a service was performed involving a female crew member; on 20 May 1971 Penelope Sutton was a member of the crew when the inshore rescue boat B-3 was launched to investigate a Swedish motor cruiser reported to be at anchor and flying a distress signal. The incident was a false alarm, as the courtesy Red Ensign flown forward of the cruiser had been misinterpreted.

Atlantic 21 *American Ambassador* (B-554) on exercise. *Rick Tomlinson*

Key dates

Opened	1860-1902; ro1965
RNLI	1860
AWLB withdrawn	8.1902
Inshore LB	5.1965

Current lifeboat details

Inshore lifeboat

Type	Atlantic 75
Official Number	B-726
Name	*Giles*
Donor	Sunday Express lottery and RNLI funds
Placed on station	11.7.1996
Launch	Tractor and do-do carriage

Location history

1860 A lifeboat house was built, situated on the main Promenade facing the beach; it was used until 1902, and is still standing, at the corner of Lifeboat Road and Marine Terrace, used as a restaurant.

1965 An inshore lifeboat station was established in May; between 1965 and 1995 the ILBs were housed in a lean-to shelter by the harbour slipway leased from the Council.

1995 A new lifeboat house was built for the Atlantic 75 and its launching vehicle, situated close to the harbour adjacent to the previous boathouse and facing the launching slipway used by the inflatable ILBs; it provides drying/changing room, workshop, toilet facility, souvenir sales outlet and crew room.

Medals and awards

Ten medals have been awarded, nine Silver and one Bronze.

Notable rescue

On 30 December 1994 the D class inshore lifeboat D-390 *Tiger D*, manned by helmsman Stuart Roberts, Wayne Evans and Carl Evans, was launched to a surfer who was in difficulty in very rough seas off Coney beach. The weather conditions were beyond the Force 7 operating limit of the ILB and the decision to launch was not taken lightly by the station's Honorary Secretary.

With waves about 4 metres high, progress to the casualty was difficult and dangerous and the ILB was constantly being filled with water. By using a high degree of seamanship and calling on all his boathandling skills, Helmsman Roberts was able to reach the casualty within 2 or 3 minutes, and positioned the ILB head to sea to break through the waves that were washing over the ILB, despite the possibility of it being capsized.

On the third attempt the ILB crew managed to pull the surfer into the boat. However, the elastic cord was still attached to the surfboard, and the force of dragging the man on board shot the surfboard into the ILB and nearly knocked out the Helmsman. Fortunately, his bump cap, which was dented, protected his head.

Returning to the station, Helmsman Roberts managed to keep the ILB just ahead of the following seas and ran her straight up on to the sandy beach. People watching from the beach had seen the ILB repeatedly engulfed in broken water and were all amazed that she and her crew could withstand such punishment.

For this outstanding service the Silver Medal was awarded to Stuart Roberts for superb seamanship, and the Thanks on Vellum was accorded to crew members Carl Evans and Wayne Evans.

Right The lifeboat house built in 1995 for the Atlantic 75 and launching vehicle, situated close to the harbour and adjacent to the previous ILB house.

Below Atlantic 75 *Giles* (B-726) on exercise off the harbour wall in 1996.

Key dates

Opened	1966
RNLI	1966
Inshore LB	5.1966

Current lifeboat details

Inshore lifeboat

Type	D class inflatable
Official Number	D-402
Name	Warwick
Donor	The Warwick Lifeboat Appeal
Placed on station	24.7.1990
Launch	Trolley

Location history

1966 An inshore lifeboat station was established in May; the ILB was kept in a boathouse at Aberavon Beach, near the Beach Hotel, on the Promenade. An extension was later added to house the launching tractor; this building was demolished in 1997.

1997 The station was moved to the Coastguard station, where temporary facilities were established.

1998 A new ILB house was built close to the Coastguard station.

Medals and awards

No medals have been awarded.

Notable rescue

On 4 March 1995 the D class inshore lifeboat D-402 *Warwick* was launched to the converted ship's lifeboat *Panama*, which was in distress in worsening conditions half a mile west of Port Talbot Harbour. On reaching the casualty lifeboatman Robert Harris went on board to calm the three occupants who were becoming increasingly concerned.

The ILB stood by until a fishing vessel arrived on scene to tow the *Panama* to a mooring in the River Afan. Lifeboatman Harris manned the tow line, which parted on one occasion when the boats were hit by a series of big waves. Throughout the operation, the ILB escorted both vessels.

The ILB house built in 1998 near the Coastguard station on Aberavon beach, with D class inflatable *Warwick* (D-402) being washed down after a routine exercise in February 1999.

For his efforts the Thanks on Vellum was accorded to Robert Harris, and framed letters of appreciation signed by the Chairman, Sir Michael Vernon, were presented to crew members Leigh Worth and Stanley May in recognition of their efforts.

Background information

There were plans to establish a lifeboat station at Port Talbot in 1902, but after further investigation this was deemed unnecessary. The nearby station at the Mumbles was improved instead.

In 1968 the Mayor presented a plaque to the station bearing the borough coat of arms. The plaque is exhibited inside the boathouse.

Mumbles

West Glamorgan

Location history

1835 The first lifeboat to cover Swansea Bay was funded by the Swansea Harbour Trust. Although it was intended for the Mumbles, it was kept at the Swansea premises of the Harbour Trust most of the time, and was certainly there in 1843. It lapsed during the 1850s, but in 1856 a new lifeboat was bought by the Harbour Trust, which in 1859 was moved to the newly opened South Dock.

1863 The RNLI took over the station and in 1865 completed a lifeboat house on the shore under the cliffs. The lifeboat was moved to the Mumbles in January 1866, launched and rehoused along a stone slipway.

1883 A lifeboat house was built on the main road approaching the pier; used until 1903, it is still standing and used by the Mumbles Amateur Rowing Club. The enamel facia panels are still intact on either side of the main door.

1903 Between 1903 and 1916 the lifeboat was kept afloat at moorings after the Mumbles Railway & Pier Company constructed a mooring slipway free of charge in 1897 for use by the station.

1916 A new slipway was built on the north of Mumbles Pier, to which a boathouse was added in 1922. This house is still in use, although it has been altered subsequently for new lifeboats, most recently for the station's Tyne class lifeboat.

Key dates

Opened	1835-c1851 and 1856
RNLI	1863
Motor LB	1924
Fast LB	1985
Inshore LB	5.1965

Current lifeboat details

All-weather lifeboat

Type	Tyne
Official Number	1096
Operational Number	47-005
Year built	1985
Name	Ethel Anne Measures
Donor	The James Frederick and Ethel Anne Measures Charity, Mumbles Lifeboat Appeal, the Lord Mayor of Birmingham Appeal and Pebble Mill Appeal
Placed on station	31.7.1985
Launch	Slipway

Inshore lifeboat

Type	D class inflatable
Official Number	D-463
Name	Nellie Grace Hughes
Donor	Bequest of Nellie Grace Hughes
Placed on station	29.11.1994
Launch	Trolley

1965 An ILB station was established in May; accommodation for the ILB was found in a building opposite the 1883 boathouse.

1995 A new ILB house was built on the same site; as well as housing the ILB, there was a changing/drying room, toilet, crew room, kitchen, office and store rooms.

Medals and awards

Eight medals have been awarded, one Gold, two Silver, and five Bronze.

Ten Silver Medals were awarded for shore-boat rescues before the station came under the auspices of the RNLI.

In 1971 the then Coxswain, Derek Scott, was awarded a Silver Medal for a rescue he performed single-handedly.

Notable rescue

On 11 October 1944 the damaged Canadian frigate *Cheboque* was towed to Mumbles Roads, and was anchored to await docking by local tugs. When a gale blew up during the night, she began to drag her anchors and radioed for help and on the evening of 12 October. The lifeboat *Edward, Prince of Wales* was launched into the strong gale, which was accompanied by squalls of rain and heavy breaking seas.

Once on the scene it was found that the frigate was under water and the Captain requested that the entire crew be taken off. In a series of hazardous approaches alongside, with the lifeboat rising and falling in the heavy swell, all 42 of the frigate's crew were successfully taken off.

After the rescue, which had taken an hour and a half, the lifeboat was in danger with such a large load, and great care was needed to ensure that nobody was washed overboard. The lee of the Mumbles Head provided some shelter enabling all the rescued to be safely landed at Mumbles. The lifeboat then made for Swansea, as she was unable to rehouse up the slipway due to the sea conditions.

For this rescue the Gold Medal was awarded to Coxswain William Gammon, Bronze Medals were awarded to Mechanic William Davies and Bowman Thomas Ace, and the Thanks on Vellum was accorded to the remainder of the crew, Charles R. Davies, Thomas A. Davies, William John Eynon, William Michael and Alfred Michael.

Background information

The station has a somewhat tragic history, as three lifeboat disasters have occurred since its establishment. The first lifeboat to be lost during service off the Mumbles was the *Wolverhampton* in January 1883, when four of her crew of 13 were lost trying to assist the barque *Amiral Prinz Adalbert*. The second disaster occurred on 1 February 1903 when the lifeboat *James Stevens No.12* capsized, resulting in the loss of six lifeboatmen. The third occurred in April 1947 when the station's first motor lifeboat, *Edward, Prince of Wales*, was lost on service to the steamship *Santampa* at Sker Point. The lifeboat's crew of eight were lost, and all of the 39 on board the steamship also died. A hatch cover from the *Santampa* is on display at Kirkleatham Old Hall Museum, near Redcar, Cleveland, together with a memorial plaque to those who were lost in the Mumbles lifeboat. There are several memorial plaques in Oystermouth Church dedicated to those lifeboatmen who gave their lives on service.

47ft Tyne *Ethel Anne Measures* (ON.1096) being launched from the lifeboat house alongside the pier on an exercise in April 1998.

Key dates

Opened	1852
RNLI	1854
Motor LB	1923
Fast LB	1986
Inshore LB	19.7.1972

Current lifeboat details

All-weather lifeboat

Type	Tyne
Official Number	1112
Operational Number	47-010
Year built	1986
Name	RFA Sir Galahad
Donor	Special appeal by Royal Fleet Auxiliary, and appeals, gifts, legacies
Placed on station	6.9.1986
Launch	Slipway

Inshore lifeboat

Type	D class inflatable
Official Number	D-438
Name	Stanley Taylor
Donor	Gift from Arthur and Georgina Stanley Taylor
Placed on station	27.4.1993
Launch	Trolley

Location history

1852 The first house was built to accommodate the Shipwrecked Fishermen & Mariners Royal Benevolent Society lifeboat at Penniless Cove, at the back of what is now the harbour against the wall leading down to the quay; it was used until 1862, and can still be seen.

1862 The first RNLI lifeboat house was built on Castle Beach, by the side of the narrow road leading from the harbour area to South Sands, facing east; this house was demolished in the 1890s.

1895 A new lifeboat house was built on the beach to the east side of Castle Hill, closer to the beach than the previous one. It was used until 1905, and in 1910 was handed over

A launch of 47ft Tyne RFA Sir Galahad (ON.1112) down what is one of the longest slipways in the country, for the station's annual Lifeboat Day in 1988.

to Tenby Corporation; it is still standing.

1905 A new lifeboat house and roller slipway were built on the north side of Castle Hill, alongside the now demolished Victoria Pier; this house is still in use today, although it has been modified and altered a number of times.

1920-3 The boathouse was adapted for the new motor lifeboat.

1962 Major alterations had to be made to the boathouse to accommodate the new wheelhouse fitted to the lifeboat.

1972 An inshore lifeboat station was established in July.

1976 A new ILB house was built, on the north side of the harbour.

1978 During maintenance work on the 1905 boathouse, many piles were found to have deteriorated since the last inspection, making the sub-structure unsafe; the lifeboat was placed afloat on moorings and the boathouse closed.

1979 The sub-structure of the boathouse and slipway was rebuilt; this work was completed in 1980.

1986 The station was adapted to accommodate the Tyne class lifeboat;

a new boarding platform, exhaust extractor system and larger-capacity fuel storage tanks were installed, and major repairs to the slipway were also carried out.

1987 A new hydraulic winch was installed in the boathouse.

1989 Infilling of the slipway toe was carried out to reduce the recovery limitation of the lifeboat; an extension was also constructed on the side of the boathouse to provide a mechanic's workshop and a souvenir sales outlet.

Medals and awards

Fourteen medals have been awarded, nine Silver and five Bronze.

One Silver Medal was awarded for a shore-boat rescue in 1834.

Background information

Tenby's 1905 launching slipway is one of the longest in the country, at 366ft 6in. However, in 1998, due to problems with this slipway and the need for a larger boathouse to accommodate the next generation of slipway-launched lifeboats, the RNLI prepared proposals to build a new lifeboat house and slipway. The proposal is to build a new station a few hundred metres to the east of the existing site, close to the site of the old Royal Victoria Pier.

Key dates

Opened	1868
RNLI	1868
Motor LB	1929
Fast LB	1987
Inshore LB	3.1994

Current lifeboat details

All-weather lifeboat

Type	Tyne
Official Number	1114
Operational Number	47-011
Year built	1987
Name	*The Lady Rank*
Donor	The Rank Foundation
Placed on station	23.6.1987
Launch	Slipway

Inshore lifeboat

Type	D class inflatable
Official Number	D-493
Name	*Isabella Mary*
Donor	Legacy of Mrs I. A. Finlayson
Placed on station	30.3.1996
Launch	Davit

Location history

1868 A stone lifeboat house was built on the eastern end of Angle Point, with a wooden launching slipway; in 1888 a new and stronger slipway was constructed to improve launching arrangements.

1908 A steam lifeboat was sent to station and was kept at moorings in Milford Haven; in December 1914 she broke away, drifted on to rocks in Chapel Bay, was badly damaged, and was withdrawn.

1910 The pulling lifeboat was withdrawn as the steam lifeboat was on station.

1915 A pulling lifeboat was sent to the station, and kept in the 1868 boathouse; this house was used until 1927, and its remains still exist although in a derelict state.

1927 A new lifeboat house and roller slipway were built on the north side of Angle Point; an unusual recovery procedure was devised in which the lifeboat was hauled up the slipway bow-first, then turned on a turntable to be backed into the boathouse ready for the next launch; this house was altered several times before it was demolished in 1992.

1987 The lifeboat house was adapted to accommodate the Tyne class lifeboat; the slipway was redecked and a new fuel tank was installed.

1991-2 A new larger lifeboat house and slipway were built on the north side of Angle Point alongside the 1927 house, the condition of which had deteriorated considerably; the new house included a new fuel storage tank, a new Biglands hydraulic winch, workshop, changing room, drying area, crew room, galley, toilet and shower facilities. The old boathouse and slipway were demolished after the new house became operational.

1994 An inshore lifeboat station was established, and a D class lifeboat was sent on 19 March initially for one season's evaluation; it is kept in a small house at the head of the lifeboat slipway.

Medals and awards

Nine medals have been awarded, four Silver and five Bronze.

Five Silver Medals have been awarded for shore-boat rescues.

Notable rescue

On 5 May 1997 the lifeboat *The Lady Rank* was launched to the motor vessel *Dale Princess*, which had anchored in North Haven, Skomer Island, to carry out some repairs. The anchors started dragging and the vessel was in danger of being driven on to a sheer cliff by gusting gale force winds and heavy seas.

Speed was essential, so to reach the casualty Coxswain Jeremy Rees took the lifeboat through the notorious Jack Sound. A force 8 northerly wind and tidal stream of 5 knots were creating very rough and confused seas, and visibility was almost zero. Coxswain Rees had to steer by compass as the radar was useless because of the clutter from the breaking seas.

When the lifeboat reached the casualty, she was lying in surf less than 30 feet from the cliffs. Despite the treacherous backwash from the cliff and numerous mooring and fishing buoys, the lifeboat was taken in near enough to connect a tow and the casualty, together with her four occupants, was saved and towed into Milford Haven.

For this rescue the Bronze Medal was awarded to Coxswain Rees in recognition of his high standard of seamanship, courage and leadership. A framed letter of appreciation, signed by the Chairman, was presented to the remainder of the crew.

The lifeboat house and slipway built in 1991-2 on the north side of Angle Point.
Tony Denton

Key dates

Opened	1822
RNLI	1855
Motor LB	1908
Fast LB	1981
Inshore LB	4.1995

Current lifeboat details

All-weather lifeboat

Type	Trent
Official Number	1198
Operational Number	14-03
Year built	1994
Name	Blue Peter VII
Donor	Blue Peter Pieces of Eight Appeal, 1993-4
Placed on station	2.9.1994
Launch	Afloat

Inshore lifeboat

Type	D class inflatable
Official Number	D-505
Name	Arthur Bygraves
Donor	Gift of Mrs Margery Bygraves
Placed on station	24.7.1996
Launch	Trolley

Location history

1822 The first lifeboat was designed by Captain Thomas Evans, RN, and built locally; it wore out and the RNLI took over the station in 1855.

1854-5 A new lifeboat house was built at the top of Goodwick Beach; it was used until 1908.

1869 A No.2 station was opened; in 1870 a lifeboat house and slipway were built in a position enabling a straightforward launch to windward.

1907 The No.1 station was closed, and in 1907-8 a new lifeboat house and slipway were built at Pen Cw for the first motor lifeboat, which was sent to the station in 1909; this house was moved to a new site in 1911 and a slipway was constructed by the Great Western Railway.

1929-30 A new lifeboat house and slipway were constructed near the passenger steamer quay, necessitated after the quay had been widened by the GWR; during construction work between 1928 and 1929 the lifeboat was kept afloat off the harbour. This house was used until 1981, and was demolished in 1993 during port improvements by British Rail.

1980 In preparation for future harbour developments, a new afloat berth and assembly/storehouse building were provided by the British Railways Board; following trials in the new berth, moorings were taken up permanently in 1981.

1995 An inshore lifeboat station was established, and the ILB went on station on 21 April; it was kept in a temporary container shed near the lifeboat mooring berth.

Medals and awards

Twenty-four medals have been awarded, one Gold, 14 Silver and nine Bronze.

Four Silver Medals have been awarded for shore-boat rescues.

Notable rescue

On 3 December 1920 the lifeboat *Charterhouse* was launched to the Dutch motor schooner *Hermina*, which was dragging its anchor outside the breakwater off Fishguard Harbour in a gale and heavy sea.

The lifeboat found the schooner grinding heavily on the rocks with seas breaking clean over her. The lifeboat was anchored to windward, then began to veer down towards the casualty, but because of the severity of the conditions there was difficulty in getting a line aboard; the seas were lifting the lifeboat almost into the ship's rigging at times. It took over an hour of considerable effort on the part of the lifeboat crew to rescue seven of the ten men on board.

The last three refused to leave, despite the lifeboatmen pleading with them, and soon afterwards the schooner was totally wrecked on the Needle Rock. Two of the men were hauled up the cliff and saved, but the third was washed away and drowned.

The lifeboat sustained considerable damage in effecting the rescue and the wet engine refused to start. The sails were therefore set, but the mizzen sail was blown away by the severe wind, and a jib had to be set. With great difficulty the lifeboat was sailed away from the cliffs, and after 3 hours in the most appalling conditions she reached her station.

For this service Coxswain John Howells was awarded the Gold Medal; Silver Medals were awarded to Tom Davies, Tom Holmes and Robert Simpson; and Bronze Medals were awarded to the remainder of the crew, T. Perkins, J. Rourke, P. Whelan, T. Duffin, J. Gardiner, W. Devereux, H. W. Mason, W. Thomas and R. Veal. The Queen of Holland presented a gold watch to Coxswain John Howells and silver watches to the other 12 members of the crew who undertook this rescue.

14m Trent *Blue Peter VII* (ON.1198) moored in the afloat berth at Goodwick. *Mark Roberts*

Key dates

Opened	1849-1932; ro1971
RNLI	1851
AWLB withdrawn	13.10.1932
Inshore LB	7.1971; second 1998

Current lifeboat details

Inshore lifeboats

Type	Atlantic 21
Official Number	B-752
Name	*Tanni Grey*
Donor	Wales and West Mercia Regional Appeal
Placed on station	25.2.1999
Launch	Tractor and do-do carriage

Type	D class inflatable
Official Number	D-467
Name	*Kathleen Scadden*
Donor	Miss J. F. Gibson
Placed on station	3.9.1998
Launch	Land Rover and Trolley

Location history

1849 The first lifeboat house was built on the south side of the mouth of the River Teifi on the shore below Penrhyn Castle, near the Black Rocks.

1876 A new lifeboat house and stone slipway were built on the same site; they were completely renovated in 1881, and altered again in 1905, on both occasions for new lifeboats. This house was used until 1932 and is still standing, used as a store.

1880 A small breakwater was constructed to protect the lifeboat house and launching site.

1971 An ILB station was established in July at Poppit Sands, at the mouth of the River Teifi, where a small ILB house was built; this was demolished in June 1986.

1986-7 A new lifeboat house was built at Poppit Sands to accommodate the new C class ILB and its launching tractor; this house was demolished in 1997.

1997-8 A new double inshore lifeboat house was built to accommodate both Atlantic and D class ILBs, launching tractor and Land Rover, and provide improved crew facilities.

Medals and awards

Four medals have been awarded, two Silver and two Bronze.

One Silver Medal has been awarded for a shore-boat rescue.

Notable rescue

On 15 August 1980 the D class inshore lifeboat D-194 was launched to four people and a dog in a motor cruiser that had been overcome by heavy seas on Cardigan Bar. To reach the casualty, Helmsman Robert Reynolds showed great skill in negotiating breaking seas on the bar. The ILB was swamped six times by large waves some 16 feet in height, but reached the scene speedily.

To take off the survivors the Helmsman had to drive the bow of the ILB on to the motor cruiser. During

The original service board from the earliest days of the station, displayed inside the lifeboat house.

the first two attempts two survivors were saved, and they were landed on the beach. The ILB then returned to take off the remaining couple.

For this rescue the Bronze Medal was awarded to Helmsman Reynolds for superb boathandling and his coolness throughout the service.

The lifeboat house at Poppit Sands completed in 1998 for Atlantic and D class inshore lifeboats, with the crew facilities in the larger part on the right.

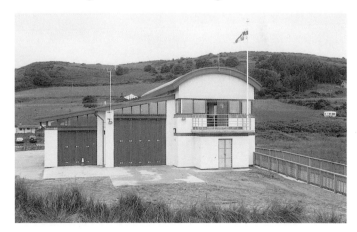

The launch from the beach at Poppit Sands of the Relief Atlantic 21 *Clothworker* (B-586) on exercise in July 1998.

Key dates

Opened	1864
RNLI	1864
Motor LB	1947
Fast LB	1992
Inshore LB	5.1967

Current lifeboat details

All-weather lifeboat

Type	Mersey
Official Number	1172
Operational Number	12-15
Year built	1990
Name	*Frank and Lena Clifford of Stourbridge*
Donor	Legacy of Mr Frank Clifford of Stourbridge
Placed on station	8.4.1992
Launch	Carriage

Inshore lifeboat

Type	D class inflatable
Official Number	D-476
Name	*Corydd*
Donor	Messrs Sinclair, Roche & Temperley
Placed on station	3.5.1995
Launch	Trolley

Location history

1864-5 The first lifeboat house was built, situated at the top of a steep incline above the slipway into the harbour; it was the only practicable spot available, and a winch was supplied to haul the boat up to the house. It was used until 1904 and has since been converted into public toilets.

1904 A new lifeboat house was built on the opposite side of the harbour to the first house, behind the small inner pier; it was adapted in 1960 to accommodate a new all-metal carriage, and again in 1970 for the Oakley class lifeboat.

1967 An inshore lifeboat station was established, and a small house was built alongside the lifeboat house.

1990-1 The lifeboat house and slipway were rebuilt for the Mersey class lifeboat.

Medals and awards

Four medals have been awarded, all Bronze.

Notable rescue

On 7 August 1966 the lifeboat *St Albans* was launched to search for some boys who had been reported missing, and was taken by Coxswain David Evans as close to the shore as possible during the search, despite the treacherous nature of the rocky coastline.

After half an hour shouts were heard, and the searchlight picked up a boy stranded on a ledge 20 feet up the cliff. With the lifeboat anchored as close as possible, two volunteers swam to the cliffs with a rope, which was used to take the youth on board. The swimmers then recovered a body and another boy, severely injured, who did not survive.

For this service Bronze Medals were awarded to the two swimmers, Mechanic George Evans and David Rees, and also to Coxswain Evans.

Background information

The station's former 37ft Oakley class lifeboat, *Bird's Eye*, is on display at the Sea Watch Centre in Moelfre, Anglesey. This lifeboat served at New Quay from 1970 to 1990, and saved 42 lives.

Above Launch of 12m Mersey *Frank and Lena Clifford of Stourbridge* (ON.1172).

Right The lifeboat house built in 1904, and extensively modified and rebuilt in 1991 for the 12m Mersey class lifeboat.

Key dates

Opened	1843
RNLI	1861
Motor LB	1932
AWLB withdrawn	31.10.1964
Inshore LB	5.1963

Current lifeboat details

Inshore lifeboat

Type	Atlantic 75
Official Number	B-704
Name	*Enid Mary*
Donor	Bequest of Miss Margaret Rosalind Phillips
Placed on station	30.3.1994
Launch	Tractor and do-do carriage

Location history

1843 The first lifeboat was kept on a carriage in a boathouse near the sea, under the charge of the Harbour Master; this lifeboat had been removed before the RNLI established a station in 1861.

1861 The first RNLI lifeboat house was built in Queens Road, set back from the seafront on a site given by the Town Council; it was used until 1875.

1875 A new lifeboat house was built on the same site, and was used until 1964; it has since been used by an ice-cream manufacturer, a funeral director to garage cars, and more recently by BBC Wales.

1963 An inshore lifeboat station was established; the ILB was housed in a former fisherman's shed on the Harbour Quay, formed by an archway under the road at the harbour; in 1982-3 it was enlarged and improved, and was used until 1994, subsequently reverting to its original use.

1994 A new lifeboat house was built for the Atlantic 75 and launching tractor, at the end of the Quay.

Medals and awards

Two medals have been awarded for shore-boat rescues, one Silver and one Bronze.

Notable rescue

On 26 July 1954 the lifeboat *Aguila Wren* was launched to the fishing vessel *Lindy Lou*, which was in difficulties between Towyn and Aberdovey in a rough sea with a moderate gale blowing. An army launch was towing the casualty towards Aberdovey.

After a rough passage the lifeboat met the two boats between the Fairway and the Bar Buoys. The tow then parted, and the army launch made for Aberdovey while the fishing vessel anchored. The lifeboat stood by for over an hour, but as the conditions were worsening the casualty's crew prepared to leave the vessel.

The lifeboat approached the vessel, which was surging about in confused cross seas, and at the first attempt all three men were safely taken on board. The fishing vessel was left at anchor and the lifeboat returned to Aberystwyth.

For this rescue the Thanks on Vellum was accorded to Coxswain Baden Davies.

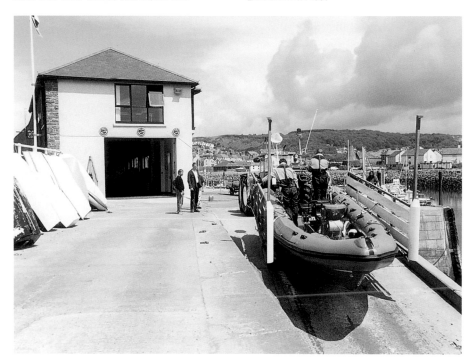

Above Recovery of Atlantic 75 *Enid Mary* (B-704) after an exercise.

Right The lifeboat house built in 1875 in Queens Road; it was used until 1964 and has since been used by BBC Wales.

Key dates

Opened	1966
RNLI	1966
Inshore LB	6.1966

Current lifeboat details

Inshore lifeboat

Type	D class inflatable
Official Number	D-479
Name	May
Donor	Gift of Dr May Reed, Bucks
Placed on station	13.6.1995
Launch	Trolley

Location history

1966 An inshore lifeboat station was established in June; the ILB was kept in a timber boathouse at the south end of Borth beach, near the Coastguard look-out post.

1986-7 A new purpose-built brick ILB house was constructed on the same site as the previous house, which was demolished; the new house included a crew room, store, drying area, shower room and an area for the sale of souvenirs.

Medals and awards

No medals have been awarded.

Notable rescue

On 11 July 1991 the D class inshore lifeboat D-344 *Onslaught* was launched in a south-westerly force 6 wind and confused breaking seas to two men cut off by the tide beneath Borth Head. On reaching the scene, the lifeboatmen found the two on a partly submerged rock close to a cliff face.

To reach them the ILB was anchored to windward and seaward, then veered down towards the rock.

It took four attempts before the men were safely taken on board. The ILB then returned to Borth where it was beached on the slipway and the casualties were safely landed.

For this rescue the Thanks on Vellum was accorded to Helmsman Ronald Davies in recognition of his high standard of seamanship and leadership. Framed letters of appreciation signed by the Chairman were presented to crew members Louis Paul De La Haye and Andrew William Doyle in recognition of their valuable support and the efficient manner in which they carried out their duties during this service.

D class inflatable *May* (D-479) on her trolley outside the ILB house at Borth.

Key dates

Opened	1837-1931; ro1963
RNLI	1853
AWLB withdrawn	1931
Inshore LB	11.1963

Current lifeboat details

Inshore lifeboat

Type	Atlantic 21
Official Number	B-559
Name	Long Life III
Donor	Allied Breweries Long Life Beer Promotion, and legacy of Mrs D. M. Kempton
Placed on station	3.11.1983
Launch	Tractor and do-do carriage

Location history

1837 The first lifeboat was purchased with help from the RNIPLS, and was managed by the Harbour Authority; a stone house was built about a mile from the harbour mouth.

1853 The RNLI took over the station.

1858 A new lifeboat house was built for the lifeboat and carriage.

1886 A new lifeboat house with boundary walls and entrance gate was constructed at the eastern end of the town; it was enlarged in 1904, and used until 1931 when the station was closed. It was subsequently used as a commercial garage, then converted into a private house.

1903 A slipway was constructed from the roadway to the beach, enabling a launch into the River Dovey; this slipway is still intact.

1963 An inshore lifeboat station was established in November; the ILB was housed in the workshops of the Outward Bound Sea School.

1991 A new ILB house was constructed to house the Atlantic 21 and launching tractor; facilities also included a souvenir sales outlet, drying room, toilet and crew room.

1995 A first floor was constructed in the boathouse to improve facilities and provide a crew room, galley and store.

Medals and awards

Two medals have been awarded, one Silver and one Bronze.

Notable rescue

On 10 August 1974 the Atlantic 21 inshore lifeboat B-514 *Guide Friendship I* was launched after a report that a man had been seen to fall overboard from the cabin cruiser *Lady Jane*, in a strong WNW wind and rough sea. A man was found in the water suffering from exposure and shock, clinging to a lifejacket, and he was picked up by the ILB. He informed the ILB crew that there were three children still on board the cruiser, so the ILB began a search of the area.

Meanwhile, on board the cruiser the eldest child, Jayne Edmunds, having already thrown a lifejacket to her father as he fell overboard, then fired distress signals, instructed her friends to put on lifejackets and supported one of them in the water after the cruiser was wrecked.

The ILB crew spotted the wreckage of the sunken cruiser on an isolated sandbank near the South Bank at the entrance to the River Dovey. Heavy surf was breaking round the sandbank and because of the rough sea the lifeboat became difficult to manoeuvre. Crew member David Williams volunteered to enter the heavy surf, and without a line waded and swam to the three children. With the help of another crew member he brought them ashore through heavy surf on to a nearby beach where the ILB had landed.

For this service the Bronze Medal was awarded to David Williams in recognition of his courage, initiative and determination. Helmsman Anthony Mills and crew member Andrew Coghill were accorded the Thanks on Vellum for their part in this service. Jayne Edmunds was awarded an inscribed wristwatch in recognition of her action.

Because of the steepness of the launching area, a powerful offshore lifeboat tractor is needed to transport the lifeboat and her carriage across the beach.

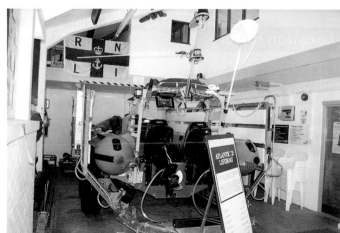

Above The ILB house built in 1991 on the banks of the River Dovey to house the Atlantic 21 and launching tractor.

Right Relief Atlantic 21 B-511 inside the ILB house in 1996.

Right Atlantic 21 *Long Life III* (B-559) launching across the beach at Aberdovey in 1988.
Tony Denton

Key dates

Opened	1861
RNLI	1861
Motor LB	1933
Fast LB	1990
Inshore LB	5.1965

Current lifeboat details

All-weather lifeboat

Type	Mersey
Official Number	1164
Operational Number	12-006
Year built	1990
Name	Andy Pearce
Donor	Bequests of Mr Andrew Stephen Pearce and Mr Ralph C. Merriott
Placed on station	23.11.1990
Launch	Carriage

Inshore lifeboat

Type	D class inflatable
Official Number	D-508
Name	John Saunderson
Donor	Gift of Dr Barbara Saunderson
Placed on station	2.10.1996
Launch	Land Rover and trolley

Location history

1861 A lifeboat house was built close to the railway station; this house was used until 1903.

1903 A new lifeboat house was constructed in Lloyd Street, between the West and East Shore, to enable a launch from either location; this practice was abandoned in the 1950s when a new sea wall was built on the West Shore, since when the lifeboat has been launched from the East.

1963 The boathouse was modified for the 37ft Oakley class lifeboat.

1965 An inshore lifeboat station was established in May; the ILB was kept in the 1903 boathouse.

1982-3 The boathouse was extended to accommodate the towing vehicle for the ILB, and a crew room was provided.

1991 Alterations were made to the boathouse to accommodate the Mersey class lifeboat; this included the installation of new steel concertina-type main doors, a new boarding/viewing platform and a new 600-gallon fuel storage tank.

Medals and awards

One Bronze Medal has been awarded.

Notable rescue

On 27 March 1919 the lifeboat *Theodore Price* was launched to the schooner *Ada Mary* of Liverpool, which had lost both sails in a fierce north-westerly gale with a very heavy sea. She dropped both anchors in Colwyn Bay, but requested assistance when one of the anchor cables parted.

The lifeboat battled her way through very heavy seas to reach the casualty, and was swamped several times by huge seas. Once on the scene she was manoeuvred alongside the casualty and was able to rescue two men, who were exhausted after their efforts to save the schooner.

On the return passage the lifeboat was unable to make headway in the prevailing conditions. The Coxswain was therefore compelled to put into Colwyn Bay for shelter. The lifeboat was beached there, and the two rescued men were landed.

For this rescue the Bronze Medal was awarded to Coxswain John Owen.

Background information

The first Coxswain at the station was Hugh Jones. He was a copper-miner and it was the duty of his daughter, in the event of a service call, to rush to the top of the shaft, halfway up the Great Orme, and signal her father to come to the lifeboat. Her method was to rap with a stone in a certain manner.

In 1990 lifeboatmen from Llandudno gave a considerable amount of help to various areas along the North Wales coast that had been flooded during hurricane force north-westerly winds and very high tides. The worst-affected areas of Towyn and Pensarn suffered severe flooding. Between 26 February and 1 March the lifeboatmen strove tirelessly for up to 16 hours each day using the station's ILB to help over 200 people to safety. A special framed certificate was presented to the station in recognition of the services carried out by them under extremely difficult circumstances.

Recovery of 12m Mersey Andy Pearce *(ON.1164) on the East Shore Promenade at Llandudno in June 1995.*

Key dates

Opened	1852
RNLI	1854
Motor LB	1939
Fast LB	1992
Inshore LB	7.1967

Current lifeboat details

All-weather lifeboat

Type	Mersey
Official Number	1183
Operational Number	12-24
Year built	1992
Name	Lil Cunningham
Donor	Gift of Miss Betty H. I. Cunningham, Derby, in memory of her sister
Placed on station	23.6.1992
Launch	Carriage

Inshore lifeboat

Type	D class inflatable
Official Number	D-485
Name	Stafford with Rugeley
Donor	Stafford and Rugeley Branch Appeal
Placed on station	11.7.1995
Launch	Trolley

Location history

1852 The Shipwrecked Fishermen and Mariners' Royal Benevolent Society built a house for the station's first lifeboat close to the beach between the River Clwyd and the sea on the west side of the river, with doors at both ends.

1856 A new lifeboat house was built by the RNLI at Foryd, on the western side of Rhyl, for the station's first Tubular lifeboat (see below); this house was used until 1868.

1868 A new brick lifeboat house was built on the west bank of the River Clwyd, close to Foryd Harbour. This house was used for the No.2 lifeboat between 1878 and 1899; the Tubular lifeboat was kept on the beach, near the Pier, under canvas until a wooden lean-to shed was built for it.

1897 A new wooden lifeboat house was built on the east side of the Pier and a short slipway on piles was erected; this house was used until it was badly damaged in a storm in January 1955 and was demolished soon afterwards. The lifeboat was placed temporarily on moorings in the river until a new house was completed.

1956 A new brick and concrete lifeboat house was built to accommodate the lifeboat, carriage and tractor; this house is still in use, with some modifications to both it and the launch slipway on to the beach.

1967 An inshore lifeboat station was established in July; the ILB was kept in the boathouse until 1983.

1983 An ILB house was built alongside the 1956 boathouse.

Medals and awards

Two medals have been awarded, one Silver and one Bronze.

Notable rescue

On 17 September 1962 the lifeboat *Anthony Robert Marshall* was launched to the hovercraft *VA3-001*, which was in difficulties in a WNW gale with heavy seas breaking over the promenade and into the lifeboat house, making launching difficult.

Despite the rolling and pitching of the casualty, the lifeboat was taken alongside and the three crew were taken off. Within minutes the hovercraft, with 250 gallons of kerosene on board, crashed into the Promenade.

The Fire Brigade stood by the vessel, and in spite of the risk of an explosion, two shore helpers boarded her to make sure that no survivors were on board.

This was the first service ever made by a lifeboat to a hovercraft, and the Silver Medal was awarded to Coxswain Harold Campini and the Thanks on Vellum was accorded to the rest of the lifeboat crew, Mechanic William Hunt, Assistant Mechanic George Povah and crew members Ian Armstrong, Bruce Herbert, R. I. Thomas and D. C. A. Williams, as well as head launcher Dennis Jones, who had boarded the hovercraft. Framed letters of appreciation were presented to the shore helpers and a collective Thanks on Vellum was presented to the station to be hung in the boathouse.

Background information

Rhyl was one of the few stations to operate a Tubular-type lifeboat. This design had a double hull, similar to a modern catamaran, with two floats meeting at each end with a grating deck in between. It was an adaptation of the pontoon system, and had great stability, but there was no shelter for the crew, who experienced considerable exposure. The first of Rhyl's Tubular lifeboats, which had an iron hull, arrived in 1856. She was replaced in 1893 by a steel-hulled boat. The third and last was the *Caroline Richardson*, on station from 1897 to 1939. Rhyl's Tubular lifeboats are credited with saving 42 lives in more than 70 years.

The lifeboat house built on the beach at Rhyl in 1956.

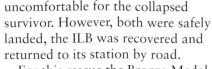

Key dates

Opened	1966
RNLI	1966
Inshore LB	6.1966

Current lifeboat details

Inshore lifeboat

Type	D class inflatable
Official Number	D-510
Name	Marjorie Helen
Donor	Bequest of Eric Bulling, Wimborne, Dorset
Placed on station	16.10.1996
Launch	Land Rover and trolley

Location history

1967 An inshore lifeboat station was established and the ILB was kept in a garage in the car park on the foreshore close to Flint Castle.

1981 A new slipway was constructed by the local council to improve launching facilities.

1985 A new ILB house was built close to the previous one, providing improved crew facilities. The ILB can be launched from a number of different sites depending on where the casualty is located. The trolley is fully road-going and the station's Land Rover is used to transport the boat to slipways up and down the River Dee, including Mostyn and Connah's Quay.

Medals and awards

One Bronze Medal has been awarded.

Notable rescue

On 26 February 1983 the Liverpool Coastguard informed the station's Honorary Secretary that a vessel had run aground 1 mile south-east of Mostyn Dock, in a strong north-westerly wind and rough sea. The D class inshore lifeboat D-252 was towed on her trailer by road to Mostyn, about 5-6 miles from Flint,

down the estuary of the River Dee, and was launched there despite the fact that it was dark and the conditions were close to the operating limits for the D class inflatable.

The casualty, the cabin cruiser *Heron II*, was reached in about 15 minutes; she was aground with her anchor out and was taking in water. It would not be possible to tow her off the sand, so the ILB prepared to go alongside and take off the crew of two.

On the second attempt both were successfully taken off; one of them had collapsed and so had to be carried on to the ILB by the lifeboat's crew. The return passage to Mostyn was difficult, as the ILB headed through waves 6 feet high, making it

uncomfortable for the collapsed survivor. However, both were safely landed, the ILB was recovered and returned to its station by road.

For this rescue the Bronze Medal was awarded to Helmsman Robert Alan Forrester in recognition of his courage, leadership and seamanship; framed letters signed by the Chairman were presented to crew members Denis James Smith and Terrence Henry Jacklin.

Background information

Between 1957 and 1966 a privately operated rescue boat was used at Flint, serving the dangerous estuary of the River Dee, and this boat is credited with saving at least 19 lives.

Right The ILB house at Flint built in 1985 and subsequently extended to improve crew facilities.

Below D class inflatable *Marjorie Helen* (D-510) in the River Dee after her Naming Ceremony on 16 November 1996.

Key dates

Opened	1966
RNLI	1966
Inshore LB	6.1966

Current lifeboat details

Inshore lifeboat

Type	D class inflatable
Official Number	D-473
Name	*Thomas Jefferson*
Donor	Gift of Mrs Marion Jefferson, in memory of her husband
Placed on station	21.12.1994
Launch	Land Rover and trolley

Location history

1966 An inshore lifeboat station was established in June, and the ILB was kept at the local Sailing Club; a purpose-built boathouse, situated on the Promenade opposite the Old Baths, was later used.

1992 A new ILB house was constructed in Coronation Gardens, immediately behind the previous one, thus reducing the risk of flooding. The old boathouse had been seriously damaged by flooding in severe storms in February 1990 and was subsequently demolished. As well as housing the lifeboat and launching vehicle, the new building includes a crew room, office, workshop, galley and toilet.

Medals and awards

No medals have been awarded.

Notable rescue

If needed, the inshore lifeboat from West Kirby can be towed by road to a variety of launch sites depending on the location of the casualty, making it an ideal rescue tool. This capacity proved particularly useful on 14 January 1991 when the D class inshore lifeboat D-322 was taken some 14 miles from her station to the lake in Walton Hall Park, Liverpool, to effect a rescue.

As it was the middle of winter, the lake had frozen over and a 13-year-old boy had been playing on the ice when it broke and he fell through into the freezing water. Although he managed to scramble on to an island in the middle of the lake, police, firemen and ambulance crews were unable to reach him, so the RNLI was alerted. West Kirby's Land Rover towed the ILB on its trailer to the Park, escorted by police through the Mersey Tunnel.

The ILB was lifted over the park railings and placed in the water. With two crew in the bows smashing the ice as they went, they reached the island and took on board the boy, was suffering from mild hypothermia, and his dog.

Above The ILB house built in 1992 in Coronation Gardens, on the Promenade at West Kirby.

Below D class inflatable *Thomas Jefferson* (D-473) on exercise, with Hoylake's lifeboat in the background. *John Truran*

Key dates

Opened	1802-14, 1824-post 1851 and 1868
RNLI	1868
Motor LB	1924
Fast LB	1988

Current lifeboat details

All-weather lifeboat

Type	Tyne
Official Number	1147
Operational Number	47-032
Year built	1988
Name	Sir William Hillary
Donor	Legacy of Mr Alan James Woolfenden, Gawsworth, Ches, with a donation from Mr Geoffrey W. Sargeant and other gifts
Placed on station	25.11.1988
Launch	Slipway

Location history

1802 The first lifeboat, funded by the Duke of Atholl, was sent to the station; it was used until it was wrecked in December 1814 after breaking from its moorings.

1824 Another lifeboat, provided through local subscription, was built for the station; it was kept in Mr Winram's Shipbuilding Yard, near the Pier, and was used until the 1850s.

1868 A new lifeboat house was built at the end of the Harris Promenade, to the north of the town.

1874 A No.2 lifeboat was placed on station, and was kept afloat inside the breakwater at the entrance to the harbour until 1895.

1892 The 1868 lifeboat house, together with the site, was sold to Douglas Council; the lifeboat was kept temporarily in an enclosure in Walpole Avenue until a new site was found and a new boathouse built.

1895 On 12 January the afloat (No.2) lifeboat was damaged beyond repair on the rocks after her mooring chain broke; she was not replaced and it was decided to abolish the station, leaving only one lifeboat at Douglas.

1896 A new lifeboat house was built near Battery Point, in the Harbour Board yard, with a launching slipway into the harbour reached by pushing the lifeboat from its house across the road on skids.

1924 A new lifeboat house for the station's first motor lifeboat was built opposite the site of the previous house, in Approach Road; this house is still in use, having been altered for subsequent motor lifeboats.

1986 A new Biglands winch was installed in the lifeboat house.

1988 A crew/instruction room and improved storage facilities were provided in the boathouse.

1989 The boathouse was adapted to accommodate the Tyne class lifeboat; the slipway rollers in the keelway were replaced, and external bilgeways and a keelway liner were provided.

Right The memorial plaque commemorating the life of Sir William Hillary mounted outside the lifeboat house on the South Quay of Douglas Harbour.

Below The lifeboat house built in 1923-4 on the South Quay, with 47ft Tyne *Sir William Hillary* (ON.1147) on the slipway. *John Truran*

Medals and awards

Fourteen medals have been awarded, four Gold and ten Silver.

Two medals have been awarded for shore rescues, both Silver.

Background information

Douglas is the home of the founder of the RNLI, Sir William Hillary, who moved there in 1808. In 1823 he wrote and published *An Appeal to the British Nation on the Humanity and Policy of forming a National Institution for the Preservation of Lives and Property from Shipwreck*. In this he set out his ideals for forming a national body whose sole responsibility would be the preservation of human life from shipwreck.

Hillary was not only the prime mover in the creation of a national lifeboat institution, but was also heavily involved in life-saving work in his home town. On 10 September 1824 the embryonic National Institution for the Preservation of Life from Shipwreck received a request from Hillary for a lifeboat for Douglas 'on account of the frequent gales and wrecks in Douglas Bay'. Although the one supplied was subsequently wrecked, between 1824 and 1851 it is reported that it saved 91 lives. In 1825 Hillary was awarded the Gold Medal as founder of the RNLI and won three other Gold Medals for gallantry.

The life of Hillary has not been forgotten. The Tower of Refuge, which was constructed in Douglas Bay in 1832 as a result of his efforts, can still be seen; it was intended as a refuge for shipwrecked sailors and is now a notable landmark in the Bay. In addition, the current Douglas lifeboat is named after him, and on 5 January 1997 a service was held to commemorate the 150th anniversary of his death. A Vellum certificate was presented to the station to record the occasion. His tomb can be seen in St George's churchyard in Douglas.

Key dates

Opened	1896
RNLI	1896
Motor LB	1936
Fast LB	1976
Inshore LB	5.1966

Current lifeboat details

All-weather lifeboat

Type	Trent
Official Number	1234
Operational Number	14-26
Year built	1998
Name	*Gough-Ritchie II*
Donor	Mrs James Ritchie
Placed on station	21.5.1998
Launch	Afloat

Inshore lifeboat

Type	D class inflatable
Official Number	D-462
Name	*Frances*
Donor	Gift of Rose Dixon
Placed on station	13.7.1994
Launch	Trolley

Location history

1896 A lifeboat house was built with doors at both ends and a stone launchway over the rocks for the carriage; altered several times, it is still in use today.

1950 The lifeboat was placed on permanent moorings in the outer harbour.

1966 An inshore lifeboat station was established in May; the inshore lifeboat was kept in the 1896 boathouse.

1976 Bulk storage facilities were installed on the quay for the new fast afloat lifeboat.

1986 A new fore and aft piled berth was provided in the harbour, parallel to Alfred Pier.

Medals and awards

No medals have been awarded.

Notable rescue

On 17 May 1981 the lifeboat *The Gough-Ritchie* was launched to the yacht *Melfort*, aground on rocks at Derby Haven in a gale and rough sea.

On reaching the scene, the lifeboat's Y class inflatable was launched with two crew, while the lifeboat was moored alongside the breakwater. One man was saved by breeches buoy, but the casualty began to break up, preventing further attempts.

The inflatable was taken in to the wreck, but was unable to help as it was pounded by heavy seas, one of which capsized it, throwing the two men into the water; they were saved by the lifeboat's crew. Another of the yacht's occupants was swept down to the breakwater and saved.

The lifeboat was then positioned at the edge of the rocks on which the casualty had foundered, and a line was thrown to the remaining man on board, who was pulled through the water to safety.

Soon the body of another of the yacht's crew was found, and the two survivors were landed at Castletown. The lifeboat then returned to station.

For this rescue the Thanks on Vellum was accorded to Coxswain/Mechanic Norman Quillin and crew members Eric Quillin and William Halsall in recognition of their skill.

The Naming Ceremony of D class inflatable *Frances* (D-462) outside the 1896 lifeboat house on 11 September 1994. *Jim Wallbridge*

Key dates

Opened	1884
RNLI	1884
Motor LB	1925
AWLB withdrawn	22.6.1992
Inshore LB	1992

Current lifeboat details

Inshore lifeboat

Type	Atlantic 21
Official Number	B-594
Name	*Herbert and Edith*
Donor	Anonymous gift
Placed on station	16.3.1993
Launch	Slipway

Location history

1884 A lifeboat house was constructed in the harbour; used until 1925, it remains unaltered in use as a public shelter.

1900 A slipway was constructed on the headland at the back of the harbour to improve launching arrangements; the lifeboat was taken to it on its carriage, but could be launched from other sites if necessary.

1925 A new lifeboat house was built, with a slipway and cradle, at the back of the harbour for the station's first motor lifeboat.

1972 Major alterations to the lifeboat house and slipway were completed to accommodate a Rother class lifeboat.

1992 The offshore lifeboat was withdrawn on 22 June and the station was temporarily closed while modifications to the slipway were made, a new launching trolley was manufactured, and a new lifting beam for the Atlantic 21 inshore lifeboat was installed; the station re-opened on 24 July with an Atlantic 21.

1996 The boathouse was refurbished and a two-storey extension was constructed incorporating crew changing room, toilet, shower, office and souvenir outlet.

Medals and awards

One Bronze Medal has been awarded.

Notable rescue

On 9 September 1970 the lifeboat *Matthew Simpson* was launched to the coaster *Moonlight*, which was reported to be in difficulties 5 miles north of Chicken Rock in a force 8 gale, gusting to force 10. The lifeboat could not find the coaster in the reported location, so began to search the adjacent coastline.

One of the coaster's life-rafts was spotted in the water, but it was found to be empty. The search continued and after more than 2 hours another life-raft was seen with two men inside it. With great skill the lifeboat was manoeuvred alongside and secured, and the two survivors were safely taken on board.

The men said that the other two men from the *Moonlight* had been washed away and drowned, so the lifeboat returned to Port Erin. The rescued men were safely landed, and immediately rushed to hospital in Douglas suffering from severe shock and exposure, from which they both recovered.

For this rescue the Bronze Medal was awarded to Coxswain Alfred Maddrell BEM, with an additional £5 monetary award to the Coxswain and six remaining crew members. The Peel lifeboat also took part in this service, and the Thanks on Vellum was accorded to the Coxswain, William Gorry.

Background information

In 1993 the 37ft 6in Rother class lifeboat *Osman Gabriel*, stationed at Port Erin from 1973 until June 1992, was sold to the Estonian Lifeboat Service (Eesti Vetelpaasteuhingu). Because of the difficulty in obtaining sufficient funding, the British Embassy in Tallin was approached for assistance. The Foreign Office agreed to the ambassador's recommendations that funds should be made available to buy the lifeboat from the RNLI. The necessary finance was forthcoming, so the lifeboat went to Estonia and joined five rescue cruisers that were already part of Estonia's lifeboat fleet. She was renamed *Anita*, and is now stationed at Haapsalu, a small town on the western coast.

The lifeboat house built in 1925 at the back of the harbour, modified in 1992 for the Atlantic 21. *Jim Wallbridge*

Key dates

Opened	1829-c1843 and 1885
RNLI	1885
Motor LB	1937-5.1972
Fast LB	1992
Inshore LB	6.1972-6.1992

Current lifeboat details

All-weather lifeboat

Type	Mersey
Official Number	1181
Operational Number	12-22
Year built	1992
Name	Ruby Clery
Donor	Bequest of Miss Ruby Alexandra Clery, St John's Wood, London
Placed on station	10.6.1992
Launch	Carriage

Location history

1829 A lifeboat station was established by the Isle of Man District Association and operated two lifeboats; the first was wrecked in 1836, and its replacement became unserviceable by c1843.

1886 A lifeboat house was built beneath the outer wall of Peel Castle, with a slipway parallel to the breakwater; this house was used until 1991.

1913 A new slipway was built closer to the lifeboat house to make launching easier.

1961 Major repairs were carried out to the slipway.

1972 The offshore lifeboat was withdrawn on 7 May, and an inshore lifeboat station was opened on 20 June; the ILB was kept in the 1886 boathouse until June 1992.

1976 Further extensive repairs to the slipway were undertaken.

1990-1 A new concrete launching slipway was constructed.

1992 A new lifeboat house was built on the site of the 1886 house, which was demolished; the new house includes accommodation for the Mersey class lifeboat and tractor coupled in-line, as well as a workshop, souvenir outlet, toilet, crew room, galley and drying room.

Medals and awards

No medals have been awarded.

Notable rescue

On 17 October 1994 the lifeboat *Ruby Clery* was launched to the fishing vessel *Three Sisters*, which was sinking 20 miles north-west of Peel. An RAF helicopter was first on the scene, and landed a winchman with a salvage pump, joined soon after by four men from HMS *Blackwater*.

The effect of the pump was limited, so once on the scene Coxswain David Eames decided to transfer crew member Frank Horne, a professional fisherman, on to the casualty. A tow was then established to gently move the casualty head to sea. A few minutes later she suddenly rolled on to her starboard side and started to sink. The tow rope was immediately cut.

Crew member Horne managed to get out of the vessel's fish hold when she started to roll, but three other men were trapped, so Horne helped to pull them to safety; it was only due to his actions that they were freed. All nine men on board the casualty then entered the water and were picked up by inflatables from HMS *Blackwater*. Some were transferred to the lifeboat, which then returned to her station.

For his part in this service the Thanks on Vellum was accorded to lifeboatman Frank Horne, and Vellum service certificates were presented to the rest of the crew.

Background information

The earliest rescue of note performed by the Peel lifeboat took place on 7 October 1889, when the lifeboat *John Monk* was launched to the sailing barque *St George*, of Christiana, which had been disabled in a severe north-westerly gale. Despite the terrible weather the lifeboat managed to get alongside and save the ship's crew of 21, as well as the Master's wife and nine-month-old baby. The Coxswain, Charlie Cain, and crew received a considerable amount of praise for this rescue, and medals were presented to each of the 17 crew by the Norwegian Government. The presentation, which took place within the walls of Peel Castle, was attended by an estimated 10,000 people.

12m Mersey *Ruby Clery* (ON.1181) being launched on exercise in 1996. *Steve Dutton*

Kippford

Key dates

Opened	1966
RNLI	1966
Inshore LB	5.1966

Current lifeboat details

Inshore lifeboat

Type	D class inflatable
Official Number	D-370
Name	41 Club II
Donor	The Association of Ex-Tablers Clubs - 41 Club
Placed on station	11.8.1988
Launch	Trolley

Location history

1966   An inshore lifeboat station was established in May, operational during the summer months only; the ILB is kept in a small house at the top of a narrow lane leading down to the beach.

1977   A replacement boathouse was built by the crew.

Medals and awards

No medals have been awarded.

The ILB house used to house Kippford's D class inflatable.

Kirkcudbright

Key dates

Opened	1862
RNLI	1862
Motor LB	1928
AWLB withdrawn	18.4.1989
Inshore LB	7.1988

Current lifeboat details

Inshore lifeboat

Type	Atlantic 21
Official Number	B-585
Name	Peter and Grace Ewing
Donor	Bequest of Mrs Jan Dewar Paton
Placed on station	13.4.1991
Launch	Slipway

Location history

1862   A lifeboat house was built in the town in St Cuthbert's Street, at Creekhead; used until sold in 1892, it has since been converted into a doctor's clinic.

1892-3   A new lifeboat house and slipway were constructed at Cutlers Pool on the Torrs Shore, about 3 miles out of the town and nearer the mouth of the River Dee.

1965   The lifeboat house was adapted for the 37ft Oakley class lifeboat.

1969   The narrow roadway leading to the boathouse was rebuilt with the help of the Army.

1988   An Atlantic 21 was sent to the station on 24 July for 12 months of evaluation trials, which proved successful.

1989   The lifeboat house and slipway were adapted to accommodate the Atlantic 21 inshore lifeboat, and the offshore lifeboat was withdrawn.

Medals and awards

No medals have been awarded.

Notable rescue

In the late evening of 26 November 1984 the lifeboat *Mary Pullman* was launched to the fishing vessel *Leon Jeannine*, which was aground and breaking up in a southerly gale and rough seas. She had been reported to be aground on Kirkcudbright Bar, but nothing was sighted by the lifeboat as she cleared the river. The casualty was then spotted on the Milton Sands in 6-foot breaking seas.

The lifeboat approached ready to take off the three men on board, but the first approach alongside the stern of the casualty failed as the men froze, and could not leave the vessel. On the second approach, however, they were grabbed by the lifeboat's crew and safely taken on board.

The Thanks on Vellum was accorded to Acting Coxswain/Mechanic Stephen Unsworth, while Vellum service certificates were presented to the rest of the crew.

The lifeboat house and slipway built in 1892-3 at Cutlers Pool, about 3 miles out of Kirkcudbright.

Key dates

Opened	1877
RNLI	1877
Motor LB	1922
Fast LB	1989

Current lifeboat details

All-weather lifeboat

Type	Tyne
Official Number	1151
Operational Number	47-033
Year built	1989
Name	*Mary Irene Millar*
Donor	Legacies of Mrs Mary Irene Millar, Miss Mary Milne Stewart and Mrs Muriel Johns in memory of her husband Captain Bertram Johns, with other gifts
Placed on station	16.3.1989
Launch	Afloat

Location history

1877 A lifeboat house was constructed on the north pier, with doors at the south (seaward) end. The lifeboat was moved out of the house on rollers and lowered into the inner harbour by a crane a short distance from the boathouse; a ladder was located under the crane to enable the crew to board the lifeboat once it was afloat.

1900 Following an accident with the crane on 19 December 1899, in which the lifeboat was seriously damaged, the new lifeboat was kept afloat in the harbour during the winter months, and in the boathouse during the summer, until 1907.

1907 A new crane was provided; the lifeboat was kept permanently in the boathouse, and a door was made at the north end of the house.

1914 A cradle and rails were provided from the 1907 crane to the boathouse to ease the movement of the lifeboat over the pier; this arrangement was used until 1922, and the cranes and trolley rails were removed for scrap in 1940.

1922 The station's first motor lifeboat was placed on moorings in the harbour, and the lifeboat has been kept afloat ever since.

1992/3 An extension to the boathouse was constructed to improve crew facilities; it provides a souvenir outlet, a galley, crew room, toilet, washing and shower facilities, a general-purpose store and a look-out training room.

Medals and awards

Three medals have been awarded, one Silver and two Bronze.

Notable rescue

On 31 January 1953 the passenger steamship *Princess Victoria*, sailing from Stranraer for Larne with 125 passengers and 49 crew, foundered approximately 4½ miles north-east of Mew Island in a full northerly gale increasing to hurricane force, snow squalls and a very rough sea. The vessel started to become unmanageable as more water was shipped, and she radioed for assistance.

The lifeboat *Jeanie Speirs* was launched and fought her way through mountainous seas. Despite being given an inaccurate location for the casualty, she arrived on the scene and began to search the wreckage of the vessel for survivors. Two were picked up from life-rafts, but the lifeboat crew could find no one else.

This was a very tragic event; in total, 133 were lost and only 41 people survived, 31 of whom were saved by the Donaghadee lifeboat, which had also launched to the vessel. It was the worst peacetime disaster involving a British merchant vessel for 25 years.

For this rescue the Bronze Medal was awarded to Coxswain William McConnell and the Thanks on Vellum was accorded to Mechanic James Mitchell. Coxswain McConnell was also awarded the British Empire Medal as well as The Mrs G. M. Porter Award for the bravest deed in 1953.

The lifeboat house on the north pier built in 1877.

The small harbour at Portpatrick, once the Scottish terminal for the Irish ferry, with 47ft Tyne *Mary Irene Millar* (ON.1151) at moorings.

Key dates

Opened	1974
RNLI	1974
Inshore LB	4.6.1974

Current lifeboat details

Inshore lifeboat

Type	D class inflatable
Official Number	D-538
Name	Tom Broom
Donor	Stamford Branch Appeal
Placed on station	19.10.1998
Launch	Trolley

Location history

1974   An inshore lifeboat station was established on 4 June; the ILB was operational only during the summer and housed in a Marley 'M' plan ILB house, on the beach at Agnew Park, west of the ferry terminal.

1994   A new ILB house was built on the same site providing housing for the D class inflatable and launching vehicle, a workshop and petroleum store on the ground floor, and crew facilities on the first floor.

Medals and awards

No medals have been awarded.

Notable rescue

On the morning of 9 September 1984 the D class inshore lifeboat D-287 was on exercise when it became clear to the crew that a specially converted Volkswagen Beetle needed towing to safety after it had entered the water in Loch Ryan. The weather was cold and wet, and there was a fresh north-westerly breeze, force 5.

The occupants of the Beetle were attempting to 'drive' it across the Irish Sea to Larne for a television programme. On entering the water, however, the engine failed and the car began to drift towards a moored yacht.

The ILB, manned by Helmsman Terry Simpson and crew members Eric McCune and Glyn Jones, came alongside; two crew members entered the water and attached a tow rope. The car was then brought safely back to Wig Bay slipway.

Another attempt at the crossing was made in the afternoon of the same day, with the same the result, the ILB having to tow the car back to the shore.

The ILB house built in 1994 at Agnew Park, to the west of the ferry terminal, on the site of an earlier ILB house.

Girvan

Strathclyde

Key dates

Opened	1865
RNLI	1865
Motor LB	1931
Fast LB	1983

Current lifeboat details

All-weather lifeboat

Type	Mersey
Official Number	1196
Operational Number	12-37
Year built	1993
Name	Silvia Burrell
Donor	Legacy of Miss Silvia Burrell, of Edinburgh, a life governor of the RNLI
Placed on station	29.8.1993
Launch	Afloat

Location history

1865   A lifeboat house was built on a site given by the Duchesse de Coigny, facing the beach; it was used until 1910.

1910   The lifeboat house was moved and reconstructed on a new site; used until 1931, it was demolished in the 1960s to make way for the beach Pavilion Development.

The shore facility at Girvan built in 1991-2 overlooking the harbour.

1931 The lifeboat was placed afloat at moorings in the harbour.

1960 Following the completion of the new harbour jetty, alongside moorings were taken up at the head of the jetty on the south side, to improve boarding arrangements; a gear store was built near the foot of the jetty, backing on to Knockcushan Street.

1992 A new shore facility was constructed on the site of the previous building; it includes a store and changing area, a self-contained souvenir outlet, crew training room, galley, toilet and washing facilities.

Medals and awards

No medals have been awarded.

Notable rescue

On 25 December 1902 the lifeboat *James Stevens No.18* was launched to the fishing boat *Optimist*, which was trying to enter the harbour in a strong gale and a very heavy sea. It was very difficult for her to cross the bar, so the lifeboat went to her assistance.

The Master of the boat realised that his vessel was in danger, so ran for Woodland Bay. Here the lifeboat stood by the vessel and four lifeboatmen were put on board to help to anchor her. Once this had been done, the entire crew were taken off by the lifeboat and safely landed.

Top 12m Mersey *Silvia Burrell* (ON.1196) leaving the harbour with the shore facility in the background. *Rick Tomlinson*

Middle Girvan lifeboatmen on board *Silvia Burrell*. *Rick Tomlinson*

Bottom *Silvia Burrell* at sea. *Rick Tomlinson*

Current lifeboat details

All-weather lifeboat

Type	Arun
Official Number	1134
Operational Number	52-38
Year built	1987
Name	*City of Glasgow III*
Donor	The City of Glasgow Appeal with other gifts and legacies
Placed on station	25.10.1987
Launch	Afloat

Location history

1871 A lifeboat house was built on a site in Portland Street given by the Duke of Portland, to whom the harbour belongs. The lifeboat was rolled out to the launch site and lowered by crane into the coaling basin. This house was used until 1904.

1904 Moorings were taken up in the Inner Harbour beyond the Gut Bridge, initially on a trial basis; a gear store was situated beyond the harbour buildings, underneath the old sail-loft.

1905 It was decided that the lifeboat should be kept afloat all the year round. The lifeboat house was sold to Ayr County Council; it was later demolished and a Police Station built on the site.

1929 New shore facilities were built on the Shipbreakers breakwater quay.

1949 The shore facilities were transferred to a site adjacent to the Inner Basin close to the lifeboat moorings.

1981 The lifeboat store was extended to provide a crew room.

1987 A new crew assembly building was constructed on the quayside to provide a workshop and store, a fuel store, and improved crew facilities; the mooring berth was dredged to enable an Arun class lifeboat to be moored.

1996 An extension to the boathouse was built to provide, on the ground floor, an improved workshop and souvenir sales outlet, and on the first floor a crew room and galley.

Medals and awards

Three medals have been awarded, two Silver and one Bronze.

Notable rescue

On 12 September 1980 the lifeboat *Connel Elizabeth Cargill* was launched in a westerly storm and a very rough sea to the Dutch dredger *Holland I*. The dredger had been working off Irvine Harbour fairway beacon and was in danger of breaking her moorings in winds gusting to force 10, and waves of up to 20 feet were sweeping across her main deck.

The lifeboat cleared the harbour entrance and ploughed through the confused seas for 3 miles to reach the casualty. Several times she was hit by huge waves that broke over her, and at one point she rolled so violently to starboard that the side of her wheelhouse was nearly in the water.

Once on the scene the lifeboat found the dredger on the edge of the surf line with just one stern mooring holding her in place. The lifeboat had to be taken alongside five times to rescue her crew of five one by one. Each approach was very hazardous as the lifeboat could have been trapped by the dredger should the stern mooring line have broken.

The return passage was difficult because of the rough sea conditions, and full power was required to drive through the heavy confused seas off the harbour entrance. Once this was safely achieved the survivors were landed at the lifeboat station.

For this rescue the Silver Medal was awarded to Coxswain/Mechanic Ian Johnson in recognition of his courage, leadership and fine seamanship, and Medal service certificates were presented to the rest of the crew.

52ft Arun *City of Glasgow III* on exercise off the harbour in the summer of 1995 with Coxswain Ian Johnson on the flying bridge.

Key dates

Opened	1964
RNLI	1964
Inshore LB	1964

Current lifeboat details

Inshore lifeboat

Type	Atlantic 75
Official Number	B-739
Name	Peggy Keith Learmond
Donor	Gift of Mrs Margaret Keith (Peggy) Learmond, Edinburgh
Placed on station	4.3.1998
Launch	Tractor and do-do carriage

Location history

1964 An inshore lifeboat station was established in May; the ILB was operated from a small house at Barrfields slipway, on Greenock Road, to the north of the town facing Great Cumbrae Island.

1981 A new Marley ILB house was built on the same site for the Atlantic 21 inshore lifeboat.

1997 A new ILB house was built on the same site for the Atlantic 75 and launching tractor, providing greatly improved crew facilities.

Medals and awards

One Silver Medal has been awarded.

Notable rescue

On 24 July 1983 the Atlantic 21 inshore lifeboat B-547 *Independent Forester Liberty* was launched to a motor cruiser that had capsized just over a mile from the lifeboat station.

On arriving at the scene it was ascertained that two men had already been picked up from the water, but a young girl was still trapped in the cabin of the capsized boat. Removing his life-jacket and bump cap, crew member Arthur Hill entered the water and ducked down about 3 feet to get under the cabin top. He found the girl trapped

forward in a small air pocket, and after reassuring her attempted to push her under the water and out from under the boat. On the second attempt he succeeded, and she was quickly taken on board the ILB once away from the upturned boat.

For this rescue the Silver Medal was awarded to crew member Arthur Hill in recognition of his courage, determination and cool assessment of a difficult situation. Helmsman John Strachan was accorded the Thanks on Vellum for his leadership and judgement.

Background information

Largs was one of the first ILB stations in the UK, and the first in Scotland, to operate an Atlantic 21 rigid-inflatable ILB. The prototype, B-500, was sent for trials in 1972; these proved very successful and the station has operated Atlantic class inshore lifeboats ever since.

Above The lifeboat house built in 1997 at Barrfields slipway for the Atlantic 75 and launching tractor.

Below Atlantic 75 *Peggy Keith Learmond* (B-739) on exercise. *RNLI*

Key dates

Opened	1965
RNLI	1965
Inshore LB	6.1965

Current lifeboat details

Inshore lifeboat

Type	Atlantic 21
Official Number	B-581
Name	*Andrew Mason*
Donor Gift of Mrs Janet Wilson Smith
Placed on station	26.2.1990
Launch	Tractor and do-do carriage

Location history

1965 An inshore lifeboat station was established in June; the ILB was kept in a small house at Rhu Marina, on the northern outskirts of Helensburgh and was launched into the mouth of the Gareloch.

1977 A new ILB house and launchway were built at Rhu Marina to accommodate an Atlantic 21; it was used until 1996, then demolished to make way for a new house.

1996-7 A new slipway was built over the existing slipway, to provide improved launching and recovery of the ILB, and a new and larger ILB house was built on the same site as the previous house; the new building included housing for the lifeboat and launching vehicle on the ground floor and improved crew facilities on the first floor.

Atlantic 21 *Andrew Mason* (B-581) launching on exercise at Rhu Marina from the lifeboat house built in 1997.
Tony Denton

Andrew Mason on exercise off Rhu Marina in 1997.
Tony Denton

Medals and awards

No medals have been awarded.

Key dates

Opened	1970
RNLI	1970
Inshore LB	6.1970

Current lifeboat details

Inshore lifeboat

Type	Atlantic 21
Official Number	B-527
Name	*Percy Garon*
Donor	Civil Service and Post Office Lifeboat Fund
Placed on station	11.1.1998
Launch	Tractor and do-do carriage

The lifeboat house built in 1997 close to the Old Pier at Lamlash, with Atlantic 21 *Percy Garon* (B-527) on her launching carriage.

Location history

1970   An inshore lifeboat station was established at Lamlash; the ILB was housed in a small garage adjoining the marine workshops at the back of the quay.

1985   A new ILB house was built near the Old Pier on the seaward side of the main road, and used until 1997.

1997   A new and larger ILB house was built on the same site for an Atlantic 21 and launching vehicle.

Medals and awards

No medals have been awarded.

Background information

The first lifeboat on Arran was stationed at Kildonan in the south-east corner of the island between 1870 and 1901. The lifeboat house built there in 1870 is now used as a store by a local hotel. The Kildonan lifeboats are credited with launching 17 times and saving 27 lives.

Strathclyde

Tighnabruaich

Key dates

Opened	1967
RNLI	1967
Inshore LB	5.1967

Current lifeboat details

Inshore lifeboat

Type	Atlantic 75
Official Number	B-743
Name	*Alec and Maimie Preston*
Donor	Mr and Mrs Alec Preston, Burnley, Lancs
Placed on station	8.4.1998
Launch	Tractor and do-do carriage

Location history

1967   An inshore lifeboat station was established in May; the ILB was kept in a house in the grounds of Tighnabruaich Hotel, facing south towards the Kyles of Bute.

1981   A new ILB house was built on the same site; it was used until 1998.

1998   A new ILB house was built for the Atlantic 75 and its launching tractor on the seaward side of the road through the village; ground floor facilities included housing for the inshore lifeboat and launching vehicle, a workshop, and oil and petrol stores.

Medals and awards

No medals have been awarded.

Above The Naming Ceremony of Atlantic 75 *Alec and Maimie Preston* (B-743) outside the 1998 ILB house on 8 August of that year. *Jim Wallbridge*

Below Alec and Maimie Preston is launched at the end of the ceremony. *Jim Wallbridge*

Key dates

Opened	1967
RNLI	1967
Motor LB	1967
Fast LB	1989

Current lifeboat details

All-weather lifeboat

Type	Arun
Official Number	1144
Operational Number	52-42
Year built	1988
Name	Murray Lornie
Donor	Trustees of the Ben Vorlich Trust, Jersey, bequest of Miss E. A. Grierson and other gifts
Placed on station	20.7.1989
Launch	Afloat

Location history

1967 During the winter of 1966/67 the cruising lifeboat *Grace Paterson Ritchie* was based at Ullapool conducting trials to ascertain the possibility of opening a new station in the area. As a result, and following a review of future requirements, it was decided that a lifeboat should be stationed at Lochinver, kept afloat at moorings in the harbour.

1969 A mechanic's workshop and store were built in the harbour.

1991 The Highland Regional Council undertook a large redevelopment of the harbour, including the construction of a finger jetty and fish-market building, as well as a new berth for the station's lifeboat.

1994 A new single-storey shore facility was constructed adjacent to the lifeboat berth, including a crew room, changing room, workshop, store, and toilet and shower facilities (see below).

Medals and awards

No medals have been awarded.

Background information

The crew facilities constructed adjacent to the lifeboat berth in 1994 were funded from a legacy left to the RNLI by Mrs Eugenie Boucher in 1992. The building at Lochinver is was one of eight boathouses funded by this legacy, all of which are known as 'Penza' lifeboat houses, named after the town in south-east Russia, approximately 350 miles from Moscow, which was the home of Mrs Boucher until the 1920s, when she moved to England, married Roy Boucher, a solicitor and businessman, and lived in Bristol in a house called 'Penza'. The seven other 'Penza' boathouses are at St Ives, Aldeburgh, Plymouth, Criccieth, Kilmore Quay, Newcastle and Clogher Head.

Above 52ft Arun *Murray Lornie* (ON.1144) moored in the berth constructed in 1991.

Below The shore facility constructed in 1994 adjacent to the lifeboat berth in the harbour.

Key dates

Opened	1860
RNLI	1860
Motor LB	1929
Fast LB	1988

Current lifeboat details

All-weather lifeboat

Type	Arun
Official Number	1149
Operational Number	52-43
Year built	1989
Name	The Queen Mother
Donor	Legacy of Miss Sarah Sinclair Gray, Dunoon, and RNLI funds
Placed on station	24.3.1989
Launch	Afloat

Location history

The Thurso lifeboat station has always been located at Scrabster, which is situated on the western side of Thurso Bay north of Thurso town.

1860 A lifeboat house with a launchway was built in Scrabster Harbour; this house was used until 1906, when it was sold.

1876 The launchway into the harbour was altered and extended.

1906 A new lifeboat house and roller slipway were built at the end of the Harbour Quay just outside Scrabster Harbour; this house was completed in 1909, and a new winch was installed in 1910. It was used until 1956 when, on 10 December, it was completely destroyed by fire together with the lifeboat, *Dunnet Head (Civil Service No.31)*, which was inside.

1957 A new lifeboat house and slipway were built on the same site; this house was used until 1988, and is now used as crew facilities.

1970 The lifeboat house was adapted for the Solent class lifeboat.

1981 Extensive repairs were necessary to the slipway due to movement of the concrete toe and general deterioration of the structure.

1984 Major slipway repairs were undertaken to remedy serious defects caused by wave action.

1988 The lifeboat was placed on permanent moorings in Scrabster Harbour following the building of a new berthing pier for the Orkney ferry, which provided a sheltered mooring outside the Terminal Building.

1989 The lifeboat house was adapted to house an emergency relief Tyne class lifeboat; a crew room and foul weather clothing drying cupboard were also built into it.

Medals and awards

Four medals have been awarded, two Silver and two Bronze.

Five Silver Medals have been awarded for shore-boat rescues.

Notable rescue

On 18 March 1931 the lifeboat *H. C. J.* was launched to the schooner *Pet*, of Chester, which had gone ashore at Brims Ness. The call for help was received late in the evening, so the lifeboat was working in total darkness and a heavy swell, but was able to approach the casualty after a flare was sighted by the lifeboatmen.

The lifeboat anchored to windward and veered down towards the stranded vessel. Submerged rocks prevented her from going alongside, but a line was fired to the casualty and one man was taken off by breeches buoy.

The other three men on board were all elderly, and because of the risk of pulling them through the water in the breeches buoy, it was decided that the lifeboat would have to go to the casualty. So despite the considerable risk of being holed by rocks, the Coxswain took the lifeboat towards the schooner.

In shallow water that often left only a foot between the lifeboat's keel and the rocks, she eventually came alongside the casualty, which was grinding heavily on the rocks. The three remaining men were then safely taken off, and the lifeboat was taken into deeper water, having not once touched any of the many rocks among which it had been operating. The four survivors were landed at Wick, and by the next day the *Pet* had begun to break up.

For this rescue the Bronze Medal was awarded to Coxswain Angus McPhail, and the Thanks on Vellum was accorded to Second Coxswain Adam McLeod.

The lifeboat house and roller slipway built at Scrabster Harbour in 1957 to replace the boathouse on the same site destroyed by fire in 1956.

Key dates

Opened	1860
RNLI	1860
Motor LB	1922
Fast LB	1984

Current lifeboat details

All-weather lifeboat

Type	Arun
Official Number	1093
Operational Number	52-27
Year built	1983
Name	Charles Brown
Donor	Gift of Mr David Robinson
Placed on station	5.4.1984
Launch	Afloat

Location history

1860 The station was located along what is now the harbourside wall, where a lifeboat house was built; this was used until 1883, then demolished to make way for a railway line extension.

1884 A new lifeboat house was built; this was used until 1922, and is now occupied by a local garage.

1921 A new lifeboat house was built inside the West Pier of the Harbour for the station's first motor lifeboat. As there was not room for a conventional slipway into the harbour, the new house had an internal lifeboat platform, or cradle, which was lowered into the water by hoists; the boat floated or slid off into the water depending on the state of the tide. This system was used between 1921 and 1961; the house has since been demolished.

1961 Moorings were taken up in the Inner Harbour, with a small workshop located on the quayside above the mooring berth.

1995 A pontoon berth was installed to improve boarding arrangements; a new shore facility was built on the adjacent quayside to replace the previous building, including a changing room, workshop, toilets, shower, fuel store, crew room and office.

Medals and awards

One Bronze Medal has been awarded.

Two Silver medals were awarded in 1890 for a shore rescue.

Notable rescue

In the early hours of 21 February 1968 the relief lifeboat *George and Sarah Strachan* was launched to go to the aid of the fishing boat *Mistletoe*, which was aground at the mouth of the River Spey. She was pounding and rolling heavily about 350 yards from the beach in a heavy confused swell. It was intensely cold and the lifeboat became coated with ice.

Attempts were made by the crew to get a line on board and to tow the casualty to safety, assisted by other fishing-boats that were already standing. Various attempts failed, and the *Mistletoe* now had waves breaking right across her deck. Coxswain George Jappy then succeeded in bringing the lifeboat alongside and manoeuvring it into a position to enable the fishing-boat's crew of six to jump to safety. Once they were all on board, the lifeboat returned to Buckie where the survivors were safely landed.

For this rescue Coxswain Jappy was awarded the Bronze Medal, and medal service certificates were presented to the remainder of the crew.

52ft Arun *Charles Brown* (ON.1093) at moorings in Buckie Harbour alongside the pontoon installed in 1995, reached from the crew facility by gangway; Buckie Shipyard is in the background.

Charles Brown on exercise off Buckie Harbour in 1996.

Opened	1974
RNLI	1974
Motor LB	1974
AWLB withdrawn	8.9.1984
Inshore LB	19.9.1985

Current lifeboat details

Inshore lifeboat

Type	Atlantic 21
Official Number	B-578
Name	The Rotary Club of Glasgow
Donor	Rotary Club of Glasgow
Placed on station	14.8.1989
Launch	Mobile crane

Location history

1974 An all-weather lifeboat station was established in March; the lifeboat was kept afloat at moorings in the Harbour, and was withdrawn in September 1984.

1985 An inshore lifeboat station was established in September; a building provided by the Council on the road to the Eastern Pier was converted to house the Atlantic 21 and launching vehicle.

The system of launching employed at Macduff is unique; because there was no available site adjacent to a quay on which the ILB house could be built, it had be launched by mobile crane. The crane was used to tow the ILB to a suitable quay from which she could be launched. It was then used to lift her off the trolley, and lower her into the water.

Medals and awards

No medals have been awarded.

Background information

The station at Macduff took over from stations located in the neighbouring villages of Banff and Whitehills. The former was established in 1860 and was operational until 1924, when the lifeboat was transferred to Whitehills.

A lifeboat house and slipway was completed there in 1933, but the lifeboat was withdrawn in 1969 and the station closed.

The offshore lifeboat at Macduff also provided cover following the temporary closure of the Fraserburgh station between 1970 and 1979. Inside the ILB house at Macduff is the first service board from the Banff lifeboat station, which was originally known as Banff & Macduff.

Above Atlantic 21 *The Rotary Club of Glasgow* (B-578) on the road-going trolley used to take her to a suitable location at which she can be launched, towed by the mobile crane.

Right The Rotary *Club of Glasgow* on exercise off the harbour in 1998.

Key dates

Opened	1806-c1850 and 1858
RNLI	1858
Motor LB	1915
Fast LB	1985

Current lifeboat details

All-weather lifeboat

Type	Tyne
Official Number	1109
Operational Number	47-007
Year built	1985
Name	City of Edinburgh
Donor	City of Edinburgh Lifeboat Appeal
Placed on station	3.11.1985
Launch	Afloat

Location history

1806 The first lifeboat, organised by the Harbour Commissioners, was supported by a sixpence per man toll on all vessels entering the harbour. A second boat replaced the original in 1831, but this was broken up during the early 1850s and the station lapsed until the RNLI took over.

1858 The RNLI re-opened the station, its first in Scotland, and a lifeboat house was built in the Harbour by the Harbour Commissioners. Re-roofed in 1875, it was used until 1883, when it was used by a firm of marine engineers, and was demolished during the mid-1990s.

1883 A new lifeboat house was built on a site adjacent to the 1858 house; it was used until 1917, then became a store and was demolished during the mid-1990s.

1894 In October the boathouse was lengthened by the Harbour Commissioners at a cost of £40.

1913-6 A new lifeboat house and slipway were constructed for the station's first motor lifeboat, situated in front of the previous house; this house was altered for new lifeboats in 1954, 1961 and 1969-70, and was used for the lifeboat until 1997.

1970 The station was temporarily closed following the lifeboat disaster in January; it was re-opened in June 1978.

1981-2 The boathouse was extended to provide toilet facilities and crew room.

1985 A major adaptation was made to the station to accommodate a Tyne class lifeboat, in conjunction with routine upkeep and maintenance work.

1997 A new berth was completed in October, and the lifeboat was placed at permanent moorings in the Harbour, adjacent to the boathouse on the north side of North Pier.

Medals and awards

Twelve medals have been awarded, one Gold, four Silver and seven Bronze.

Three medals have been awarded for shore-boat rescues, one Gold and two Silver.

Background information

Fraserburgh lifeboatmen have lost their lives on service on three occasions. On 28 April 1919 the lifeboat *Lady Rothes* was launched in a heavy northerly gale and tremendous sea to HM Drifter *Eminent*, but she was caught broadside by a huge wave and overturned. Most of the crew were thrown overboard, but clung to the upturned hull as it was swept ashore. Of those on board, Coxswain Andrew Noble and Acting Second Coxswain Andrew Farquhar were drowned.

On 9 February 1953 the lifeboat *John and Charles Kennedy* was launched to escort fishing boats into the harbour. While off the North Pier a heavy swell broke aboard her and she was capsized; one man was flung out and swept ashore alive, but the other six perished: Coxswain Andrew Ritchie, Mechanic George Duthie, Bowman Charles Tait, Assistant Mechanic James Noble and crew members John Crawford and John Buchan.

The station suffered a third disaster on 21 January 1970, when the lifeboat *The Duchess of Kent* was capsized with the loss of five of her crew of six while on service to the Danish fishing vessel *Opal*: those who died were Coxswain John Stephen, Mechanic Frederick Kirkness and crew members William Hadden, James R. S. Buchan and James Buchan. Assistant Mechanic John (Jackson) Buchan was flung clear and saved by a Russian trawler. When the funerals took place on 25 January over 10,000 people attended, including HRH The Duke of Kent, President of the RNLI. Following this capsize, the station became temporarily non-operational.

47ft Tyne *City of Edinburgh* (ON.1109) moored in the harbour on the north side of the North Pier, with the lifeboat house and slipway in the background.

Key dates

Opened	1865
RNLI	1865
Motor LB	1912
Fast LB	1988

Current lifeboat details

All-weather lifeboat

Type	Tyne
Official Number	1127
Operational Number	47-019
Year built	1987
Name	Babs and Agnes Robertson
Donor	Gift of The Robertson Trust, founded by the Misses Robertson of whisky blenders Robertson & Baxter Ltd, Glasgow
Placed on station	14.1.1988
Launch	Afloat

Location history

1865 The first lifeboat house was built in Greenhill Road on the east side of the North Harbour. Rebuilt and enlarged in 1900-1, it was used until 1908, and has since been demolished.

1908 The slipway into the South Harbour used for launching was removed, so the lifeboat was kept afloat on moorings in the harbour.

1911 A new lifeboat house and roller slipway were built on a site to the west of the South Harbour, and from 1912 housed a second lifeboat, which became the No.2; five tenement houses were bought and demolished to make room for the new house. The moored lifeboat became the No.1 lifeboat in 1912, but was withdrawn in 1928 and the No.1 station was closed. The lifeboat house was altered in 1938, 1964, 1969 and 1978 for new lifeboats, and was used until 1998.

1980-1 The boathouse was extended to provide toilet facilities.

1998 The lifeboat was placed in a berth to the west of the North Harbour in July; temporary shore facilities were installed on the quayside in the Harbour, after agreement with the Harbour Commissioners.

Medals and awards

Thirteen medals have been awarded, one Gold, two Silver and ten Bronze.

Eight Silver Medals have been awarded for shore-boat rescues.

Notable rescue

The most outstanding life-saving act in the station's history took place between 23 and 26 January 1942, when the lifeboat *Julia Park Barry of Glasgow* went out four times to three ships aground in Peterhead Bay. Throughout the services, gales were blowing with gusts of over 100mph, and there were blinding snow storms and horrendous seas.

On 23 January the lifeboat launched to the steamship *Runswick*, which had been damaged in a collision. Two other steamships, the *Saltwick* and *Fidra*, had also been damaged, and all three were escorted to anchor in Peterhead Bay.

The following day the *Runswick* was driven on to rocks by the gale, so the lifeboat launched to her aid. Despite the weather, the lifeboat managed to save the crew of 44.

On 25 January the other two steamers went ashore. The lifeboat stood by at her station as neither crew was in immediate danger, and Coastguards were attempting a rescue; however, their attempts had to be abandoned when they became exhausted.

The lifeboat was then launched and found the *Fidra* almost submerged on the rocks. The lifeboatmen succeeded in getting a line aboard, and despite the heavy swell one, two or three men jumped aboard with each approach. She was alongside for 50 minutes, during which time the 26 crew were rescued.

By daybreak the *Saltwick* was on the beach, with seas breaking over her, so the lifeboat was again launched. During her approach she struck a reef of rocks and was damaged, and one heavy sea nearly washed several crew members overboard. However, she managed to go alongside and take off 36 of the *Saltwick*'s crew, then got clear, again striking the rocks as she left.

For these outstanding rescues, the Gold Medal was awarded to Coxswain John Buchan McLean, the Silver Medal to Mechanic David Wiseman, and Bronze Medals to Alexander Hepburn, William Strachan, Alexander Strachan, William Summers, Alexander Gowans and George Cordiner. It was a series of arduous and exhausting services in which great risks were run and high courage, splendid seamanship, great determination and endurance shown. In 75 hours the crew had less than 12 hours rest, and stood by the casualties for 54 hours, during which time 106 lives were saved.

47ft Tyne **Babs and Agnes Robertson** *(ON.1127) moored in the North Harbour in 1998.*

Key dates

Opened	1802-20 and 1841
RNLI	1925
Motor LB	1926
Fast LB	1976
Inshore LB	1968

Current lifeboat details

All-weather lifeboat

Type	Arun
Official Number	1135
Operational Number	52-39
Year built	1988
Name	Mickie Salvesen
Donor	Bequest of Mrs Mary 'Mickie' Salvesen
Placed on station	28.8.98
Launch	Afloat

Inshore lifeboat

Type	D class inflatable
Official Number	D-536
Name	Margaret II
Donor	Bequest of Mrs M. Minett, Caterham, Surrey
Placed on station	22.7.1998
Launch	Davit

Location history

1802 The first lifeboat, funded by Alexander Baxter (Consul General for Russia), was stationed at the North Pier, where a boathouse was built in 1810 located to the north of the Round House.

1811 A slipway was built on the North Pier between the Inner (Shelter) Jetty and Abercrombie Jetty, to improve launching; a new slipway was built in 1872 at the same location.

1820 On 2 March the lifeboat was badly damaged on service, so was broken up; the boathouse was let to a local steamship company until 1841.

1841 The station was re-established and a new lifeboat was supplied. The boathouse was renovated and a carriage supplied to ease launching; this house was used until 1853 and was then converted into a storehouse.

1853 A new lifeboat house was built on the road to the North Pier, on the harbour side of Pilot's Square.

1874 The lifeboat house was moved to a new site at the north-east corner of North Footdee Square, at the edge of the beach; this was known as the beach lifeboat.

1875 A second lifeboat was bought for the station, and a new lifeboat house was built over the water at Pocra Quay. The lifeboat floated in the water of the harbour inside her own house, but as she banged about inside, a new house was built on Pocra Jetty near the Aberdeen, Leith & Clyde Shipping Company's wharf in 1877; this was known as the harbour lifeboat.

1890 The 1877 lifeboat house was moved to Shelter Jetty in the lower harbour basin; the lifeboat was launched from a carriage into the channel from the slipway below the Lower Jetty.

1891 A hoisting apparatus with a hand-operated windlass was built in the 1890 house, which was used to lift the boat out of the water when she was not being used; this house and the hoisting gear were dismantled when the RNLI took over the station.

1925 The RNLI took control of the station, and the first motor lifeboat was placed afloat at Pocra Jetty. Moorings were later moved to St Clement's Bridge Jetty, and the No.2 lifeboat was kept on a carriage in the house at Footdee.

1962 The No.2 station was closed on 30 June; the house at Footdee has since been demolished.

1968 An inshore lifeboat station was established in August.

1973 The lifeboat was moved to the north side of Victoria Dock and moored on the inner side of the approach jetty to St Clement's Bridge. A wooden hut was built for the gear, while a purpose-built facility and pontoon berth were built later, and used until 1997.

1994 A Schat davit was installed on the quay for launching and recovering the inshore lifeboat.

1997 A new combined shore facility and ILB house was constructed at Dock Island, providing housing for the ILB and improved crew facilities.

Medals and awards

Ten medals have been awarded, four Silver and six Bronze.

Five medals have been awarded for shore-boat services, one Gold and four Silver.

Notable rescue

Between 21 January and 1 February 1937 the worst gales in living memory blew at Aberdeen; they were so bad that one of the harbour breakwaters was washed away. The station's motor lifeboat, *Emma Constance*, was called out three times, and the No.2 pulling lifeboat *Robert and Ellen Robson* was launched once. During this period the most notable service took place on 26 January, when the *Emma Constance* was launched to the coastal steamer *Fairey*, which was in difficulties and drifting towards the heavy surf 2 miles south of Belhelvie. A gale was blowing from the south-east with a very heavy sea, the night was very dark and it was intensely cold and snowing hard.

The lifeboat stood by the steamer while another trawler attempted to tow her, but this failed, and it was obvious that the casualty would not make it to Aberdeen. As the steamer drifted close to the surf, the crew indicated that they wished to be taken off. The lifeboat had been repeatedly swept by heavy seas, but went alongside the steamer and rescued some of the crew on this first pass.

On the second approach the rest of the casualty's crew jumped, but one man fell between the steamer and lifeboat. He was promptly grabbed by John Masson and, at the risk of being dragged overboard himself, hauled aboard the lifeboat. The actual task of saving the seven crew from the *Fairey* had only taken a few minutes, and soon afterwards she drifted right into the heavy surf where her crew would have been drowned.

With the bar at Aberdeen harbour too dangerous to cross, the lifeboat was forced to go to Macduff, which was the only port available. She arrived there at 4.30 the following morning, having been at sea for some 12 hours.

For this rescue the Silver Medal was awarded to Coxswain Thomas Sinclair, and Bronze Medals to Mechanic Alexander Weir and crew member John Masson; the Thanks on Vellum was accorded to Second Coxswain George A. Flett, Second Assistant Mechanic James Cowper, Assistant Mechanic Robert J. B. Esson, John M. Noble and Alexander S. Masson in recognition of their meritorious conduct during this service.

Background information

The Aberdeen lifeboat station was established by the Aberdeen Shipmasters' Society in 1802, but in 1810 control was passed to the Aberdeen Harbour Commissioners who became responsible for life-saving. In 1875 a second station was established, and up to 1925 the Aberdeen lifeboats are credited with saving 589 lives. At the beginning of 1925, at the request of the Harbour Commissioners, the RNLI assumed control of the lifeboats and of the rocket life-saving apparatus at Torry and the North Pier, the Commissioners agreeing to contribute £500 a year towards their

upkeep. It was the last important station to be taken under the management of the national body after a host of stations had joined it during the latter half of the 19th century. The life-saving apparatus at North Pier and Torry was operated by the RNLI until 1962 when, together with the second lifeboat, it was removed.

Top The combined shore facility and ILB house constructed at Dock Island in 1997.
Gary Markham

Below 52ft Arun *Mickie Salvesen* (ON.1135) moored alongside at Victoria Dock.
Gary Markham

Right Launching Relief D class inflatable D-334 on an exercise from Dock Island in 1995.

Key dates

Opened	1965
RNLI	1965
Inshore LB	6.1965

Current lifeboat details

Inshore lifeboat

Type	Atlantic 75
Official Number	B-720
Name	Frederick Robertson
Donor	Anonymous gift
Placed on station	12.12.1995
Launch	Tractor and do-do carriage

Location history

1965 An inshore lifeboat station was established in June; the ILB was kept in a small Hardun house situated at the back of the Sailing Club in the middle of the bay, and the ILB was launched over the beach.

1982 A new Marley pre-cast ILB house was built in the Harbour; it was extended in 1987 and moved to a new site in the Harbour in 1991 to allow work by the local Drainage Authority. It was used until 1995.

The two-storey ILB house and launching ramp built in 1995 on the beach, with Atlantic 75 *Frederick Robertson* (B-720) and launching tractor outside.

1995 A new two-storey ILB house and launching ramp were built on the beach to accommodate an Atlantic 75 and its launching tractor.

Medals and awards

No medals have been awarded.

Queensferry

Lothian

Key dates

Opened	1967
RNLI	1967
Inshore LB	7.1967

Current lifeboat details

Inshore lifeboat

Type	Atlantic 75
Official Number	B-735
Name	Donald and Ethel Macrae
Donor	Bequest of Mrs Jean Alison Sim
Placed on station	8.5.1997
Launch	Trolley

Location history

1967 An inshore lifeboat station was established in July; the ILB was housed in the converted old Toll House situated at Hawes Pier, South Queensferry, beneath the Forth railway bridge, the southern terminal of the old ferry crossing.

1989 A new ILB house was built on the same site, including a crew/ instruction room, changing room, store and toilet facilities; it was extended in 1998 for an Atlantic 75. The boat is launched down the old ferry slipway into the Firth of Forth

Medals and awards

No medals have been awarded.

Background information

When the station was established in 1967 it was known as South Queensferry, but from 1 January 1969 the name was changed to Queensferry. It was one of the first stations to operate the rigid-inflatable Atlantic 21 inshore lifeboat.

The ILB house built at Hawes Pier in 1989, beneath the Forth railway bridge, with Atlantic 75 *Donald and Ethel Macrae* (B-735) outside.

Key dates

Opened	1860-1925; ro1967
RNLI	1860
AWLB withdrawn	10.1925
Inshore LB	4.1967

Current lifeboat details

Inshore lifeboat

Type	D class inflatable
Official Number	D-452
Name	*Blue Peter III*
Donor	Blue Peter TV Appeal, 1993-4
Placed on station	8.3.1994
Launch	Trolley

Location history

1860 A lifeboat house was built to the east of the town; in 1871 a slipway was constructed from the house to the beach to improve launching.

1904 A new lifeboat house was built on the same site, on the corner of Victoria Road overlooking the beach on the road to the harbour. This house was used until 1925 when the station was closed; it became the Victoria Café for a number of years.

1967 An inshore lifeboat station was established in April; the ILB was funded by a BBC Blue Peter Appeal, and was kept in a small garage at the basement of Harbour Terrace, close to the Harbour.

1991 The 1904 boathouse was purchased by the RNLI and refurbished to accommodate the ILB.

1997 The boathouse was extended to house an Atlantic 75 and tractor in-line; separate crew facilities were built on an adjacent site overlooking the launching slipway and beach.

Medals and awards

Two medals have been awarded, both Bronze.

Notable rescue

On 26 July 1973 the D class inshore lifeboat D-216 *Blue Peter III* was launched to bathers who were reported to be in difficulties in East Bay, to the east of the Harbour and about 500 yards from the lifeboat station.

Although the wind was only force 2, there was a swell of some 15 feet by the rocks, making an approach by the ILB extremely hazardous. A man was struggling in the heavy swell close to the rocks, and was hauled aboard the ILB with some difficulty. As he was taken on board, the ILB was hit by two very heavy seas that injured the survivor and one of the lifeboatmen, and slightly damaged the boat.

The ILB and its crew recovered, then spotted another person floundering in the water, but by the time the ILB had reached his position he had disappeared. No trace of him could be found, despite an extensive search carried out after the survivor had been landed and an extra crew member taken on board.

For this rescue Bronze Medals were awarded to Helmsman Benjamin Pearson and crew member Alexander Russell in recognition of their courage and determination, and the Thanks on Vellum was accorded to crew member James Pearson. The three crew also received Blue Peter's gold badge, its highest award for outstanding achievement, on 20 December 1973.

Above The lifeboat house built in 1904 and the launchway on to the beach, with the 1997 crew facility on the right.

Right Relief D class inflatable D-418 being launched on exercise across the beach in 1997.

Key dates

Opened	1808-post 1821 and 1865
RNLI	1865
Motor LB	1934
Fast LB	1993
Inshore LB	7.1968

Current lifeboat details

All-weather lifeboat

Type	Trent
Official Number	1207
Operational Number	14-09
Year built	1995
Name	Sir Ronald Pechell Bt
Donor	Bequest of Dora, Lady Pechell, with local appeal and other gifts and legacies
Placed on station	17.12.1995
Launch	Afloat

Inshore lifeboat

Type	D class inflatable
Official Number	D-397
Name	Banks' Staff III
Donor	Appeal to Banks' staff
Placed on station	5.12.1989
Launch	Trolley

Location history

1808 The first lifeboat was sent to the station; there are few details of its operation, and it was sold c1821, after which the station closed; in 1827 the old boathouse was being used as committee room.

1864-5 A new lifeboat house was built on the harbour quay; it was used until 1901 then demolished.

1901 A new lifeboat house was constructed on the same site; this house was used until 1931, then became a gear store and crew room.

1931 The lifeboat was placed afloat at moorings on the south side of Victoria Harbour, close to the lifeboat house.

1968 An inshore lifeboat station was established in July; the ILB is kept in the 1901 lifeboat house.

1993 Following problems with silting of the harbour entrance, a low-water mooring berth for the lifeboat was provided at Torness Harbour, approximately 4 miles south of Dunbar and across the bay from Skateraw; the lifeboat is kept here when crossing the harbour entrance at Dunbar would not be possible.

1996 The lifeboat house was refurbished to improve the crew facilities, which include a changing/drying room, crew room, store, souvenir sales outlet, shower and toilet; an extension to the rear port side of the boathouse was also constructed to house the inshore lifeboat and its launching vehicle.

Medals and awards

Two medals have been awarded, one Silver and one Bronze.

Three Silver medals have been awarded for shore rescues.

Notable rescue

On 13 October 1905 the lifeboat *William Arthur Millward* was launched to go to the aid of the steamship *King Ja Ja*, of Swansea, which was in danger close to the rocks a few miles west of Cockburnspath. The lifeboat was dragged to the harbour mouth where, with wind and sea against her and a very strong swell, she was launched.

The steamer's machinery had broken down, so the lifeboat stood by for 4 hours while it was repaired, then returned to Dunbar. However, within an hour she had to go out again to the vessel, which was in trouble in a worsening northerly gale and much larger waves that were causing her anchor to drag.

The second launch was more difficult than the first, and the casualty had drifted to a position some 10 miles from Dunbar. During the passage the lifeboat shipped heavy seas that drenched all those on board. Once alongside, it took an hour to save the six men by lines fired over the vessel. The return journey took a further 3 hours, and the steamer was subsequently wrecked near Thorntonloch.

For this rescue the Silver Medal was awarded to Coxswain Walter Fairbairn.

Background information

In 1906 it was decided that a lifeboat should be placed at Skateraw, to the south of Dunbar; the station was established in 1907, a lifeboat house was built and the lifeboat manned from Dunbar. In 1944 the lifeboat was withdrawn and the station closed; the lifeboat house was demolished in the 1960s.

14m Trent *Sir Ronald Pechell Bt* (ON.1207) moored at Dunbar Harbour prior to her Naming Ceremony on 7 September 1996.

Key dates

Opened	1911
RNLI	1911
Motor LB	1936
AWLB withdrawn	12.7.1974
Inshore LB	4.6.1974

Current lifeboat details

Inshore lifeboat

Type	Atlantic 21
Official Number	B-572
Name	Dorothy and Katherine Barr
Donor	The Robert Barr Charitable Trust
Placed on station	12.2.1988
Launch	Slipway

Location history

1909-11 A slipway was built in the harbour, with the lifeboat sitting out in the open at the top.

1914-5 A lifeboat house was built at the top of the slipway; this house is still in use today.

1964 The lifeboat house was adapted to house the 37ft Oakley class lifeboat.

1980-1 The lifeboat house was re-sheeted and converted to house the inshore lifeboat.

1982 An electric winch was installed for recovery of the Zodiac Mk IV inshore lifeboat.

1985 The station was adapted to operate an Atlantic 21, which was launched from a cradle lowered down the slipway.

1987 Modifications were carried out to the launching trolley and slipway to improve the launching capability at low water.

1998 Improved crew facilities were provided in the lifeboat house.

Medals and awards

Four Silver Medals have been awarded, all for shore-boat rescues in the 1830s.

Notable rescue

On 9 September 1976 the D class inshore lifeboat D-235 was launched to the yacht *Glorfindel II*, which was in danger of being swamped in St Abbs outer harbour in a northerly storm force 10 wind, heavy swell and rough seas. Although moored in the outer harbour, the yacht could not be moved from her position because of the severity of the weather.

The ILB was launched after the owner of the yacht had asked to be taken off with the anchor cable in danger of parting. Considerable skill was needed to get the ILB clear of the slipway, but once away it was immediately alongside the yacht. The three occupants were taken off with some difficulty, as the ILB's propellers were in danger of being fouled by nets and lobster creels washed off the pier, and safely landed in the inner harbour.

For this service a framed letter of thanks, signed by the Chairman, Major General Ralph H. Farrant CB, was presented to Helmsman Alistair Crow and crew member James Wilson for the skill, determination and fine seamanship they displayed.

Above Launching Relief Atlantic 21 *Clothworker* (B-586) on exercise down the slipway.

Right Atlantic 21 *Dorothy and Katherine Barr* (B-572) off St Abbs.
Rick Tomlinson

Key dates

Opened	1994
RNLI	1994
Motor LB	1996
Fast LB	1996
Inshore LB	9.1994

Current lifeboat details

All-weather lifeboat

Type	Arun
Official Number	1067
Operational Number	52-15
Year built	1980
Name	*Hyman Winstone*
Donor	Gift of Mrs Marie Winstone
Placed on station	11.11.1998
Launch	Afloat

Inshore lifeboat

Type	D class inflatable
Official Number	D-499
Name	*Jean and Paul*
Donor	Gift of Mrs Jean Cudbym, Belfast
Placed on station	8.6.1996
Launch	Trolley

Location history

1994 On 26 September an inshore lifeboat was placed on station; it was kept in premises belonging to HM Coastguard in Olderfleet Road.

1996 On 19 January an all-weather lifeboat arrived; it was placed on station on 19 March and was kept afloat at moorings in Larne Lough.

1997 Premises adjacent to HM Coastguard buildings were extensively refurbished to provide permanent shore facilities, including accommodation for the ILB, the boarding-boat, Land Rover, as well as crew changing facilities.

Medals and awards

No medals have been awarded.

Background information

Larne is a relatively young lifeboat station, although several attempts had been made to establish a station before 1994. In January 1956, when the question of forming a station was raised but not pursued, it came to light that various investigations had been made over the years but nothing had been done. In March 1994, following a further investigation, the RNLI's Committee of Management resolved that a lifeboat station be established in Larne Harbour.

The Larne crew on board 52ft Arun *Hyman Winstone* during crew training at the RNLI Depot at Poole in 1998. Front, l-r: Will McCauley, Rob Rice, Paul Johnstone, Karen Black. Back, l-r: Frank Healy (Coxwain), Jeff Bell and Norman Surplus. *RNLI, Derek King*

Key dates

Opened	1965
RNLI	1965
Inshore LB	5.1965

Current lifeboat details

Inshore lifeboat

Type	Atlantic 21
Official Number	B-584
Name	*Youth of Ulster*
Donor	Generosity of the people of the Province of Ulster
Placed on station	21.11.1990
Launch	Trolley

Location history

1965 An inshore lifeboat station was established in May.

1984 A new lifeboat house was constructed by North Down Borough Council at the harbour for the ILB, which is launched down a short concrete slipway into the sheltered harbour waters.

Medals and awards

No medals have been awarded.

Atlantic 21 *Youth of Ulster* (B-584). *Rick Tomlinson*

Key dates

Opened	1910
RNLI	1910
Motor LB	1910
Fast LB	1979

Current lifeboat details

All-weather lifeboat

Type	Arun
Official Number	1107
Operational Number	52-33
Year built	1985
Name	City of Belfast
Donor	The City of Belfast Appeal
Placed on station	7.12.1985
Launch	Afloat

Location history

1910 The lifeboat has always been kept at moorings in the harbour, off the South Pier; a small crew room is located on the quayside.

Medals and awards

Two medals have been awarded, both Bronze.

Notable rescue

For two outstanding wartime rescues carried out in 1940 in the lifeboat *Civil Service No.5*, Coxswain Samuel Nelson was awarded the Bronze Medal. The first of the two rescues took place early on the morning of 21 November when the lifeboat was launched to the steamship *Coastville*, which had gone on to the rocks in Belfast Lough in a heavy gale, with seas breaking over her.

It was impossible to drop anchor and veer down towards the casualty because of the rocky nature of the location, so Coxswain Samuel Nelson took the lifeboat alongside through heavy broken water; seven out of the crew of nine were rescued, the other two being saved from the shore. The rescued men were landed at Bangor, and the lifeboat then returned to her station.

The second rescue took place a fortnight later, on 6 December, when the lifeboat was launched to the steamship *Hope Star*, of Newcastle, which had gone ashore in Ballyholme Bay and was lying in shallow water surrounded by rocks.

Coxswain Nelson took the lifeboat alongside through the heavy seas and succeeded in rescuing nine of the 43 men on board. The others refused to leave, so after landing the nine men the lifeboat returned and stood by in gale force winds. She returned to her station after the weather improved having been on service for 8 hours.

As well as the Bronze Medal being awarded to Coxswain Nelson, the Thanks on Vellum was accorded to Mechanic David Nelson and to Bowman Alexander Nelson for their part in these two rescues.

Background information

The station's former lifeboat, *Sir Samuel Kelly*, is on display in the car park close to the lifeboat station.

Above The small harbour at Donaghadee with 52ft Arun *City of Belfast* (ON.1107) at moorings.

Below The crew facility at the harbour close to the lifeboat moorings.

Key dates

Opened	1986
RNLI	1986
Inshore LB	10.10.1986

Current lifeboat details

Inshore lifeboat

Type	Atlantic 21
Official Number	B-593
Name	*Valerie Hull*
Donor	Bequest of Mrs M. C. Hull
Placed on station	27.1.1993
Launch	Davit

Location history

1986 An inshore lifeboat station was established in October; the ILB was kept in a small building on the south side of the harbour, and launched down a slipway. This house was used until 1990.

1990 The station was redesignated to Atlantic 21 status in June.

1992 A new Schat davit was installed on the quayside on the north pier, and a new ILB house was built to house the Atlantic 21; it includes a workshop, changing room, fuel store, crew room, office, toilet and shower facilities.

Medals and awards

No medals have been awarded.

Launching Relief Atlantic 21 B-569 on exercise at Kilkeel in 1997.

Clogher Head

Louth

Key dates

Opened	1899
RNLI	1899
Motor LB	1931
Fast LB	1993

Current lifeboat details

All-weather lifeboat

Type	Mersey
Official Number	1190
Operational Number	12-31
Year built	1993
Name	*Doris Bleasdale*
Donor	Bequest of Miss Doris Bleasdale
Placed on station	3.3.1993
Launch	Carriage

Location history

1899 A corrugated galvanised iron lifeboat house was built on a concrete foundation on the beach, with a short slipway, and a roadway to the county road; a tractor house was added later. Both buildings were used until 1992, then demolished.

1992-3 A new lifeboat house was built to accommodate the 12m Mersey class lifeboat with main doors at either end to allow the lifeboat to be driven completely through. It also provides a storage room, souvenir sales outlet, shower and toilet, a crew room, drying area and workshop/storage area. This is one of the eight 'Penza' lifeboat houses (see Lochinver entry).

Medals and awards

Five medals have been awarded, one Gold and four Silver, all for shore-boat or shore rescues, carried out before the station was established by the RNLI.

The Naming Ceremony of 12m Mersey *Doris Bleasdale* (ON.1190) on the beach outside the lifeboat house on 4 September 1993.
Jim Wallbridge

Current lifeboat details

Inshore lifeboat
Type   Atlantic 75
Official Number   B-747
Name   Rockabill
Donor   RNLI general funds (named
                  after a lighthouse off Skerries)
Placed on station   22.6.1998
Launch   Tractor and do-do carriage

Location history

1854 A lifeboat house was built for the station's first lifeboat; this house was altered in 1866 for a larger lifeboat and was used until 1903.

1903 A new lifeboat house was constructed on the seafront; it was used until 1930 when the station was closed following the placing of a motor lifeboat at Howth. The house has since been rebuilt as a private residence.

1981 An inshore lifeboat station was established in July; the ILB was kept in a stone-built house on the seafront, north of the main pier at the end of Harbour Road. This house was used until 1997.

1997 A new ILB house was built on the same site near the pier for an Atlantic 75 and launching tractor.

Medals and awards

One Gold Medal has been awarded, and two Silver Medals for a shore rescue.

Notable rescue

On 15 November 1858 the Austrian brig *Tregiste*, of Trieste, ran ashore during an easterly gale between Lambay Island, near Dublin, and the mainland. The Skerries lifeboat was taken overland on her carriage to the strand south of the town of Rush, from where she was launched. However, despite considerable exertions on the part of the lifeboat's crew of 13, under the command of Henry Hamilton, of Balbriggan, they could not pull the boat to the casualty, so returned to Rogerstown. Here the lifeboat was kept afloat in the river and the crew were kept in readiness to put out again.

The brig survived the night, riding out the gale, although the sea remained as violent as before. On 16 November a large steamer attempted to rescue those on board but could not get near enough, so the casualty had to survive a second night in the gale, her crew working hard at the pumps to ensure she remained afloat.

Early in the morning of 17 November the wind lessened and the lifeboat was able to put out again, with the same crew who had remained on stand-by. This time, after a considerable struggle, they reached the vessel more than 2 hours after putting out. Once near the casualty, the entire crew of 13 were successfully taken off, in twos and threes, over the vessel's stern. They were then safely landed at Rogerstown, and the brig's hull was subsequently towed to Dun Laoghaire Harbour.

For this rescue the Gold Medal was awarded to Henry Hamilton, who already held the Silver Medal and clasp for services at Balbriggan, and additional monetary rewards were paid to the crew. *The Lifeboat* of April 1859 said that this was 'an unusually gallant service, and reflected the highest credit on the bravery and perseverance of Mr Hamilton and his intrepid crew.'

Background information

The dangers of lifesaving work in the 19th century are clearly shown by events at Skerries. On two occasions the pulling lifeboats from the station were capsized while on service.

The first occasion was 1 February 1873, when the lifeboat *Admiral Mitchell* was launched on service to the schooner *Sarah*, of Runcorn. The night was bitterly cold with showers of snow and sleet, and it is thought that the crew became numbed and lost all their oars when a cross sea capsized the lifeboat and threw out the Coxswain and six of the crew. The Coxswain was the only man to regain the boat, which was capsized twice more, and of the crew left on board by this time, only four survived, six being drowned. The crew of the *Sarah* were also all lost. The Institution voted £250 to the local fund and there is a memorial in the local cemetery to those who were lost.

The second occasion was the night of 23-24 October 1881. The lifeboat *Laura Platt* was launched to the barque *S. Vaughan*, of Windsor, Nova Scotia, and while she was being towed by a trawler, the tow rope broke and a sea struck the lifeboat on her quarter. She was capsized, but none of the 13 on board were lost.

Launch of Atlantic 75 *Rockabill* (B-747) from the ILB house built in 1997.
Sam Shiels, RNLI Skerries Branch

Key dates

Opened	1817-post 1843 and 1851
RNLI	1962
Motor LB	1930
Fast LB	1986
Inshore LB	4.1967

Current lifeboat details

All-weather lifeboat

Type	Arun
Official Number	1113
Operational Number	52-35
Year built	1986
Name	*City of Dublin*
Donor	City of Dublin Appeal
Placed on station	22.8.1986
Launch	Afloat

Inshore lifeboat

Type	D class inflatable
Official Number	D-530
Name	*Marguerite Joan Harris*
Donor	Bequest of Marguerite Joan Harris
Placed on station	23.4.1998
Launch	Trolley

Location history

1817 The early lifeboats in Dublin Bay were funded and operated by the Corporation for Preserving and Improving the Port of Dublin (known as the Dublin Ballast Board). The first lifeboat was placed at Howth by the Ballast Board; all of their lifeboats were taken over by the RNLI in January 1862.

1862 The RNLI took over the station, and a lifeboat house was constructed at the end of the West Pier jetty. The house was altered for a larger lifeboat in 1871 and was used until 1899; in 1900 it was handed over to the Board of Public Works.

1899 The lifeboat was placed afloat on moorings in the harbour in a berth at the end of the East Pier.

1900 Arrangements were made for using a yawl to board the lifeboat when rough weather prevented the crew from reaching her by pier.

1933 A new gear store and crew room was constructed at the end of the East Pier; this was used until 1984, but some of the station's service boards are still inside.

1967 An inshore lifeboat station was established.

1982 During the re-development of the harbour, a slip was built in readiness for a new ILB house.

1983-4 A new ILB house was built in the harbour and new moorings for the all-weather lifeboat were provided nearby.

Medals and awards

Two medals have been awarded, one Silver and one Bronze.

Nine medals have been awarded for shore-boat rescues, six Silver and three Bronze.

Notable rescue

On 14 July 1964 the reserve lifeboat *H. F. Bailey* was launched to the motor fishing vessel *Roscairbre*, of Dublin, which was in grave danger near the cliffs at the north side of Freshwater Bay. A southerly gale was blowing, there was a very rough sea and a heavy south-easterly swell.

The lifeboat had to travel almost 3 miles to reach the casualty, which was found lying head to wind in about 2 fathoms of water. Seas were breaking over her and she was dragging her anchor. The lifeboat attempted to tow her clear of the cliffs, but the first attempt failed and was abandoned.

As the casualty was getting into a very dangerous position, another tow was attempted. The lifeboat went alongside through broken water, and a tow rope was safely passed across. Once this was secured, the tow began and this time it was successful. The fishing vessel was pulled clear of the cliffs and into safe water, then towed to Howth. Here she was secured, having been saved together with her crew of three.

For this rescue the Bronze Medal was awarded to Coxswain Joseph McLoughlin, and Medal service certificates were presented to the other five members of the crew.

The ILB house built in 1983-4 in the harbour for the station's D class inshore lifeboat.

52ft Arun *City of Dublin* (ON.1113) moored in Howth harbour in 1995.

Key dates

Opened	1817
RNLI	1862
Motor LB	1919
Fast LB	1967
Inshore LB	3.1986

Current lifeboat details

All-weather lifeboat

Type	Trent
Official Number	1200
Operational Number	14-05
Year built	1994
Name	Anna Livia
Donor	Proceeds of the Dublin Bay Lifeboat Fund, with other gifts and legacies
Placed on station	29.6.1995
Launch	Afloat

Inshore lifeboat

Type	D class inflatable
Official Number	D-441
Name	Irish Diver
Donor	Irish Underwater Council
Placed on station	20.5.1993
Launch	Trolley

Location history

1817 The first lifeboat was placed at Dun Laoghaire by the Dublin Ballast Board; a granite boathouse was built by the Board of Works, but it was in an unsuitable position when the RNLI took over in January 1862 and was abandoned.

1862 A new lifeboat house was built, close to the East Pier, when the RNLI took over the station; this house was used until 1911 when the No.1 lifeboat was withdrawn.

1890 A second lifeboat was considered necessary, and was kept at moorings in the harbour.

1901 A new lifeboat house and slipway were built, initially for the No.2 lifeboat, between the Carlisle Pier and the National Yacht Club for a launch into the harbour. The house was altered in 1917 and 1938 for new lifeboats, and was used until the 1960s; it was demolished in 1963, although the slipway remained intact until 1998.

1963 Moorings close to the Mail Boat Pier (formerly the Carlisle Pier) were taken up, with a boarding-boat close to the shore facility constructed on the site of the 1901 boathouse.

1986 An inshore lifeboat station was established in March; the ILB was kept in the 1862 boathouse, situated between the Yacht Club and the East Pier, which was refurbished and altered for the purpose.

1998 Construction of a new shore facility began on the site of the 1901 boathouse, adjacent to the Yacht Club.

Medals and awards

Two medals have been awarded, one Silver and one Bronze.

One Gold Medal was awarded in 1829, and ten medals have been awarded for shore and shore-boat rescues, one Gold and nine Silver.

Notable rescue

On 24 December 1895 the No.2 lifeboat Civil Service No.7 was wrecked while proceeding to the assistance of the steamship Palme, of Finland, and the entire crew of 15 were drowned. The lifeboat capsized about 600 yards from the distressed vessel, and although every effort was made to help the unfortunate lifeboatmen, and also the Palme, nothing could be done.

The No.1 lifeboat Hannah Pickard was then launched to the Palme, with a crew of only nine, supplemented by six further volunteers from HMS Melampus. However, she also capsized while under sail, but fortunately all regained the lifeboat, which successfully righted itself. She was then driven ashore at Vance's Harbour, Blackrock.

The following day the crew of the Palme, 20 in all, were successfully rescued by the steamship Tearaght under the command of Captain Thomas McCombie. In recognition of his intrepid conduct, McCombie was awarded the Gold Medal by the RNLI.

Following the lifeboat disaster, a fund was opened locally and £17,000 was raised; to this the RNLI added a sum of £2,200 and, as is usual, defrayed all the funeral and other expenses.

There is a memorial to the 15 lifeboatmen lost in the Civil Service No.7 overlooking the harbour, close to the lifeboat moorings, as well as a memorial tablet on the roof of the 1862 boathouse.

14m Trent Anna Livia (ON.1200) moored in the harbour close to the Mail Boat Pier.

Key dates

Opened	1865-1925; ro1990
RNLI	1865
AWLB withdrawn	1925
Inshore LB	5.1990

Current lifeboat details

Inshore lifeboat

Type	D class inflatable
Official Number	D-412
Name	BP Service
Donor	Gift of BP Oil (Ireland) Ltd
Placed on station	16.3.1991
Launch	Trolley

Location history

1865 A lifeboat house was built; it was used until 1911 and has since been demolished.

1885 A slipway was built at the north side of the harbour to improve launching arrangements; in 1887 the slipway was extended by 21 feet.

1911 A new lifeboat house was built on land to the seaward side of the harbour; this was used until 1925 when the station was closed.

1990 An inshore lifeboat station was established in May; the 1911 lifeboat house was repurchased to house the ILB.

The lifeboat house built in 1911 and converted in 1990 to house the D class inflatable.

1992 The boathouse was refurbished to provide a boat storage area, souvenir outlet, drying cabinet, toilet and shower on the ground floor, and a crew room and operations room on the first floor.

Medals and awards

No medals have been awarded.

Rosslare Harbour

Wexford

Key dates

Opened	1896-1921 and 1927
RNLI	1896
Motor LB	1927
Fast LB	1984

Current lifeboat details

All-weather lifeboat

Type	Arun
Official Number	1092
Operational Number	52-26
Year built	1983
Name	St Brendan
Donor	RNLI general funds
Placed on station	1.6.1984
Launch	Afloat

Location history

1896 The lifeboat station was established, and the lifeboat was kept afloat in the Harbour.

1921 The station was closed following the placing of a motor lifeboat with a permanent crew at the village of Fort, located at Rosslare Point. However, during December 1924 and January 1925 gales and heavy seas overwhelmed the area and the Fort station had to be abandoned; the Fort and lifeboat station, together with all the buildings on the Point, were eventually washed away.

1925 The lifeboat was kept at Wexford until 1927.

1927 The station at Rosslare Harbour was re-opened and the lifeboat was kept moored to the west of the pier; a row of houses, called Lifeboat Terrace, was built close to the harbour for the lifeboatmen, some of whom were full-time, and a boarding-boat was kept on the beach.

1980 The lifeboat moorings were moved to the west of the new West Pier.

1985 A new mooring pen alongside the East Pier was constructed, together with new shore facilities that included a lifeboat store, workshop, assembly room, toilet and shower facilities.

1996 Because of extensive port developments, the lifeboat moorings were relocated to a new berth between the East and West Piers in the harbour area; a dolphin was installed for the boat to moor alongside, an access bridge was built, and a new boarding gangway was provided. As a result of the harbour developments, the lifeboat is now virtually hidden from view from the shore except from within the immediate port area.

Medals and awards

Seven medals have been awarded, three Silver and four Bronze.

Seven medals have been awarded for shore and shore-boat rescues, one Gold and six Silver. (These totals do not include medals awarded to the Wexford lifeboatmen.)

Notable rescue

On 7 December 1978 the relief lifeboat *Sir Samuel Kelly* was launched to the fishing boat *Notre Dame du Sacre Coeur*, which was sinking 3½ miles off the Tuskar Rock. A storm force 10 to violent storm force 11 was blowing, and a very heavy sea was running.

After clearing the shelter of the harbour, progress was difficult due to the severity of the seas, which were estimated at 33 feet in height. Once the casualty had been reached, the lifeboat circled her while the Coxswain assessed the situation.

The lifeboat was then taken alongside the starboard quarter of the fishing vessel, and one fisherman was dragged aboard by two lifeboatmen. A second run was made alongside the port quarter, enabling a second fisherman to be saved. The fishing boat was then abandoned as it was clearly sinking and the lifeboat returned to harbour at reduced speed, where the two survivors were landed.

For this rescue the Bronze Medal was awarded to Second Coxswain Seamus McCormack in recognition of the courage, leadership and seamanship he displayed, and Medal service certificates were presented to the rest of the crew.

The most famous rescue performed by the Rosslare Harbour lifeboat was the saving of seven men from the Liberian tanker *World Concord* in November 1954; this rescue was carried out in conjunction with the St Davids lifeboat, and a full description can be found in the entry for that station.

Background information

Lifeboats have been stationed at various points around Rosslare Bay, including the present location at Rosslare Harbour. The first station to cover the area was established in 1838. The first lifeboat was transferred from Newcastle (Down) and operated from Rosslare Point at the south side of the entrance to Wexford Harbour, but was replaced during the following year by a new one; the station lapsed during the 1850s. The station was re-established at Rosslare Point in 1858 and a second larger lifeboat was stationed afloat in the same year. The first of these stations was known as Rosslare Fort and the other as Wexford. In 1866 both stations were known as Wexford, the afloat boat as No.1, the shore-based boat as No.2. The No.2 station continued in operation until 1897, and the No.1 until 1925.

One of the most famous incidents in the history of the station occurred in February 1914 when the lifeboat took part in the rescue of survivors from the schooner *Mexico*, which had been driven aground on Keeragh Island during a storm. The Fethard lifeboat was also launched, but capsized with the loss of nine of her crew of 14 (see Fethard entry). The lifeboat from Rosslare was towed to the scene by a local tug, and Kilmore Quay and Dunmore East lifeboats were also launched. The Rosslare boat succeeded in rescuing ten men. For their efforts Silver Medals were awarded to Wexford Coxswain Edward Wickham, crew members James Wickham (later Coxswain at Rosslare Harbour) and William Duggan, and Kilmore Quay Coxswain Walter Power; the Chief Inspector of Lifeboats, Commander Thomas Holmes, who directed rescue operations, was also awarded the Silver Medal. In the village of Burrow, where most of the lifeboatmen lived, a memorial to all those who took part in this rescue was unveiled in 1982.

The memorial at Burrow, near Wexford, erected in 1981 to commemorate the lifeboatmen from Rosslare who went to the aid of the survivors of the Norwegian schooner *Mexico*, wrecked in February 1914. Four lifeboats put out to the schooner, and the Fethard lifeboat was lost, with nine members of her crew drowned.

The mooring pen near the ferry terminal for 52ft Arun *St Brendan* (ON.1092), with the shore facility nearby.

Key dates

Opened	1847-c1850s and 1884
RNLI	1847
Motor LB	1937
Fast LB	1992

Current lifeboat details

All-weather lifeboat

Type	Mersey
Official Number	1187
Operational Number	12-28
Year built	1992
Name	*Mary Margaret*
Donor	Bequests of Denis Adolph
	Sydney Williams and
	Mary Margaret Williams
Placed on station	2.12.1992
Launch	Carriage

Location history

1847 The lifeboat supplied by the RNIPLS was kept in a Coastguard boathouse close to the high-water mark; it was in need of repair by the early 1850s, and was removed.

1884-5 The station was re-opened and a new lifeboat house was constructed near the harbour; it was used until 1992.

1989 The tractor house was adapted to accommodate a new Talus tractor.

1992-3 A new lifeboat house was built for the 12m Mersey class lifeboat on the site of the earlier house; to retain some of the original character, the stone from the previous house was used in part to build the new one.

Medals and awards

Three medals have been awarded, two Silver and one Bronze.

Seven medals have been awarded for shore-boat rescues, all Silver.

Notable rescue

On 19 December 1957 the lifeboat *Ann Isabella Pyemont* was launched to the French trawler *Augusta*

Maurice, of Lorient, which was in difficulty near Ballyteige Bay, 5 miles from Kilmore, in a fresh SSW gale with occasional gusts of force 10.

As the lifeboat approached she had to reduce speed as heavy seas were breaking around the casualty, which was listing heavily to port. To approach the vessel the lifeboat was taken between two trawl boards that were swinging hazardously over the side. Once alongside, two fishermen scrambled on board before the lifeboat was hit by a heavy sea and swept away from the casualty.

The lifeboat was taken alongside again, and this time lines were put aboard the trawler. The lines held the lifeboat steady long enough for six more men to be saved, but the skipper then cast off the securing ropes and the lifeboat was once more forced to move away.

At the third attempt the ninth man from the trawler scrambled aboard, then the lifeboat was taken alongside long enough to enable the Bowman to grab the skipper, who was also dragged to safety. By this time the trawler was less then half a mile from the beach, but with the crew of ten all safe the lifeboat returned to her station and landed the survivors.

For this rescue the Silver Medal was awarded to Coxswain Mark Bates, and the Thanks on Vellum was accorded to the rest of the crew, Second Coxswain J. Bates, Bowman J. Blake, Motor Mechanic J. Kehoe, Assistance Motor Mechanic C. Bates, and crew members R. Barry and N. Wickham.

Background information

On 24 December 1977 the lifeboat *Lady Murphy* was launched following a reported sighting of distress flares. During the search the lifeboat capsized twice with the loss of crew member Finton Sinnott. Acting Second Coxswain Joseph Maddock and Acting Assistant Mechanic Dermot Cullerton were also injured during the capsize. The Coxswain and Mechanic, helped by other crew members, rescued one crew member who was washed out of the lifeboat during the first capsize and three of the four crew members washed out during the second.

Following this service the Silver Medal was awarded to Coxswain Thomas Walsh and the Bronze to Acting Mechanic John James Devereaux, and the Thanks on Vellum was accorded to the remainder of the crew, Acting Second Coxswain Maddock, Acting Assistant Mechanic Culleton, David Culleton and Eugene Kehoe. A special Certificate Inscribed on Vellum was awarded posthumously to Finton Sinnott.

The lifeboat house built in 1992-3 for the station's 12m Mersey and Talus MB-H launching tractor.

Key dates

Opened	1886-1914; ro 1996
RNLI	1886
AWLB withdrawn	1914
Inshore LB	7.1996

Current lifeboat details

Inshore lifeboat

Type	D class inflatable
Official Number	D-528
Name	*Arthur Harris*
Donor	Bequest of Marguerite Joan Harris
Placed on station	14.3.1998
Launch	Trolley

Location history

1886 A lifeboat house was built near the Quay and was used until the station was closed in 1914; in 1915 it was handed over to the people of Fethard, and was used as a store until 1995.

1996 An inshore lifeboat station was established in July; the ILB was kept in the 1886 boathouse, which was refurbished.

Medals and awards

No medals have been awarded.

Background information

On 20 February 1914 the lifeboat *Helen Blake* was launched to the three-masted schooner *Mexico*, of Christiana, which was totally wrecked on the South Keeragh Island. While proceeding to the casualty, the lifeboat was capsized and nine of her crew of 14 were lost. The five survivors landed on the island and helped the eight men from the *Mexico* ashore with ropes.

Many attempts were then made to bring the survivors to the mainland. On 23 February the Dunmore East lifeboat took off two lifeboatmen, and the Wexford lifeboat, towed by the tug *Wexford*, took off seven of the *Mexico*'s men and the other three lifeboatmen. One of the *Mexico*'s crew died of exposure during the days spent on the Island.

The Fethard lifeboatmen lost were Coxswain Christopher Bird, Bowman Thomas Hendrick, and crew members Michael Hendrick, James Morrissey, Patrick Roche, Patrick Cullen, William Bird, William Banville and Patrick Stafford. The reaction to the tragedy was immediate: the RNLI Committee of Management voted £50 for immediate necessities and a further £2,000 towards local funds.

The King of Norway conferred Silver Medals on the five surviving members of the Fethard crew, as well as Commander Thomas Holmes, Chief Inspector of Lifeboats, Coxswain Walter Power of Dunmore East, Coxswain Edward Wickham of Wexford, and crew members James Wickham and William Duggan of the Wexford lifeboat. The RNLI accorded the Thanks on Vellum to G. L. Bassett (Fethard Honorary Secretary), Captain Busher (of the tug *Wexford*), and to each of the five survivors of the Fethard crew.

This disaster was one of the greatest losses suffered by RNLI lifeboats in Ireland, and resulted in the closure of the station. The lifeboat house was handed over to the people of the village, and a plaque placed on the boathouse wall to show that it was for the use of the local fishermen. In addition, an impressive memorial to the lifeboatmen was erected in Fethard centre, at the side of the main road.

The memorial in Fethard village to the lifeboatmen who were lost on 20 February 1914 when the lifeboat was wrecked on service.

The lifeboat house built in 1886 and used until the station was closed in 1914. It was re-acquired by the RNLI to house the station's D class inshore lifeboat in 1996.

Key dates

Opened	1859-1969; ro 1997
RNLI	1859
Motor LB	1930
AWLB withdrawn	25.3.1969
Inshore LB	26.4.1997

Current lifeboat details

Inshore lifeboat

Type	Atlantic 21
Official Number	B-553
Name	Kirklees
Donor	Kirklees Lifeboat Appeal
Placed on station	14.9.1998
Launch	Trolley

Location history

1859 A lifeboat house was built on the north side of Dungarvan Bay.

1863 The lifeboat house was rebuilt at Ballinacourty; used until 1900, it has since been used as a store.

1899 A new lifeboat house and slipway built at Crowe Point on the south side of Dungarvan Bay, to the west of Helvick Harbour, was completed in 1901; the house was used until 1930, then demolished c1964; only the foundations remain.

1930 The station was moved to Helvick Head harbour where the motor lifeboats lay afloat at moorings; a gear store was built at the edge of the harbour. The station was closed in 1969, but the gear store is still standing.

1997 An inshore lifeboat station was established; the Atlantic 21, sent on evaluation, was operated from a compound at Helvick Pier, with a Portacabin used as crew room.

1998-9 A new ILB house was built at Helvick Head harbour.

Medals and awards

Three Silver Medals have been awarded for shore and shore-boat rescues.

Background information

The station was known as Dungarven (Ballinacourty) from 1859 until 1900; it was then named Dungarven Bay (Helvick Head) until in 1903 it was again renamed as Helvick Head (Dungarven Bay) until its closure in 1969. Since being re-opened in 1997, it has been called Helvick Head.

Atlantic 21 B-528 under a tarpaulin in the temporary compound at the head of the slipway into the harbour at Helvick Head. *Tony Denton*

Key dates

Opened	1839
RNLI	1857
Motor LB	1931
AWLB withdrawn	5.1984
Inshore LB	25.5.1984

Current lifeboat details

Inshore lifeboat

Type	Atlantic 21
Official Number	B-561
Name	Marjory Turner
Donor	Gift of the late Mr V. S. Turner
Placed on station	30.6.1985
Launch	Tractor and do-do carriage

Location history

1839 The first lifeboat was kept under a tarpaulin, next to the Coastguard house, on the west bank of the River Blackwater; by the 1850s it was rotten and neglected.

1857 A lifeboat house was built on the site on Green Park where the lifeboat had been kept. This house was used until 1876, and in 1878 was sold to the Town Commissioners; it was demolished in 1964.

1876 A new lifeboat house was built about 200 yards east of the previous one, backing on to the Mall in the centre of the seafront on the beach; it has been in use ever since, albeit much altered.

1984 The lifeboat house was adapted for launching an Atlantic 21 from a cradle on rails placed on the old slipway; in 1988 the internal layout of the boathouse was altered to provide improved crew facilities.

1995 The lifeboat house was renovated and the slipway rails were removed so that the Atlantic could be launched using tractor and carriage.

Medals and awards

Three medals have been awarded, one Gold, one Silver and one Bronze.

Three Silver Medals have been awarded for shore or shore-boat rescues.

Notable rescue

On 17 December 1905 the lifeboat *Mary Luckombe* was launched to the aid of the schooner *Annetta*, of Dungarvan, which had run ashore at Youghal, opposite the railway station, in a strong SSE gale with a very heavy sea, while bound for Youghal with a cargo of coal.

The rocket apparatus team was unable to get a rocket-line to the casualty because of the force of the wind. However, the lifeboat was able to reach the schooner, whose stranded crew had taken to the rigging and were totally exhausted. The only way to reach them was to drive the lifeboat over the sunken vessel, and despite the considerable dangers caused by the sea breaking continually over the lifeboat, the three crew were saved.

One of the men in the rigging had to be abandoned on the first two attempts to reach him as the breaking seas and large quantity of wreckage forced the lifeboat back. However, on the third occasion he was saved, although the lifeboat was considerably damaged and her rudder was smashed. The Master and one other member of the crew, who were on the weather side of the rigging, were drowned before the lifeboat reached them.

For this rescue the Silver Medal was awarded to Coxswain Michael Hannagan and extra monetary rewards were made to him and each of the lifeboat crew.

Above The lifeboat house built in 1876, and modified and extended in 1995 for the Atlantic 21 and launching tractor. *Tony Denton*

Below The lifeboat house on the west bank of the River Blackwater, with Atlantic 21 *Marjory Turner* (B-561) and her launching tractor outside. *Tony Denton*

Right Marjory Turner being launched on an exercise in 1998. *Tony Denton*

Key dates

Opened	1996
RNLI	1996
Inshore LB	4.1996

Current lifeboat details

Inshore lifeboat

Type	Atlantic 75
Official Number	B-729
Name	*Rose West*
Donor	Bequest of Miss Rosemary Dora Bodenham West
Placed on station	9.10.1996
Launch	Tractor and do-do carriage

Location history

1996 An inshore lifeboat station was established in April to provide additional cover on the west coast of Ireland, especially the Shannon Estuary. An ILB house was built just outside the Marina lock, facing Scattery Island, with easy access to the harbour's deep-water approach channel. The house includes accommodation for the Atlantic 75 and launching tractor, a workshop, changing/drying room, souvenir sales outlet, crew room, office, toilet facilities and fuel store.

Medals and awards

No medals have been awarded.

Atlantic 75 *Rose West* (B-729) inside the ILB house on her launching carriage.

Aran Islands

Galway

Key dates

Opened	1927
RNLI	1927
Motor LB	1927
Fast LB	1987

Current lifeboat details

All-weather lifeboat

Type	Severn
Official Number	1217
Operational Number	17-06
Year built	1996
Name	*David Kirkaldy*
Donor	Mr David Kirkaldy
Placed on station	6.6.1997
Launch	Afloat

Location history

1927 The lifeboat was kept afloat at moorings at Killeary Bay, Kilronan, the main settlement on the Island of Inishmore, the largest of the three Aran Islands; shore facilities were provided at the side of the harbour.

1990 A derelict boathouse, situated adjacent to the present boathouse, was renovated to provide improved crew facilities.

Medals and awards

Eleven medals have been awarded, all Bronze.

Ten medals have been awarded for shore and shore-boat rescues, nine Silver and one Bronze.

The crew store facing Killeary Bay at Kilronan on the Island of Inishmore, overlooking the lifeboat moorings.

Notable rescue

On 16 January 1962 the lifeboat *Mabel Marion Thompson* was launched to the motor vessel *June*, of Groningen, which had taken refuge and run aground on the reefs off Mutton Island in a south-westerly force 7 wind gusting to force 9 and a rough sea.

The lifeboat had to travel 24 miles from her station to reach the

casualty, which was found to be listing 20 degrees to port with her bows on a rock. But as the weather was improving, the Master decided not to abandon her, so the lifeboat put into Galway Docks. She set out again in the evening when the weather began to deteriorate, towing a small boat to assist with a rescue. An extra man with knowledge of the area was also taken, as well as the owner of the casualty.

The gale was now gusting with rough seas, and visibility was much reduced by squalls of hail and rain. The casualty's crew had taken refuge on Mutton Island, and Coxswain Coleman Hernon manoeuvred the lifeboat as close to the Mutton Island lighthouse as possible. Using the small boat, made fast by line, crew members Thomas Joyce and Bartley Mullen took turns rowing to the lighthouse in order to rescue six of the survivors from the island, who were then taken on board the lifeboat.

Patrick Quinn took the place of Bartley Mullen and seven further attempts were made to return to the island; eventually the remaining two men were successfully taken off, although the small boat was swamped on several occasions. Throughout the rescue the lifeboat was manoeuvred by Coxswain Hernon with considerable skill in broken water and strong gale conditions, which added a considerable element of danger.

For this rescue Bronze Medals

17m Severn *David Kirkaldy* (ON.1217) moored in Kilronan Harbour in 1998. *Gary Markham*

were awarded to Coxswain Coleman Hernon, Assistant Mechanic Bartley Mullen and crew members Thomas Joyce and Patrick Quinn.

Background information

Between 1927 and 1995 the station was known as Galway Bay. Since 1 August 1995 it has been named Aran Islands, reflecting more accurately its location and to avoid confusion with the inshore lifeboat station established at Galway.

Key dates

Opened	1996
RNLI	1996
Inshore LB	3.1996

Current lifeboat details

Inshore lifeboat

Type	Atlantic 75
Official Number	B-738
Name	Dochas
Donor	Galway City Appeal
Placed on station	3.9.1997
Launch	Davit

Location history

1996 An inshore lifeboat station was established in March to provide inshore cover for a large area of Galway Bay, supplementing the existing Aran Islands station at

Kilronan; the ILB was kept in a temporary house in the Dock area of the city, and a crew store was placed on the quayside, with an electric launch davit built on the quay.

1997 A permanent inshore lifeboat house was constructed on the

The ILB house built in 1997 at Galway Docks, with the launch davit used to lower the Atlantic 75 into the water. *RNLI*

dockside over the revetment, adjacent to the launching davit, to house the Atlantic with a motor room for the davit.

Medals and awards

No medals have been awarded.

Key dates

Opened	1988
RNLI	1988
Inshore LB	3.1988; second 1997

Current lifeboat details

Inshore lifeboats

Type	Atlantic 75
Official Number	B-751
Name	*Benjamin Dowing Fairbridge*
Donor	Legacy of Mrs M. A. H. Fairbridge
Placed on station	12.1.1999
Launch	Tractor and do-do carriage

Type	D class inflatable
Official Number	D-525
Name	*Holme Team IV*
Donor	Landlord and regulars of The Fleece Inn, Holmfirth
Placed on station	19.5.1998
Launch	Land Rover and trolley

Location history

1988 An inshore lifeboat station was established on 15 March for one season's evaluation.

1989 In March the station became fully operational during the summer only.

1992 A new purpose-built ILB house was constructed on the quayside to house the ILB and launching vehicle; it included a workshop, drying room, crew room and kitchen.

1998 A new ILB house to accommodate the Atlantic 75 and launching tractor was constructed at the end of Beach Road.

Medals and awards

No medals have been awarded.

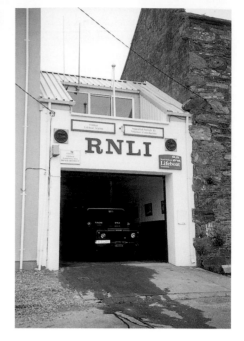

The lifeboat house built on the quayside in 1992, and used for the D class inflatable. *RNLI*

Achill Island

Mayo

Key dates

Opened	8.1996
RNLI	1996
Motor LB	1996
Fast LB	1996

Current lifeboat details

All-weather lifeboat

Type	Arun
Official Number	1057
Operational Number	52-10
Year built	1978
Name	*Soldian*
Donor	Lerwick Lifeboat Appeal, including Brent and Ninian Pipeline Consortium Chevron Petroleum (UK) Ltd, The Aberdeen Students' Charities Campaign and other legacies and gifts
Placed on station	26.1.1998
Launch	Afloat

Location history

1996 Moorings were taken up in Achill Sound for an all-weather lifeboat, near the keep of a small 15th-century tower house on the Atlantic Drive, just to the south of Kildavnet pier; the boarding-boat is moored off the pier, and temporary Portacabins used to store the crew's gear.

Medals and awards

No medals have been awarded.

52ft Arun *Soldian* (ON.1057) moored in Achill Sound, opposite Castle Kildavnet. *Tony Denton*

Key dates

Opened	1989
RNLI	1989
Motor LB	1989
Fast LB	1989

Current lifeboat details

All-weather lifeboat

Type	Severn
Official Number	1235
Operational Number	17-15
Year built	1998
Name	Bryan and Gordon
Donor	Legacies from Mr Bryan Clifford Griffiths and Mr Gordon William Griffiths, who were brothers
Placed on station	14.8.1998
Launch	Afloat

Location history

1989 Moorings for the all-weather lifeboat were taken up at Ballyglass, a fjord-like inlet opening to the north into Broad Haven Bay, about 4 miles north-east of Belmullet town, one of the most remote villages in Ireland.

1994 A new crew facility was built close to the lifeboat's moorings; a former C class inflatable is used as the boarding-boat.

Medals and awards

A Bronze Medal has been awarded for a shore rescue.

Notable rescue

On 25 October 1997 the lifeboat *Mabel Williams* was launched to search for four persons reported overdue in their 16ft curragh. The crew of a local fishing vessel reported voices in a cave west of Horse Island, 18 miles from Ballyglass.

On arrival at the scene the lifeboat's Y class inflatable was launched with John Gaughan and Cathal Reilly on board; when they were 650 feet into the cave they also heard voices. The casualties were spotted on a ledge 20 feet above sea level, but unreachable because of heavy breaking swell.

Two local divers, Michael Heffernan and Joseph Barratt, volunteered to assist the lifeboat crew and entered the cave in an IMES rescue boat intending to swim to the rear of the cave with a line. Both divers appeared to clear the breaker before being dragged by the backwash. At this point the recall signal was felt on the line, which was quickly retrieved. Joseph Barratt was recovered but Michael Heffernan was not, and it was assumed he had reached safety.

At 0030 a request for a professional diving team was made to the Garda Underwater Unit in Dublin. While waiting for the divers, the lifeboat and several fishing vessels sat just outside the entrance to the cave 2-3m from the cliff face in an effort to illuminate the inside of the cave.

At daybreak an attempt to swim from the IMES rescue boat went wrong. The boat was caught in the breaking swell and thrown the 100m to the back of the cave, landing upside down on the ledge 6-7m above sea level. The engine was destroyed but the divers and crew survived unhurt.

At this point the rescue team made contact with the three survivors and learned that Will Ernst von Below (owner of the curragh) and Michael Heffernan were dead. Eight people were now marooned in the cave, without a line to the cave entrance or any inflatable to get out. So Ciaran Doyle swam through vicious seas to the entrance carrying 300m of rope secured to one of the fishing boats.

Once Doyle was in the cave, the IMES rescue boat was gently pulled down from the ledge to sea level. The casualties and rescue team then climbed aboard it and were towed to safety, although it came close to capsizing on three occasions. The casualties, having spent 17 hours on the ledge, were severely hypothermic and were landed to an ambulance.

For this rescue the Bronze Medal was awarded to Ciaran Doyle of the Garda Underwater Unit; the Thanks on Vellum was accorded to Joseph Barratt and Michael Heffernan (posthumously) from Grainne Uaile Sub Aqua Club; and framed letters of appreciation signed by the Chairman were presented to Assistant Mechanic John Gaughan and crew member Cathal Reilly.

17m Severn *Bryan and Gordon* (ON.1235) arriving on station in July 1998. *Gary Markham*

There are many small displays of lifeboat-related items to be seen throughout the British Isles. The following lists those places where actual lifeboats can be seen on display, and does not include details of every museum or display centre where lifeboat-related material can be seen.

Arklow
The former Clogher Head lifeboat *Charles Whitton* is undergoing restoration at Tyrrells Boatyard for possible display at Clogher Head.

Bamburgh
The Grace Darling Museum contains items relating to Grace Darling and has a replica of the coble used in the rescue of the *Forfarshire*. Tel 01668 214465

Barrow
The former Barrow lifeboat *Herbert Leigh* is displayed outside the New Dock Museum, North Road. Tel 01229 870871

Blackgang Chine
The former Flamborough lifeboat *Friendly Forester* is on display at the Blackgang Sawmill & St Catherine's Quay Museum on the south side of the Isle of Wight. Tel 01983 730330

Buckie
The former Anstruther lifeboat *The Doctors* is on display outside The Drifter Centre near the harbour. Tel 01542 834646

Cardiff
The former Moelfre lifeboat *Watkin Williams*, in which a Gold Medal rescue was performed, is displayed outside the Industrial & Maritime Museum, Bute Street. Tel 01222 481919

Charlestown (Cornwall)
The former Scarborough lifeboat *Amelia* is on display outside the Shipwreck & Heritage Museum, near St Austell. She may be joined by the former Selsey lifeboat *Charles Henry*, which was displayed outside

Merry Hill Shopping Centre, Dudley. Tel 01726 69897

Chatham Naval Dockyard
The Chatham Historic Dock Yard is the home of the National Lifeboat Collection, which consists of the following lifeboats: the first 37ft Oakley lifeboat *J. G. Graves* of Sheffield; the former Holyhead lifeboat *St Cybi (Civil Service No.9)*; the former Sennen Cove lifeboat *Susan Ashley*; the former Torbay lifeboat *Edward Bridges (C.S.&P.O. No.37)*; the former North Sunderland and Youghal lifeboat *Grace Darling*; the unique 28ft Harbour class lifeboat *Helen Blake*; the former Margate lifeboat *North Foreland (Civil Service No.11)*; the former Yarmouth and Falmouth lifeboat *B. A. S. P.*; the last Flamborough lifeboat *The Will and Fanny Kirby*; the prototype Waveney 44-001; and the pulling lifeboats

37ft Oakley *The Doctors* (ON.983) displayed outside Buckie Drifter Centre.

Lizzie Porter, *St Paul*, and *James Leath*. In addition there are displays relating to the history of lifeboats and the RNLI. For further information contact the Visitor Centre for the Dock Yard, tel 01634 812551

Cobh
The former Llandudno lifeboat *Lilly Wainwright* is stored at Verone Shipyard for future display.

Cromer
The centrepiece of the Lifeboat Museum is the former Cromer lifeboat *H. F. Bailey*, in which Coxswain Henry Blogg performed some notable medal-winning rescues. There are also many other items relating to the Cromer station in general and the exploits of Blogg in particular.

Donaghadee
The former Donaghadee lifeboat *Sir Samuel Kelly*, on loan from the Ulster Folk & Transport Museum, Cultra, is on display in a car park close to the harbour.

Duxford
At the Imperial War Museum, Duxford Airfield, Cambs, is the former Bembridge lifeboat *Jesse Lumb*, fully restored and on display in a hangar. Tel 01223 835000

Fraserburgh
At Sandhead, the former Fraserburgh lifeboat *Lady Rothes* is being restored for display at Fraserburgh.

Gorleston-on-Sea
The former Great Yarmouth and Gorleston lifeboat *John and Mary Meiklam of Gladswood* is displayed inside the lifeboat house.

Hartlepool
The former Filey lifeboat *Robert and Dorothy Hardcastle* is kept at the Power Station and used for display and fundraising purposes in the North East.

Harwich
Inside the Old Lifeboat House, on the Green, is the former Clacton lifeboat *Valentine Wyndham-Quin*.

Holywood (Co Down)
The lifeboat *William and Laura* is in storage at the Ulster Folk & Transport Museum, Cultra, and not at present on display to the public. Tel 01232 428428

Irvine
At the Scottish Maritime Museum is the former Longhope lifeboat *TGB*, and the pulling lifeboat *Jane Anne*, which is undergoing restoration for future display. Tel 01294 278283

Kirkleatham
The former Redcar lifeboat *Sir James Knott* is on display at Kirkleatham Old Hall Museum, near Redcar. Tel 01642 479500

Land's End
The lifeboat *James and Catherine MacFarlane*, which served at The Lizard station in Cornwall, is on display outside at the Land's End Exhibitions complex. Tel 01736 871501

Littlehampton
The former Broadstairs lifeboat *Frances Forbes Barton* is under restoration for possible future display near the lifeboat house.

Lynmouth
The lifeboat *Docea Chapman*, renamed *Louisa II* to commemorate the famous overland launch that started in Lynmouth, is on display inside the Tourist Information Centre.

Mevagissey
The former Cadgwith lifeboat *Guide of Dunkirk* is being restored for display in the harbour.

Milford Haven
Outside on a launching carriage in the Docks is *Calouste Gulbenkian*, an early 37ft Oakley class lifeboat.

Moelfre
The former New Quay lifeboat *Birds Eye* is displayed inside the Sea Watch Centre with a small display relating to the local lifeboats.

Newport (Isle of Wight)
At the Classic Boat Museum are three former Isle of Wight lifeboats: the *Queen Victoria*, originally stationed at Bembridge has been fully restored and is on display, while the former Ryde lifeboat *Selina* and former Bembridge lifeboat *Langham* are under restoration for future display.

Pitsea, Basildon
The former Wick lifeboat *Princess Marina* is displayed at the National Motorboat Museum.

Polperro
The former Looe lifeboat *Ryder* has been fully restored and is displayed at the Polperro Heritage Museum of Smuggling and Fishing. Tel 01503 72423

Poole
Displayed outside at the RNLI's Depot is the first 48ft Oakley lifeboat *The Earl and Countess Howe*. In the Old Lifeboat House on the Quay is the former Poole lifeboat *Thomas Kirk Wright*.

Porthleven (Cornwall)
At the Shipwreck Centre is the former Blyth lifeboat *Dash* undergoing restoration for future display.

Reading
The former Newbiggin lifeboat *Mary Joicey* is displayed at the Child Beale Wildlife Trust.

Redcar
In the Zetland Museum, 5 King Street, on the Promenade is *Zetland*, the oldest surviving lifeboat in the world, which was built by Henry Greathead in 1802. There are also other exhibits relating to lifeboats at Redcar. Tel 01642 494311

Station	County	Opened	RNLI	Closed	Station	County	Opened	RNLI	Closed
Johnshaven	Grampian	1891	1891	1928	Port Errol	Grampian	1877	1877	1922
Kessingland	Suffolk	1855	1867	1936	Port Logan	Dumfries &			
Kildonan	Isle of Arran	1870	1870	1901		Galloway	1866	1866	1932
Killough	Down	1901	1901	1914	Portavogie	Down	1965	1965	1981
Killybegs	Donegal	1941	1941	1945	Porth Rhufydd	Gwynedd			
Kimmeridge	Dorset	1868	1868	1896		(Anglesey)	1891	1891	1904
Kingsdowne	Kent	1866	1866	1927	Porthleven	Cornwall	1863	1863	1929
Kingsgate	Kent	1862	1862	1897	Porthoustock	Cornwall	1869	1869	1942
Landguard					Portland	Dorset	1826		1851
Fort	Suffolk	1821		1826	Portloe	Cornwall	1870	1870	1887
Laugharne	Dyfed	1835	1835	1843	Queenstown	Cork	1866	1866	1920
Leith					Rhoscolyn	Gwynedd			
(Newhaven)	Lothian	1805		1825		(Anglesey)	1830	1830	1929
Littlehaven	Dyfed	1882	1882	1921	Rhosneigir	Gwynedd			
Liverpool	Merseyside	1802		1894		(Anglesey)	1872	1872	1924
Llanaelhaiarn	Gwynedd	1883	1883	1901	Robin Hood's				
Llanddulas	Clwyd	1869	1869	1932	Bay	North Yorkshire	1830	1881	1931
Llanddwyn	Gwynedd				Rogerstown	Dublin	1874	1874	1882
	(Anglesey)	1826	1840	1833	Rossglass	Down	1825	1825	1835
Llanelly	Dyfed	1852	1854	1863	Runswick	North Yorkshire	1866	1866	1978
Looe	Cornwall	1866	1866	1930	Ryde	Isle of Wight	1869	1894	1923
Lossiemouth	Grampian	1859	1859	1923	St Agnes				
Lynmouth	Devon (North)	1869	1869	1944	(Scilly)	Cornwall	1890	1890	1920
Machrihanish	Strathclyde	1911	1911	1930	St Andrews	Fife	1800	1860	1859
Magazines	Cheshire	1827		1863	St Annes	Lancashire	1881	1881	1925
Maryport	Cumbria	1865	1865	1949	St John's Point	Down	1835	1835	1843
Mevagissey	Cornwall	1869	1869	1930	Saltburn	North Yorkshire	1849	1858	1922
Middlesbrough	East Yorkshire	1854	1858	1895	Saltfleet	Lincolnshire	1827		1828
Montrose No.3	Tayside	1885	1885	1892	Sandgate	Kent	1876	1876	1893
Morte Bay	Devon (North)	1871	1871	1900	Sandy Cove	Dublin	1803		1855
Mostyn	Clwyd	1835	1835	1851	Scratby	Norfolk	1854		1875
Mullion	Cornwall	1867	1867	1908	Seaham				
Mundesley	Norfolk	1811	1857	1895	Harbour	Durham	1855	1870	1979
Nairn/					Seascale	Cumbria	1875	1875	1895
Moray Firth	Highland	1878	1878	1911	Seaton Carew	Durham	1823	1857	1922
New Romney	Kent	1861	1861	1928	Seaton Snook	Durham	1907	1907	1909
Newburgh	Grampian	1828	1877	1965	Shanklin	Isle of Wight	1884		1916
Newlyn	Cornwall	1908	1908	1913	Sidmouth	Devon (South)	1869	1869	1912
Newport	Dyfed	1884	1884	1895	Sizewell	Suffolk	1826		1851
North Deal	Kent	1865	1865	1932	Skateraw	Grampian	1907	1907	1943
Orford	Suffolk	1826		1835	Solva	Dyfed	1869	1869	1887
Pakefield	Suffolk	1840	1855	1922	South Shields	Durham	1789		1937
Palling	Norfolk	1852	1857	1930	Southend				
Pembrey	Dyfed	1863	1863	1887	(Kintyre)	Strathclyde	1869	1869	1930
Penmon	Gwynedd				Southport	Lancashire	1816	1860	1817
	(Anglesey)	1831	1831	1915	Southsea	Hampshire	1886	1886	1918
Penrhyndhu	Gwynedd	1844	1894	1853	Stonehaven	Grampian	1868	1868	1934
Penzance	Cornwall	1803	1853	1812	Stronsay	Orkney	1909	1909	1915
Pigeon House	Dublin	1804	1862	1816	Studland	Dorset	1826		1848
Pill	Somerset	1971	1971	1974	Sutton	Dublin	1805		1834
Point of Ayr					Sutton-on-Sea	Lincolnshire	1843	1864	1913
(Gronant)	Dyfed	1826		1894	Theddlethorpe	Lincolnshire	1828	1864	1882
Point of Ayr					Thorpeness	Suffolk	1853	1855	1900
(Talacre)	Dyfed	1894	1894	1923	Torquay	Devon (South)	1876	1876	1923
Polkerris	Cornwall	1859	1859	1922	Totland Bay	Isle of Wight	1870	1885	1884

Station	County	Opened	RNLI	Closed	Station	County	Opened	RNLI	Closed
Tyrella	Down	1838	1838	1851	Wexford	Wexford	1859	1859	1927
Ullapool	Highland	1966	1966	1967	Wexford No.2	Wexford	1866	1866	1897
Upgang	Yorkshire	1865	1865	1919	Whitburn	Durham	1830	1854	1918
Varne Lightvessel	Kent	1971	1971	1972	Whitehaven	Cumbria	1803	1865	1925
Watchet	Somerset	1875	1875	1944	Whitehills	Grampian	1924	1924	1969
West Hartlepool	Durham	1847	1869	1894	Whitelink Bay	Grampian	1878	1878	1905
West Hartlepool	Durham	1854	1869	1894	Winterton	Norfolk	1823	1857	1924
Westport	Mayo	1857	1857	1862	Woodbridge Haven	Suffolk	1825		1853
					Worthing	West Sussex	1852	1865	1930
					Yealm River	Devon (South)	1878	1878	1927

Some of these stations are mentioned in connection with current operational stations in the main body of the book.

Stations that do not have a date in the 'RNLI' column never came under the auspices of the national body, and were operated locally by other societies or associations.

Appendix 8: Glossary

Afloat berth
A place in a harbour or other sheltered site assigned to a lifeboat where it can be permanently moored

All-weather lifeboat
A lifeboat that is designed to put to sea in any weather, regardless of severity

Breeches buoy
A lifebuoy attached to a line that is fired by a rocket from a boat or the shore, to assist with the rescue of people in distress

Carriage
Used to transport a lifeboat across a beach to enable it to be launched

Casualty
A vessel, ship or person that is in distress and needs the assistance of a lifeboat

Coastguard
The government-funded organisation that keeps watch on the coastline

Coxswain
The person in command on board a lifeboat when it is at sea

Davit
A crane mounted at the side of a dock or harbour used to launch inshore lifeboats

Do-do carriage
A carriage used to transport an inshore lifeboat across a beach, specially designed to enable the ILB to drive-off and drive-on easily

'Fast' lifeboat
A lifeboat capable of speeds in excess of 13 knots

Flare
A hand-held or rocket-fired burning torch used to illuminate an area or signal to other vessels

Fibre reinforced composite
A very strong material used for the hulls of several lifeboat classes

Glass reinforced plastic
A very strong material used for the hulls of several lifeboat classes

Helmsman
The person in command on board an inshore lifeboat when it is at sea

Honorary Secretary
The person in charge of operational functions at a lifeboat station

Inshore lifeboat
A small lifeboat, usually with an inflatable tube around the hull, used for work close inshore; often abbreviated to ILB

Maroons
Signal rockets that explode in the air; they are fired to summon a lifeboat crew when it is needed

Mooring
A place for anchoring a lifeboat afloat

Pulling and sailing lifeboat
A lifeboat powered primarily by sails and oars

Pulling lifeboat
A lifeboat that is powered primarily by oars pulled by the crew to propel the boat through the water

Quadbike
A four-wheeled vehicle with controls similar to a motor cycle, used to tow inshore lifeboats on their launching trolleys

Slipway
A sloping ramp into the water down which lifeboats can be launched

Strop
A strip of rope, used in conjunction with a davit to launch an inshore lifeboat